NOETIC MAGIC

And The Coming Transformation in Human Consciousness

by

Daniel L. Wick, Ph.D.

The Mirandola Press
37 Miguel, Suite 3
San Francisco, CA 94131

**Noetic Magic
and the Coming Transformation in Human Consciousness**

Copyright © 1997 by Daniel L. Wick

Library of Congress Catalog Card Number 97-76534

ISBN: 0-966-0714-0-9

Manufactured in the United States of America

To Jeanne

Table of Contents

Part Five: The Magus as Monster

BOOK TWO: MAGIC FUTURE

How to Read this Book

If you are an unregenerate member of the "New Age" and have the slightest inclination to believe in spirit channeling, UFOs, alien abduction, and other variations on the higher nonsense, this book is not for you.

If, on the other hand, you have a genuine interest in the transformative potential of the human mind, you will find much in the following pages that will interest and intrigue you.

Noetic Magic is divided into two parts.

Part One explores *Magic Past*, tracing the Western magical tradition from its originator, Pythagoras, through Platonism, Neo-Pythagoreanism, Gnosticism, Hermetism, the Cabala, Sufism, and the Renaissance Neo-Platonists to the modern era of the Order of the Golden Dawn, W.B. Yeats and Aleister Crowley. In addition to outlining the key ideas of Western magic, Part One explores the lives of such famous magi as Apollonius of Tyana, Dr. John Dee and Cagliostro.

Part Two investigates *Magic Future*, articulating the principles of Noetic Magic, outlining its philosophical basis, its relationship to modern psychology, and its potential for assisting in the "Global Mind Change" that Willis Harman has so eloquently described in his book of the same name. The penultimate chapter, *Exercises in Noetic Magic*, contains a description of suggested noetic and meditative exercises, including self-remembering, the phenomenological reduction, and Jungian meditations on the Tarot.

Depending on your interests and knowledge, you may start with either of the book's two parts.

Bibliographical essays and references for quotations will be found at the end.

Preface

What is Noetic Magic?

Noetic Magic is magic for the modern world. It is a synthesis of esoteric Christianity (Gnosticism), esoteric Judaism (the Cabala), and esoteric Islam (Sufism) as understood in the context of modern philosophy, especially phenomenology, and the psychological principles of Karl Jung and G.I. Gurdjieff.

The term Noetic is derived from the Greek **nous** which is often loosely translated as "Reason." But **nous**, to the Greeks, signified the "ground of being" that underlies all experience. It is "a part or phase of higher Nature, and therefore objective." In modern terms, **nous** is that part of the human psyche to which it is most difficult to gain access, what Jung termed the collective unconscious, what others have called the transcendental self.

Noetic Magic seeks to connect human beings with that transcendental ground of being through altering human consciousness at will. In this sense, it is intimately linked to the higher magical tradition in the West originated by Pythagoras. Through the exercise of will, imagination, meditation and the cultivation of the "good unconscious" (*anamnesis*), Noetic Magic strives to assist us in our heroic quest for the essence of self and the loving knowledge of others.

Each man is in his Spectre's power
Until the arrival of that hour,
When his humanity awake
And cast his own Spectre into the Lake.

-William Blake

Introduction:
The Meanings of Magic

We are confined in a perceptual prison of our own devising, yet like prisoners in all ages, we rarely think to question our lot. Humanity alone is responsible for this development. It is we who created the myths of determinism, divine and mechanical. It is we who have fostered the myth of the passive mind, a mere receptacle for the impingement of sensations from "outside." The belief in a stable, continuous ego is a comfortable illusion. It permits "safe" activity; it reduces the potential perils (as well as the potential joys) of existence.

William Blake symbolized limited human consciousness as the "Spectre," that "ghost in the machine" which can only be banished by will. But will by itself is not enough to erase an illusion which has been so carefully self-perpetrated throughout centuries of human development. What is also required is a sustained effort of the imagination, a gradual, perilous awakening from self-induced sleep.

In the West, two alternatives to the illusion of limited human consciousness have arisen: Magic and Mysticism, the development of which has been intimately linked throughout history, though they offer different solutions to the problem. Mysticism is quiescent and self-denying. Its objective is to "give up the ghost," to dispel the illusion of self by achieving union with God, Nature or the Universe. Mysticism seeks not adventure and change but rather peace and permanence. It is fundamentally "god-centered." In contrast, magic is "man-centered."

Magic is active and self-affirming. It dispels the illusion of the passive ego by overcoming it. In the words of W. E. Butler, "Magic is the art of effecting changes in consciousness at will." The power which the magician so passionately pursues is ultimately power over the self.

Science has contributed more than any other single force to the current eclipse of magic. Yet science and magic are in many ways similar. Both seek power and control; both are manipulative; both are essentially man-oriented. But science has until recently been based on an arbitrary dissection of that which is "out there" into easily analyzable parts. It has served to accentuate the illusion of our separateness from the rest of the universe by making a distinction between the observer and that which is observed. Above all, science has crystallized the sensation of limited human consciousness into a perceptual dogma through the success of the principle of mechanistic determinism.

Science Moves Towards a New Metaphysics

Former Stanford University professor Willis Harman argues that science is moving away from the mechanistic model based on the metaphysic of materialistic monism (matter giving rise to mind) to a metaphysic of transcendental monism (mind giving rise to matter.) As Harman says, "In contrast with conventional science, such a more comprehensive science will include more emphasis on holistic models and will center around . . .hierarchically related causes." This revolution in thought, which Harman calls the "Second Copernican Revolution," means that "society will, in only a few generations from now, be as different from modern industrial society as that is from [the] society of the Middle Ages."

Whatever else can be said of the end of the twentieth century, there is a feeling in the air that we are on the threshold of great discoveries. There is a growing awareness of our new position in the universe:

"This new position of intellectual man, in astronomy, in biology, and in psychology, and the other sciences, opens the door to a new sense of human freedom. We have a new picture of man's place, his powers, his destiny, and his responsibility. Just as our perception of the external world transcends our internal accidents of construction, so our powers now begin to transcend our biological accidents of origin. It is time to stand up free, with awareness and confidence and choice, to shape from now on, the further development of what we will become."

Science and Magic

Although science may increasingly be approaching a magical worldview, there is still too much narrow-mindedness to give rise to optimism about the immediate future. What is needed is a revolution in thought from the bottom up, not an occasional insight from the top down. And considering the traditional hostility with which scientists have always regarded magic, it is unreasonable to place much hope in their direction.

Since the beginnings of the rationalist movement in the seventeenth century, magic has been under constant attack. Magic, it was argued, is nothing more than pagan superstition. It depends on a belief in the devil, a notion which, in 1691, the Protestant clergyman Balthasar Bekker had shown was totally lacking in scriptural support. Worse yet, magic is incapable of scientific demonstration. It claims to operate outside the traditional scientific province of cause and effect, a claim which is patently absurd. What difference did it make whether magic was universally believed in, argued Bayle and Voltaire. Universal belief proves nothing. Didn't everyone before Copernicus believe the earth to be the center of the universe?

And so the attack continued, right down to the present day. Magic, declared Sir James Frazier in his famous Golden Bough, is nothing but false science. It obeys two pseudo-scientific laws: the law of contagion (the principle that things which have once been in contact continue ever afterwards to act on each other) and the law of similarity (like produces like). These principles, according to Frazier, have no scientific foundation whatsoever. Belief in magic is sustained in primitive societies by tradition. Magic is nothing more than self-fulfilling prophecy. Freud went on to identify magic with neurosis. Like the neurotic, the magician attempts to impose his will on the outside world.

Magic is nothing more than a form of wish-fulfillment based on a belief in the omnipotence of thought.

How the magus has fallen! The demi-god of the ancient world has been magically transformed by a modern feat of intellectual prestidigitation into a neurotic.

Yet magic continues to exert its mysterious fascination over us. We are at once attracted and repelled by it. It seems to violate our reason and yet, it promises power. Is it really nothing but superstition tempered with fraud?

Dictionary definitions will not help us here. "Magic," we learn, "is the pretended art of working by the power or assistance of supernatural beings." Note the arrogance, the imputation of dishonesty in that carefully placed "pretended." Why is magic here described as an art? A "pretended art" must surely be more ignoble than a "pretended science." Magic works, says the dictionary, by the power or assistance of supernatural beings. But what does it work? How is it alleged to control these supernatural beings? Must it work only with supernatural beings? Why not supernatural forces? Or even natural forces? Clearly we must look elsewhere for enlightenment. The dictionary definition reverberates with the overtones of the rationalist disdain for magic. Moreover, there is nothing in this definition that distinguishes science from religion. Doesn't religion also work with the power and assistance of supernatural beings?

Magic and Religion

The problem of distinguishing between magic and religion is a difficult one. Bronislaw Malinowski, in his book Magic, Science and Religion, has provided a set of distinctions which may help to get us started. According to Malinowski, magic is a "body of purely practical acts performed as a means to an end," while religion is a "body of self contained acts being themselves the fulfillment of their purpose." What does this mean? It is essentially a behavioral definition of magic. Any act performed by a magician, according to Malinowski, is a means to an end. Rain dances are not performed by indigenous peoples for sheer pleasure but to bring on rain. A religious act, on the other hand, is an end in itself. A priest, for example, does not try to use the Mass for a purpose beyond itself. The priest's incantations are not magical. Through them he does not expect to cause the heavens to roll with thunder, lightning to flash and rain to fall upon the earth. If it did rain shortly after Mass, the priest would think nothing of it. He would see no connection between his saying Mass and the rain. The tribe who had performed the rain-dance would, however, perceive such a connection

This seems clear enough. Magical acts are means. Religious acts are ends. One further clarification should be made, however, and here we can no longer rely on Malinowski who remained content with behavioral distinctions.

An act is magical if, and only if, it is so intended by those who perform that act. In other words, magic is not a property of the act; it is a property of the intentions of the actors.

There is a two-step process here. The first is to perform intentionally an act of magic. The second step is to perceive a connection between that act and some later phenomenon.

There is little else in the sociological and anthropological literature that helps distinguish magic from religion. Durkheim, Weber, Hubert and Mauss all argued that the priest works for the collectivity whereas the magician works for private clients or groups of clients. Durkheim further asserted that magic is often hostile to religion, taking "a sort of professional pleasure in profaning holy things." And anthropologists and cultural historians have vainly tried to distinguish between "miracle" and magic, largely to preserve the legitimacy of the miracles of Jesus, distinguishing them from "mere" magic. But one man's miracle is another's magic. In short, the contrast between miracle and magic is a distinction without a difference.

The problem with the anthropological approach to defining magic and its differences with religion is that academics have taken too narrow a view of both magic and religion. Matters will become much clearer when we look at the fourfold distinction between folk magic and philosophical magic and between transcendental and transitive magic.

Varieties of Magic

A useful distinction is that between folk and philosophical magic. Folk magic - shamanism, witchcraft, sorcery, etc. - has existed in all societies and in all ages, often performing a valuable function in terms of tribal or group survival. Folk magic is perhaps best described as practical and functional. Philosophical magic, on the other hand, operates within a well-considered world-view and on the basis of certain clear principles. Philosophical magic is intimately related to the Western intellectual tradition, especially to the development of Western mysticism, both pagan and Christian. Most authorities have failed to distinguish between folk and philosophical magic. Consequently, by lumping all magic together under a single comprehensive category, they have contributed to the modern confusion about the nature of magic best illustrated by the widespread belief that magic and witchcraft are essentially identical. But witchcraft is merely a species of folk magic.

A further distinction is necessary, that between transitive and transcendental magic. Transitive magic aims to effect changes in the outside world. The ancient Greeks referred to transitive magic as goetia, or sorcery and carefully distinguished it from magia, magic, which they considered to be a spiritual discipline of the highest order. Magia or transcendental magic aims to effect changes in consciousness.

Folk magic is largely, though not entirely, transitive. Philosophical magic is largely, though not entirely, transcendental.

The principal tradition of transcendental magic derives from Ancient Greece, where implicit in the teachings of Pythagoras and Plato and explicit in the Neo-Pythagoreans and Hermetists, it involved active techniques for bringing into consciousness the nous, or Reason, the ground of being. In its later manifestations, including Sufism and the Cabala, noetic magic was inward and imaginative, not outward and manipulative.

These distinctions should be regarded as a convenient analytic framework of understanding, not as comprising a definitional Procrustean bed that seeks to conform all possible variations in conceptions of magic to an unvarying formula. But for a sophisticated understanding of magic, the quadrapartite division of transcendental/philosophical, transitive/folk should prove helpful.

Take, for example, the distinction made by Hellenistic culture between thaumaturgy and theurgy. Thaumaturgy, or wonder working, was transitive magic of the most spectacular kind. Doubtless the impressive effects achieved by the thaumaturge, making elephants disappear and the like, were accomplished by means similar to those employed by modern illusionists like Houdini or David Copperfield. Theurgy, on the other hand, was transcendental magic of the highest kind in which human beings invoked and, in some instances temporarily became, gods.

The medieval distinction between demonic and spiritual magic is similar. Demonic magic was transitive in its effort to compel demons to influence human action and thought. Necromancy, the summoning of the spirits of the dead to question them about the future, can be placed in this tradition as can the efforts of medieval sorcerers to affect events through incantations and potions. Spiritual magic, as practised by the Renaissance neo-Platonists, was aimed at inward transformation and was thus transcendental.

The Impossibility of True Transitive Magic

It should be emphasized from the outset that transitive magic in its pure form is impossible. Human beings cannot now and never could cause miraculous things to happen through the actions of their minds or by compelling spirits to do their bidding. In a culturally constructed form, transitive magic often does work if the members of a particular culture share the belief that certain rituals or incantations or spells really do have efficacy. But this represents merely the enormous power of suggestion when backed up by the deep cultural consensus inherent in all supernaturalist belief systems. Another form of transitive magic that does work is, of course, the magic of illusion, the kind of magic with which we are most familiar. Modern illusionists are unanimous in denying that they do anything more than deceive the eye through ingenious misdirection. In times past, however, illusionists often sought to claim supernatural sanction for their spectacular parlor tricks.

To those who would object that transitive magic may be possible through the operation of extrasensory perception, especially telepathy and psychokinesis, I would point out that even those academic researchers who are the strongest supporters of the reality of ESP can point only to very weak manifestations of these phenomena, hardly enough to justify a belief in extrasensory perception as a basis for transitive magic. And for those who still believe, in spite of overwhelming evidence to the contrary, that there are all manner of miraculous psychics around, I can only recommend that you stop reading this book and hook up with the Psychic Friends Network or similar organizations whose only interests are your supposed psychic welfare and their burgeoning pocketbooks.

Attempts to distinguish between Black and White Magic have been unsuccessful. Black Magic, it is argued, is directed toward personal gain while White Magic has as its primary purpose the service of others. In practice, however, the two are indistinguishable. No magician admits to practicing Black Magic. Only one's enemies are Black Magicians. Aleister Crowley, for example, castigated the leaders of the Theosophical Society as the founders and perpetrators of the infamous (but mythical) doctrines of the so- called Black Lodge while he, in turn, was widely regarded in occult circles as the blackest of Black Magicians. The difference between Black and White Magic (if any) is chiefly a difference in intention.

For convenience, I refer to philosophical/transcendental magic simply as "magic" while I term folk/transitive magic "sorcery" unless another more specific term (witchcraft, for example) is more appropriate.

The Philosophical Basis of Magic

The philosophy upon which magic rests can be summarized under five general principles: (1) The doctrine of correspondence (2) The doctrine of emanations (3) The belief in the primacy of will (4) The belief in the importance of the imagination and (5) The belief in a supernatural world.

The doctrine of correspondence is based on the notion that the soul is essentially a reflection, in miniature, of a higher spiritual realm. Humanity is a microcosm within the macrocosm. Because we contain within ourselves the essence of everything that exists in the universe, we are able, by concentrating on the divine spark within, to summon the supernatural to our aid. The doctrine of correspondence is most succinctly expressed in the ancient dictum: "As above, so below."

The doctrine of emanations is based on Later Pythagorean philosophy. God or Nous (Reason) is seen as the transcendent, incorporeal One. By virtue of the irrepressible nature of the One, it emanates spiritual force as the sun emanates light. The corporeal world is the last emanation of the One. Man, composed of both spirit and matter, can raise himself by an effort of will through the hierarchy of emanations to ultimate union with the One.

The belief in the primacy of will is central to magic. The magus seeks to train his will by various means, some involving extreme asceticism. Magical failures and successes are generally explained in terms of the absence or presence of will. It is chiefly this emphasis on will that distinguishes magic most clearly from mysticism.

The belief in the importance of the imagination is found in all philosophies of magic. In the words of Israel Regardie: "What we so casually call the Imagination in the ordinary man is, according to the Theurgists of all time, the inherent faculty of the soul to assimilate the images and reflections of the divine Astral." Paracelsus is even more concise: "A resolute imagination is the beginning of all magical operations." Will and imagination complement one another; in the absence of either, magic is impossible.

Most magicians have believed in the reality of a supernatural world. We should not be led into thinking that the visions induced by magicians are not real to them. On the contrary, they are exhilaratingly (and sometimes frighteningly) real. Some modern magicians, it is true, have argued that a belief in the supernatural need not be sincerely held; it can be just a "working hypothesis." In general, however, belief in a supramundane world must be counted as one of the basic tenets of magic.

Western magic, though deriving considerable impetus from Asian thought during periods of religious syncretism, differs significantly from its Eastern counterpart. As Francis King has shrewdly observed: "Eastern technique is designed to raise matter toward spirit while the Western technique is aimed at the incarnation of spirit in matter."

This difference is important. It has served to render the Western magical tradition, despite occasional ascetic excesses, far less otherworldly and life-denying than its Eastern counterpart. Indeed, Western magic is essentially life-affirming.

Despite our pitiable efforts at precision, we find, in the end, that no series of distinctions, no definition can encompass the meaning of magic as a historical phenomenon. Its true significance, like some wizard's enchanted reverie, is fluid and ever-changing. Occasionally, as we study its history, we may imagine that we have glimpsed an irreducible analogy between magic and some other mode of thought. For a moment, magic is transformed into religion or even science. But such transformations are inevitably brief and are themselves soon transformed. Magic, like man, is protean.

The ego of primitive man is not a limit but it embraces all things surrounding him and participating in his life, even those which, after a brief contact with him, detach themselves from his body.

- Castiglioni

BOOK ONE: MAGIC PAST

Chapter 1:
The Birth of Dualism and the Spirit of Magic

Magic is as old as man and older than art. The first human pictorial representations were magically inspired. Cave paintings in southern France, especially those at Lascaux, provide the prehistoric equivalent of the medieval grimoire. Among the remarkable variety of figures which cover these walls, drawings of animals are by far the most prominent. Reindeer, horse, lion, brown bear, bison, rhinoceros, and mammoth are portrayed in a variety of poses. These paintings were used by stone-age man for purposes of sympathetic magic as an aid to success in the hunt. The inaccessibility of the caves in which the paintings appear (in some cases, it takes three hours or more to get to them) strongly suggests that they were reserved for use only on special occasions. This is further borne out by the fact that the human figures in the paintings are not portrayed in natural poses killing their prey, but rather in a curious attitude of worship. Clearly these stone-age hunters displayed a reluctance to take life unless it was absolutely necessary to tribal survival. Such a love for life seems, at first thought, quite remarkable among a people popularly believed to be crude and unfeeling savages, but considering the kind of world which stone-age people perceived, the world in which they acted and thought, a profound reverence for that which lives is understandable.

It requires an act of imagination to reconstruct in our minds the way in which early humans saw their world. Their way of life and modes of perception are so different from our own as to be almost alien. It is only our common humanity which provides the link between ourselves and our stone-age ancestors and permits us to entertain the hope that we can enter imaginatively into their world.

Life was revealed in everything they perceived. The wind in the trees, the roll of the oceans, all of the manifold stirrings of nature, all movement, in fact, was evidence of the presence of life. They lived in a world of constant motion, changing shapes and colors, a world of metamorphoses, vivid and alive. How can we recapture in all of its vitality, its strangeness and its wonder this sense of a living, animate universe? In the end, perhaps we must remain content with the dry and difficult words which archaeology and anthropology have used to describe this ancient world-view: animism, hylozoism, panvitalism. However inadequate our words, there is a sense in which we can understand that, in Hans Jonas' phrase, "Unquestioned and convincing at the beginning stands the experience of the omnipresence of life."

In this animate prehistoric universe, there remained one inexplicable reality, the fact of death. Death was the absolute negation of the vital principle which suffused every aspect of existence. Death, therefore, became the first philosophical problem which human beings confronted:

"To the extent that life is accepted as the primary state of things, death looms as the disturbing mystery. Hence the problem of death is probably the first to deserve this name in the history of thought. ... Before there was wonder at the miracle of life, there was wonder about death and what it might mean. If life is the natural and comprehensible thing, death—its apparent negation—is a thing unnatural and cannot be truly real. The explanation it called for had to be in terms of life as the only understandable thing: death had somehow to be assimilated to life."

This assimilation took a variety of forms. Fundamentally, however, it involved a growing belief in immortality. Death was seen as simply another metamorphosis, differing from the others only in the sense that the transformation it effected could not be experienced in this world. Out of the fact of death, then, arose life-after-death on another plane; the spirit world was born.

The world of spirits became a fact of human experience largely through magic. Transcendental magic enabled ancient peoples to communicate with this world and transitive magic to exercise some control over it. This suggests an explanation of the Lascaux cave paintings. The human figures kneeling reverently before their kill are communicating with the spirit of the dead animal while in a trance state. Holding life so important, they are able to kill only because they do not believe they are killing the important thing, the vital principle which inhabits the animal's body, its spirit. The ritual change of consciousness which they undergo reaffirms this fact by putting them in touch with the still-living spirit.

What was the basic function of magic for our ancient ancestors? Essentially it was the means by which they communicated with the spirit world; it was, in other words, **the change of consciousness** which permitted such communication. In addition, it is clear that magic arises out of a dualistic world-view; that is to say, where a difference is perceived and a distinction made between body and soul. Magic is the means by which this dualism is mediated by establishing a change of consciousness which makes communication possible between soul and body. These fundamental characteristics are present in the tradition of transcendental magic as well, which invariably involves a change of consciousness that constitutes a means of transcending dualism.

The experience of dualism was not acute in prehistoric times. As century followed upon century, however, and elaborations of ritual were gradually built up, dualism increased its hold on the mind. Funeral cults were established and death began to rival life in importance. Yet, as Hans Jonas has said:

"This is the paradox: precisely the importance of the tombs in the beginnings of mankind, the power of the death motif in the beginnings of human thought, testify to the greater power of the universal life motif as their sustaining ground: being was intelligible only as living; and the divined constancy of being could be understood only as the constancy of life, even beyond death and in defiance of its apparent verdict."

It is impossible to say at what point death finally triumphed over life in the history of human thought. We have only the sense of the gradual growth of dualism until it achieves radical expression in the cosmogonies of Zoroastrianism and Orphism. To the Orphics, the body was the grave of the soul; only in death is the soul permitted an independent life of its own. This increasing concern with the afterlife, shared by all the civilizations of the ancient world, Egyptian, Chaldean, Assyrian, Babylonian, to a greater or lesser degree, is evidence not only of the gradual separation of the material and the spiritual into two separate planes, but also of the increasing importance of the spiritual world in relation to the material world, of the afterlife in relation to this life. Moreover, as dualism became more pronounced, the spirit world more important, the techniques for overcoming dualism and the means for communicating with the spirit world increased in importance and sophistication.

It is not surprising, therefore, that the cosmogonies of antiquity in which dualism achieved its most radical expression—the Babylonian, the Zoroastrian, the Orphic, the Pythagorean, and the Gnostic—were also responsible for the sophistication and elaboration, in both theory and practice, of that consciousness-transforming activity which we call magic. Indeed, the word magic itself is derived from the **Magi**, those priest magicians of ancient Persia, whose function it was to mediate between the material and the spiritual worlds.

Despite the interest which these older civilizations unquestionably have for the student of magic, however, we shall begin our account with the Greeks for it was in Greece that magic entered the mainstream of Western thought and if we are to understand its subsequent development, we must understand the appeal that it exerted on the Greek mind.

Chapter 2:
The Magic of Greece

Magic is native to all lands but never has it enjoyed a setting as appealing to the imagination as in Greece. The mysterious and rugged landscape of the country with its gloomy caves, its volcanic mountains, its springs and fissures, half-hidden in mist, redolent with subterranean vapors, must have proved a powerful stimulus to the souls of the unknown tribes who first settled there. Greek mythology, the most enduring creation of the ancient mind, is fundamentally magical. Witness Pluto's helmet of invisibility, the head of Medusa which turned all who looked upon it to stone, the life (or death)-conferring staff of Hermes, the tale of the Golden Fleece, and the invulnerability of Achilles to name but a few examples.

Despite the magical character of Greek myth, sorcery was unknown until it was imported from Egypt and Persia. The legend of Orpheus, who was credited by the Greeks as the inventor of magic, may be a subtle echo of this influence for Orpheus was said to have been born in Thrace which, with Thessaly, had been strongly influenced by Persia. Also, the Greeks had no word for magic until after the Medean wars.

In Greece, as elsewhere, a distinction arose between official and unofficial magic. Unofficial magic was despised as mere sorcery and perhaps, as we shall see in the case of Pythagoras, as a potential source of revolutionary political ideas.

Orpheus, though, was the prototype of all benevolent sorcerers. Gentle, charming, poetic, he was worshipped as a god by those who heard the sound of his lyre. When his bride, Eurydice, died and descended into Hades, Orpheus followed her and won her back by playing his lyre for Persephone. He had only to observe one condition on their ascent from the nether world: that he would not look back until they reached the surface. However, Orpheus, overcome with fear that Eurydice might not be following him, glanced back and saw her disappear into the infernal regions forever. Upon reaching the earth's surface, he so enraged the women of Thrace by ignoring their offers of consolation that they tore him limb from limb. His music could not be stilled, however, for his severed head continued to sing. It was buried in a cleft in the rock at Lesbos which soon became the site of a famous oracle.

Orphism, the cult of Orpheus, had a powerful impact on the religious life of Greece. It introduced a new restraint into the Dionysiac ecstasies of religious worship as well as a new conception of the body as essentially evil restrained by a soul that was divine. This dualistic world-view, common to magical religions, may have influenced Pythagoras, who also adopted (perhaps independently) the Orphic doctrine of the transmigration of souls.

Greece had its sorceresses as well. No one who has read the Odyssey can ever forget the sinister charms of the fair Circe. The prototype of the medieval witch can be found in Medea, around whose name a hundred tales of infamy arose. Pale Hecate, goddess of the moon, wielder of the whip and cord, mistress of life and death, was propitiated at every crossroads by little round cakes and lizard masks. Enchantress, witch, and goddess; in one form or another they are with us today.

The ancient Greeks were enveloped in an atmosphere of superstition, sorcery, and magic. Illness was attributed to the invasion of Keres, or little demons. Anything from the appearance of a deformed man to the flight of birds could be interpreted as a portent of things to come. Sorcerers mixed aphrodisiacs and love philters; curses were as common as they were feared.

According to Theophrastus, an avowed enemy of superstition, if a Greek encountered a red snake in his house he would pray to Dionysus; if he passed a mound of stones set up at a crossroads, he knelt down, anointed it with oil, and prayed to it; if he met a madman or an epileptic he shuddered and spat on his chest to ward off evil spirits.

Living in a magical universe as they did, it is not surprising that even during the Greek Enlightenment when it became the custom for philosophers like Theophrastus to scoff at superstition, Greeks felt a profound attraction to anything that had the air of mystery about it. There were a number of mystery cults in addition to the Orphics, the oldest and most eminent of which belonged to the Eleusinian Mysteries. Each September candidates for initiation into the Greater Mysteries trod the fourteen mile path on the Sacred Way to Eleusis. After a period of purification which included bathing and fasting, they were taken into the Hall of Initiation where they witnessed a symbolic play, probably representing Pluto's rape of Persephone, and the wanderings of Demeter which culminated in the goddess's gift of agriculture to the Greeks. Finally, the worshipers descended into a subterranean chamber where, when they raised their heads, they could see a higher chamber in which sacred relics were bathed in brilliant light. The effect of this solemn ceremony was to produce in the initiates a mystical rapture of union with God.

Other sources of the supernatural in the life of ancient Greece were the many oracles that existed all across the land. Of these, which were consulted by commoner and noble, tradesman and philosopher alike, the two most famous were the oracle of Zeus at Dodona and the oracle of Apollo at Delphi. According to legend, the site of the Delphian oracle was discovered by a shepherd named Coretas when, in searching for a lost goat, he approached a cleft in the rock from which an intoxicating vapor arose. Seized with ecstasy, he began to utter strange prophecies. A temple was erected to Apollo on that spot for it was believed that the vapors Coretas had inhaled were exuded by the body of a Python which Apollo had slain and dropped into the crevice. The priestesses of the temple at Delphi, called Pythias, sat above the cleft on a high throne, chewed laurel leaves and inhaled the sacred stench, all the while uttering prophecies which were dutifully taken down and interpreted by priests. Although many of these prophecies were stunningly ambiguous (thus inaugurating a tradition that has unfortunately persisted to the present) they were often wise and always moderate. One of their chief functions was to predict the birth of great men and, as legend has it, when it came to the birth of Pythagoras, their prophecy was accurate.

Chapter 3:
Pythagoras and
Pythagoreanism

Virtually all that has been transmitted to us about Pythagoras is legend. But legends are lies that tell the truth.

Of all the sages of antiquity, it was Pythagoras who most profoundly influenced the direction and development of magic in the Western world. This remarkable man, whom Iamblichus referred to as the divine Pythagoras, was probably born at Samos, second largest of the islands in the Ionian Sea, around 589 B.C. His name means "mouthpiece of the Pythian Oracle at Delphi" for legend has it that the famous oracle informed his father, Mnesarchus, that Mnesarchus' wife "would bring forth a son surpassing in beauty and wisdom all that had ever lived, and who would be of the greatest advantage to the human race in every thing pertaining to the life of man." Many of the followers of Pythagoras believed him to be Apollo himself; some even claimed to have caught a glimpse of his golden thigh, a sure sign to the ancients of his divine origin.

Before embarking on a discussion of his doctrines, however, let's dwell for a moment on some of the curious legends which the name of Pythagoras inspired in the Hellenic world, legends which eloquently testify to the fact that Pythagoras was looked upon by the ancient world as a worker of miracles, a magician.

One day, as he was traveling from Sybaris to Crotona, he came upon some fishermen as they were drawing in their catch from the sea. A vegetarian, Pythagoras disliked seeing any harm whatsoever done to animals; therefore, he engaged the fishermen in conversation and, after a time, he wagered that he could predict the exact number of fish they had caught. In return, the fishermen promised that if Pythagoras were correct, they would do anything he asked of them. When his prediction proved to be accurate, Pythagoras ordered the fishermen to cast the fish back into the sea. Then, seeing that the fishermen were downcast at losing the fruit of their day's labour, Pythagoras paid them for the fish and departed.

On another occasion, Pythagoras heard of a huge and vicious bear which had attacked and injured several people in the neighborhood of Daunias. He therefore sought out the bear and, despite its reputation, approached it fearlessly and began stroking its back with his hand, talking gently to it all the while in a low voice. Finally, after feeding it with maize and acorns, he ordered it not to molest any living thing. Presumably the bear complied or there would be little point to the legend.

Once, at Tarentum, he saw an ox eating green beans. Approaching the herdsman, Pythagoras suggested that he tell the ox to refrain from eating the beans since they would he harmful to him. The herdsman laughed, saying that he didn't speak the language of oxen but that if Pythagoras did, then he ought to advise the animal. Pythagoras went up to the ox and whispered in its ear, ordering it to cease eating the beans. Much to the herdsman's astonishment, the ox responded to Pythagoras' request and, according to Iamblichus, was later taken to a place near the temple of Juno at Tarentum where it was worshipped as the sacred ox of Pythagoras.

One day, as he was crossing the river Nessus with a number of companions, he stopped and addressed the river. In a loud and clear voice, the river is said to have replied, "Hail, Pythagoras!"

Many other legends are told of this unique man, including the story that Pythagoras was seen on the same day at both Tauromenium in Sicily and Metapontum in Italy, cities which were several days' travel apart. Also, he is said to have predicted earthquakes, quieted storms, calmed waters so he could pass over them, and, on one occasion, to have predicted a shipwreck on a day when the sea was calm.

The fact that so many stories and tales have grown up around

Figure 1
Fifteenth Century Woodblock Depicting Pythagoras

Pythagoras' name is some indication of the veneration in which he was held by the Ancient world. His youth, the legends tell us, was devoted to a rigorous program of intellectual and physical discipline. Then, at the age of eighteen, reportedly having mastered the whole of Greek thought up until that time, Pythagoras embarked on a quest for the secret knowledge of cultures older than his own, determined that "nothing might escape his observation which deserved to be learnt in the arcana or mysteries of the Gods."

Following the advice of Thales, Pythagoras journeyed to Egypt in order to receive instruction from the Memphian and Diospolitan priests. Passing through Phoenicia, he stopped long enough to be initiated into the mysteries of Byblus and Tyre. Realizing that these were only the pale progeny of the sacred rites of Egypt, Pythagoras sailed on the first ship he could find that was headed for that land. Unfortunately, the ship on which he so hastily embarked was manned by an unscrupulous crew which planned to sell him into slavery. However, his silent and godlike manner so impressed the sailors that when the ship arrived in Egypt, instead of selling him into slavery, they raised a temporary altar to him, showered him with gifts and then departed.

Pythagoras reportedly spent twenty-two years in Egypt and was initiated into all the mysteries of the gods. What these mysteries were, no one is quite certain. They may have involved the practice of theurgy, which was later to be revived by the neo-Pythagoreans in the last centuries of the Roman Empire. According to Porphyry, the Egyptians taught Pythagoras geometry and inspired in him reverence for the Sun God, Atum, whom he identified with Apollo, the central figure of Pythagorean philosophy, equivalent to the One.

Upon leaving Egypt, he was captured by soldiers in Cambyses' army and arrived in Babylon where he studied under the Magi, especially the sage Zaratas. Porphyry notes that Zaratas taught Pythagoras techniques of ritual purification and lectured him on the metaphysical principles of the cosmos:

"Zaratas expounded to him that there are two causes present in the universe from the beginning: the father and mother. The father is light, the mother darkness; the parts of light are hot, dry and light; those of darkness cold, moist, heavy, and slow. From this it follows that the whole cosmos consists of the male and the female. [Zaratas] said that the cosmos is a musical harmony. Thus the sun too completes an harmonious revolution. . . Zaratas had the following to say about the things born from the earth and the cosmos: there are two gods, one heavenly, the other infernal; the infernal god producing life on earth, the heavenly one forming the psyche (the life-principle in the cosmos, as against the bodily, mortal things created by the infernal deity). The psyche is a fire partaking of air, and hot and cold. Thus none of these things can destroy or pollute the psyche. This is the essence of all things."

After twelve years in Babylon, apparently feeling that he had acquired sufficient insight into the mysteries, Pythagoras, now fifty-six years of age, returned to Samos where he attempted to set up a school in order to instruct the citizens of his birthplace in all the wonders which he had learned during his long journey. The Samians, however, found Pythagoras too obscure for their tastes. Furthermore, the dictatorship of Polycrates conflicted with the ideas of human freedom in which Pythagoras had come to believe. Hoping to find an audience more receptive to his teachings, he once again embarked on a journey, this time to Croton in southern Italy.

Why did Pythagoras choose to make Croton the site of the founding of his school? We can only conjecture, but it is interesting to note that a few years before Pythagoras arrived, the Crotonians had suffered a terrible defeat at the hands of the Locrians in the battle of Sagra. Perhaps Pythagoras felt that Croton, humiliated by defeat and in a state of serious economic decline, was in need of strong spiritual leadership. He developed a socio-religious philosophy which dealt with man's relationship to the cosmos, to one another, and to the state. Pythagoras was the first humanist and the Western magical tradition which he inaugurated bears testimony to this for Western magic, in all its varied manifestations, has exhibited a profoundly humanist bent.

Our picture of Pythagoras would he incomplete if we failed to take account of his political activities. According to Iamblichus, upon his arrival in Italy, Pythagoras "inspired the inhabitants with a love of liberty," and was instrumental in freeing from tyranny Croton, Sybaris, Catanes, Phegium and several other cities in Italy and Sicily. He established laws, quieted party discord, and raised the entire region to a high level of prosperity and peace.

During this period of intense political activity, however, Pythagoras did not neglect his spiritual mission. He set up a school in Croton, a school which was open to all who would submit to his discipline including (and this is unusual in antiquity) women.

The school which Pythagoras founded and the doctrines that he taught laid the foundations for the development of higher magic in the West. The Croton school was divided into outer (exoteric) and inner (esoteric) students. All students were enjoined to lead an almost monastic life, abstaining from flesh, eggs and beans and devoting much time to silence and contemplation. The members were bound by vows of loyalty to one another as well as to the Master. A student entering the school was required to give up all of his worldly goods to the community. If, however, he was later found to be wanting in either character or intellect, he was dismissed from the school, given twice the amount of his original donation, and treated as dead by the Pythagorean brotherhood.

Information concerning the doctrines taught at the school is scanty and incomplete. It is necessary to piece together brief and biased accounts which have been left to us by Aristotle, Plutarch, Sextus Empiricus and others, all of whom lived long after the original Pythagorean school was founded. Pythagoras himself wrote nothing, nor did most of his early followers. Nevertheless some things can be said about Pythagorean doctrine with relative certainty.

Basically, the Pythagoreans believed in the opposition of two mathematical principles, the Limited and the Unlimited which combined together to form the Cosmos which, as the imposition of Limit upon the Unlimited, is essentially an infinite, eternal and divine creature, the Primordial One from which all things are generated.

This notion of a living Cosmos implied the essential unity of all life. This gave rise to the Pythagorean belief in the transmigration of souls. Pythagoras himself claimed to have undergone several incarnations, in one of which he was a courtesan, in another, Euphorbus, one of the heroes of the siege of Troy. The souls of men, as part of the divine soul, the Cosmos, were immortal, but men, ignorant of this fact, disregarded their divine nature and therefore were condemned to suffer endless bodily incarnations until they learned the means whereby they would be able to merge their individual souls into the divine soul. The method which Pythagoras taught to attain this goal was not religious but philosophical. The word philosophy itself appears to have originated with Pythagoras. Irritated at the term sophia, which he regarded as pretentious, he substituted as a description of his own activities, philosophia, meaning the love of wisdom, rather than wisdom itself. As far as the Pythagoreans were concerned, philosophy meant the use of intellect and reason to attain understanding of the universe. In this, they are most clearly distinguished from the Orphics, who also believed in the transmigration of souls, but thought that union with the universal soul could be achieved by purely religious means.

Through a combination of philosophy and happenstance, Pythagoras came to believe in the idea, commonly associated with his name, that things are numbers. Passing a blacksmith shop one day, Pythagoras was surprised to hear what sounded like regular musical intervals in the sounds which came from striking the anvil. After determining that the hammers used by the blacksmith were of different weights, he began to wonder if the tones could be expressed by numerical ratios. In order to verify this hypothesis, Pythagoras undertook an experiment (an unusual procedure among the ancient Greeks). Taking two strings of equal thickness and tension, he discovered that an octave was sounded when one string was twice as long as the other. In a similar manner, all musical intervals could be mathematically expressed. Pythagoras went on to argue that, since all moving bodies emit sounds, the movement of the heavenly bodies must produce a veritable symphony of sounds which man cannot ordinarily hear because it is always present. This was the famous "music of the spheres" and it became an important part of Pythagorean discipline to learn to listen to this divine music.

Expanding on his discovery of harmonic intervals, Pythagoras taught, not simply that all things can be expressed by number, but that all things are number. Number, to Pythagoras, was not an abstraction from reality, but reality itself. The Pythagoreans, therefore, concentrated on mathematics as the best means by which they could understand the order of the Cosmos.

But Pythagoras made a distinction between pure number and mathematical number. Pure number exists independently of the human mind and constitutes the structure of the universe. Mathematical number is merely the human symbology for pure number.

And so out of the One, pure spirit, flowed the dyad and from these emerged the ensuing combinations that make up the first ten numbers (the decad).

"From the One comes all that is good in the universe for it is the source of the odd numbers, such numbers being termed good because in the system of Pythagorean arithmetic the sides around numbers or gnomons always form squares around odd numbers."

The dyad (two) is the opposite of the One. It is the source of matter and therefore, of evil.

The triad (three) is the first number and is analogous to the cosmic psyche that animates the universe.

The tetraktys (four) represents the four elements of the universe (earth, air, water, and fire) and is second only to the One in its sacred significance to the Pythagoreans.

Five, half of the sacred ten, symbolized the five fundamental shapes: the pyramid, cube, octahedron, and dodecahedron.

Six is the first perfect number because its products add up to six $(1+2+3=6)$.

Seven is the first prime number in the sense that no two numbers multiplied within the decad equal seven. (The reason why five is excluded from possessing this honor is that five multiplied by two produces ten, the decad, whereas seven multiplied by two produces fourteen, a number outside the decad).

Eight, called "Harmonia," is the first perfect cube.

Nine is the highest number in the decad and a symbol of justice because its square root is three.

Ten (the decad) is, like the One, a symbol of unity and perfection.

The Pythagoreans were also responsible for introducing one of the most fertile ideas in the history of Western mysticism and magic: *the notion of the macrocosm and the microcosm, the idea that man is a replica, in miniature, of the workings of the Cosmos.* The Pythagoreans believed that by studying the mathematical order contained in the Cosmos, they would be able to comprehend this order within themselves and thus merge with the divine.

It is said that the Pythagorean school at Croton prospered for several years. Then a certain Cylon, who had been refused admission into the esoteric doctrines, in a spirit of revenge burned down the school, murdered several of the students and expelled the rest from Croton.

According to some accounts, Pythagoras was killed as he tried to escape from Cylon's mob, while others have it that he disappeared mysteriously and lived out the remainder of his days at Metapontum.

After the attack by Cylon, the Pythagorean sect reasserted its influence until, sometime in the fifth century B.C.E., another wave of persecutions caused the members of the Brotherhood to disperse. Recent research indicates that the Pythagorean Brotherhood, clustered into small groups, continued into the Roman era. The so-called Pythagorean revival of the first century C.E. was therefore not a revival at all but a continuation of an unbroken tradition.

The persecution of the Pythagoreans is difficult to understand, until we remember the political ideas which Pythagoras espoused. Liberty, then and now, inspires fear.

As for Pythagoras, how can we do justice to his many-sided genius? Sage, mystic, mathematician, he can justly lay claim to being the father of both science and philosophy as well as to articulating the principles of Western magic. We shall hear his name again in this history. We shall see how Plato assimilated and, to a degree, modified the teachings of Pythagoras in the fourth century B.C.E. Then, in the first century C.E., we will witness the rise of neo-Pythagoreanism in the person of Apollonius of Tyana. Not even after we come to understand how neo-Pythagoreanism merged with Gnosticism and Hermetism to form the mainstream of Western magical thought, will the name of Pythagoras be forgotten. His influence, like his genius, is universal.

Chapter 4:
Plato and the Magical Universe

The history of magic in Greece should be viewed within the context of the growth of popular irrationalism from the seventh to the fourth century B.C.E., a development which has been largely ignored by historians. The Greek city-states, politically unstable and constantly threatened by invasion, became the breeding grounds of fear and superstition.

The dualistic doctrines of Pythagoras and the Orphics gradually filtered down to the popular level, effecting a change in the traditional Greek concept of the soul. Homer had regarded the soul (*thumos*) as the life-force of the body, a concept which was still present in the later Greek word *psyche*, which denoted both "spirit" and "mind." Pythagoreanism and Orphism, however, regarded the soul as the prisoner of the body. The Orphic formula *soma-sema* (body-tomb) concisely expresses this view.

What were the consequences of the introduction of dualism into Greek thought? According to E. R. Dodds, dualism, "by crediting man with an occult self of divine origin, and thus setting soul and body at odds, . . .introduced into European culture a new interpretation of existence, the interpretation we call puritanical." Life was regarded as a form of punishment to which all souls were more or less equally subjected. Only after passing through a series of cycles of birth and rebirth and ultimately purifying itself, could the soul escape from the prison of the world. A shortcut to the release of the soul was offered by the new cults: avoid pleasure and lead the spiritual life on earth; attempt to communicate with the gods. The Orphics advocated the use of music and incantations as means of effecting the necessary change in consciousness that permitted contact with the spiritual world. The Pythagoreans believed that meditation, especially on the mystery of numbers, would achieve the same result.

On the popular level the growth of dualism and irrationalism was reflected in an increase in the practice of magic. Asclepius, once an insignificant figure, became a widely worshipped deity as a result of the growing belief in magical healing. The magical practice of *defixio*, cursing someone by inscribing his name on a potsherd and summoning demonic powers to one's aid, became increasingly popular.

The so-called Greek Enlightenment did not put a stop to these practices. Indeed, some historians have theorized that the Enlightenment actually produced an irrationalist reaction which reached its height in the fourth century B.C.E. It is clear in any event, that Plato, arguably the greatest of the Greek philosophers, was by no means free of irrationalist tendencies.

Plato was a Pythagorean. He inherited from Pythagorean thought a fascination with numbers and a belief that the universe is divine. As Kurt Seligmann has pointed out, "Plato's world is a magical one; for it is unified and all things are interrelated." Nevertheless, Plato regarded transitive magic as a danger to the state and, in the **Laws**, advocated legislation against sorcery. But he magical element in Plato has little to do with sorcery; rather, it is a certain attitude of mind, a profound yearning for the absolute, that makes Plato important in the history of both magic and mysticism.

Recent scholarship has made clear just how much Plato owed to the Pythagoreans: among other key concepts, his doctrine of the soul, the idea of the microcosm and the macrocosm, the idea of number as the essence of reality, and the One (in Platonic terms, the Good) as the ultimate determining principle. He also believed, with Pythagoras that philosophers should become kings or kings philosophers.

But Plato ignored the Pythagorean insistence on reserving philosophy for an esoteric elite. Not that Plato was a democrat. Far from it. He believed that philosophy should be reserved for the few but saw no reason why it need be confined to an esoteric Brotherhood.

In terms of its influence on the history of magic, perhaps the most important of Plato's writings is the **Timaeus**, a work written when he was about seventy years old. Apparently disillusioned with Athenian politics, Plato set out to describe the ideal state as a vision, not of the future as in the **Republic**, but of the remote past. In so doing, he provided an account of creation which proved to be enormously influential in the development of magical thought.

According to the **Timaeus** the world was created by a demiurge. The earth and all things upon it are merely the imperfect copies of the Ideal Forms existing in heaven. The world is thus a microcosm, reflecting in debased form the macrocosm of the eternal universe. This notion, expressed in the formula "as above, so below," was by no means original with Plato. We have encountered it before in Pythagoras; indeed, it is one of the metaphysical mainstays of all magic and mysticism and is probably derived from prehistoric animism.* What Plato accomplished, however, was the transfer of this doctrine of correspondence from the realms of superstition, popular religion, and esoteric Pythagorean tradition to the realm of public philosophy. He provided it with force and power; no longer did the doctrine of correspondence have merely an emotional appeal but also an intellectual one.

The **Timaeus** was one of the most influential Platonic dialogues in classical antiquity. In fact, many knew Plato only through the **Timaeus.** It provided the essentials of a complete philosophy: cosmology, cosmogony, a theory of the soul, and a theory of science. It was one of the few Platonic dialogues that survived into the Middle Ages. Most of the others lay hidden in decaying Byzantine monasteries awaiting their revival at the time of the Renaissance.

The magic of the Roman Republic need not detain us long. Magic there was, in popular form, but philosophically, the Romans contributed little to magical thought. True, magic was enshrined in the state religion, but this was largely a formal affair and the general Roman attitude toward unofficial magic can be seen by their condemnation of spells in the Twelve Tablets and their prohibition of Bacchic festivals and the cult of Dionysus. The attitude of Roman intellectuals toward

---

* Some historians mistakenly claim that this "doctrine of correspondence" originated with the Stoics. But, although the Stoics popularized the formulation "as above, so below," Pythagoras introduced the concept to Western philosophy.

magic was generally hostile. Cicero regarded magic as foreign super-stition as did Pliny (who, nevertheless propagated a host of supersti-tions of his own). It was, in fact, in the age of Pliny, around the first century C.E., that magic once more came into its own.

The reasons for this are somewhat difficult to ferret out. As A. J. Festugière has pointed out, the early centuries C.E. constituted an era of relative peace and prosperity in the Roman Empire. The barbarian hordes were kept at bay by Roman armies on the frontiers, leaving the internal life of the empire undisturbed by thoughts of war. Monuments were erected testifying to widespread satisfaction with imperial rule. Politically, economically, and militarily, the Roman Empire was at its zenith. Why, then, the growing attachment to mystery religions, why the striking increase in occult speculation?

The answer seems to lie at least partially in the fact that the intellectual legacy left to Rome by the Greeks had finally run its course. The great philosophic schools founded by the Greeks: the Platonic Academy, the Stoics, Epicureans, Cynics and Skeptics now no longer seemed to pro-vide adequate answers to the vital problems of human life. In each school, philosophic thought had hardened into dogma. A citizen living in the Roman Empire during this era was thus presented with a variety of internally consistent but mutually irreconcilable philosophic doc-trines from which to choose. Disenchantment with Greek thought led to a search for non-Greek sources of inspiration. The deductive ratio-nalism which formed the foundation of Greek philosophy was increas-ingly seen as inadequate. Why not return to a more ancient, and there-fore more profound, mode of thought than that of the Greeks? The oriental mystery religions, products of nations conquered by Rome, conquered Rome in turn.

Chapter 5.
Tales of the Magi I:
Apollonius of Tyana

The early centuries C.E. can, without fear of exaggeration, be called an age of miracles. The sturdy, traditional religion of the Roman Republic gave way to the religious syncretism of the Roman Empire. Cults based upon esoteric religious mysteries flourished: the cult of the Great Mother, the worship of Isis, Mithraism, Zoroastrianism, the worship of Baal, Atargatis, Azziz, and a hundred others. The single common characteristic shared by all of these cults was a belief in the miraculous; priests, shamans, magicians, wonder-workers of all varieties plied their trades throughout the broad expanse of the Empire, sowing the seeds of magic in all but the most skeptical minds. The names of many of these magicians are lost to us; for the most part their fame barely survived their own lifetimes. There was one man, however, whose reputation remained undimmed until Christianity achieved religious hegemony in the Roman world, a man to whom the emperor Hadrian dedicated a temple, a man whose image was included in the pantheon of the eclectic emperor, Alexander Severus, a man who was regarded by such early Fathers of the Church as Lactantius as a pagan rival to Jesus himself, Apollonius of Tyana.

Apollonius was born at Tyana, a Greek city in Asia Minor, sometime in the early years of the first century C.E. Many legends surround his birth, one of which relates that his mother, during her pregnancy, had a vision of Proteus, the god of metamorphoses, who told her that the forthcoming child would be an incarnation of him. As Philostratus remarks, this legend is particularly apt, for Proteus was endowed with the ability to read minds and to foresee the future, abilities with which, as we shall see, legend also endowed Apollonius.

Like his better-known contemporary, Jesus, Apollonius was a child prodigy. At the age of fourteen, he went to Tarsus to study under the rhetorician, Euthydemus. Disgusted by the sybaritic citizens, Apollonius journeyed to nearby Aegae where he lived at a temple dedicated to Aesculapius and discussed philosophy with representatives of all the schools. The philosophy which most attracted him was that of Pythagoras, even though the Pythagorean master at Aegae, Euxenus, had little understanding of the doctrines which Pythagoras had taught and merely repeated teachings that he had memorized by rote. Nevertheless, Apollonius learned all he could from Euxenus, until, when he was sixteen, he bought his teacher a villa and bade goodbye to him, saying, "Live here after your own fashion, but I will live like Pythagoras."

True to his word, Apollonius became a vegetarian, discarded animal clothing, wore only a simple linen robe, and allowed his hair to grow long, after the fashion of Pythagoras, the "long-haired Samian," as Iamblichus calls him. Apollonius then set himself up in the temple and became known for his wisdom and his remarkable ability to cure illness. The activities of Apollonius in the temple of Aesculapius inspired the saying, still current some two hundred years after his death: "Where are you running? To see the lad?"

Apollonius was remarkable not only for his wisdom, but for his beauty. Even as a youth he possessed a noble and lofty appearance, tall and straight with the features of a bust modeled by some divine Praxitiles, the features of a god. The prefect of Cilicia, attracted by the youth's reputation for beauty, made a special pilgrimage to the shrine of Aesculapius hoping to seduce Apollonius. The attempted seduction proved a failure and it was not long after this incident that Apollonius renounced sexual activity of any kind, thereby exceeding the demands of Pythagoras who required only that men be faithful to their wives. Philostratus writes that Apollonius was accused of unchastity by several of his enemies but that these charges were all untrue. The legend is consonant with the age for it was at about this time that a peculiar spirit of religious asceticism began to make itself felt, probably as a reaction against centuries of sybaritic self-indulgence. A similar denial of the flesh is found during this period, not only among the Christians but in the various Gnostic sects as well.

Shortly after taking his vow of chastity, Apollonius was asked by Euxenus why he hadn't written anything, since he expressed himself so clearly and wisely in ordinary speech. Apollonius replied: "Because so far I have not practiced silence." From that time forward, he resolved to keep silent for a period of five years in order to observe everything that was going on about him. Although Philostratus fails to provide a reason for this particular act of asceticism, it may very well have been that Apollonius felt he was in danger of pretending to be wiser than he really was and hoped to find humility by undergoing a period of self-enforced silence. Whatever the reason, Apollonius apparently held to his vow, even though there were times when breaking it would have made his spiritual tasks much simpler. Once, for example, as he was passing through the city of Aspendus, he encountered a mob of citizens preparing to burn the prefect of the province alive. The terrified prefect, who was clutching at a statue of the emperor Tiberius for protection, hastily explained the situation to Apollonius. It seems that a number of wealthy citizens, in an attempt to corner the market on grain, had hoarded all of the grain in the city so that there was nothing left to eat but miserable vetches. The people of the city, driven to desperation by hunger, knew nothing of this and blamed the prefect for the emptiness in their bellies. Facing the hostile mob, Apollonius silenced them with an imperious wave of his hand and indicated by gesture that they should listen to what the prefect had to say. Immediately the prefect explained what had happened, naming the men who were responsible for the famine. Before the crowd had a chance to fall upon these men and tear them limb from limb, Apollonius once again intervened and had the men brought before him. Still maintaining his vow of silence, he wrote his wishes on a clay tablet and gave it to the prefect to read. In a voice loud enough for all assembled to hear, the prefect read the following words: "Apollonius to the food-peddlers of Aspendus: the earth is mother of us all, for she is impartial, but you by your injustice have made her the mother of none but yourselves; and if you do not stop it, I shall not permit you to stand on her any longer." The hoarders, grateful for having been delivered from the mob and terrified by Apollonius who seemed to them a god, hastened to their secret hiding places and gave up all their ill-gotten grain to the starving mob. In this way, Apollonius prevented bloodshed on all sides without ever having to utter a word.

After his period of silence ended, he resolved to make a pilgrimage to the East. Hoping to surpass even Pythagoras, Apollonius planned to journey to Persia and beyond to the furthest reaches of the civilized world. He had heard many tales of the wisdom of the Indian Brahmins and, possessing an insatiable curiosity, he wished to learn anything they had to teach. Arriving at Nineveh on the first leg of his journey, he paused before the statue of Io and fell into conversation with a Ninevite named Damis. Upon learning that Apollonius was planning to travel to the East, Damis offered his services as a guide and inter-preter, saying that he spoke many languages and was well acquainted with most of the cities Apollonius would be traveling through on his way to Babylon. Apollonius replied that he, too, was familiar with all of these languages even though he had never studied them. When Damis expressed amazement, Apollonius said, "Do not wonder at my under-standing the languages which men speak, for I even know the things which they do not speak." Nevertheless, Apollonius allowed Damis to accompany him on his journey, fortunately for us, for the Assyrian kept a copious account of everything that happened to them. This ac-count is now lost to us, but it served as the chief source from which Philostratus drew his portrait of Apollonius, the only biography of the philosopher which has survived from antiquity. According to Philostratus, Damis was a poor writer but a keen observer and an ex-haustive note-taker.

As the two travelers entered the territory controlled by Babylon, they were stopped by a eunuch who asked Apollonius how he dared to travel to the sacred city without an invitation from the king. Appollonius replied: "All the earth is mine, and I may journey in it where I please." Some miles past where they had left the bemused eunuch, Apollonius and Damis encountered a small town where lived a number of Eretrian Greeks. They complained bitterly of their lot to the travellers, saying that the king of Babylon had refused to give them any aid even though they lived on such poor land that they could scarcely feed their children let alone themselves. Moved by their plight, Apollonius promised that he would see to it that the king helped them.

As they entered the city of Babylon, Apollonius and Damis passed by a huge statue of the king which, according to law, they were required to bow down before. Apollonius refused, saying that since he had not yet met the king and ascertained whether or not he was a worthy man, he could hardly be expected to worship him. Despite this breach of the law, no one arrested Apollonius or stood in his way as he went on to the palace.

The king was performing a sacrifice before the Magi when Apollonius was summoned to see him. In honor of the sun, the king was about to slaughter two fine white horses caparisoned in gold. Apollonius said to him, "Sacrifice in your way, 0 King, but let me sacrifice in mine," whereupon he threw some incense into the fire and delivered a prayer to the sun. Then, not wishing to witness the slaughter of the animals, Apollonius left the presence of the king until the sacrifice was completed.

Despite these breaches of protocol, Apollonius got on very well with the king whom he found to be a wise and just man. Much of his time, however, was spent consulting with the Magi. Unfortunately, Damis was left behind on these occasions, so we know nothing about what actually was said. When Damis asked Apollonius what he thought of the Magi, he replied: "They certainly are wise, but they are not wise on every subject."

The king asked Apollonius and Damis to stay at the palace but Apollonius refused, saying that it was not wise for philosophers to be exposed to so much luxury lest it cause their minds to wander from the pursuit of truth. Therefore, the travellers stayed with a humble family of ordinary means who lived close to the palace. The king grew daily more impressed with Apollonius and once, in order to express his gratitude to the sage, he offered him any ten gifts which he should care to select.

Delighted at their good fortune, Damis exhorted his master to take advantage of this offer. Apollonius replied that simply because they were in a foreign land far from Greece did not mean that they had ceased to be philosophers and could relax their standards. When the day arrived on which Apollonius was required to name the gifts which he wanted, however, he did not refuse the king's generosity altogether. Saying that there was one gift which would please him more than a hundred others, Apollonius told the king of the plight of the Eretrian Greeks and requested that he give them his aid and protection. The king swore to do everything in his power to help the Eretrians, "but Apollonius," he said, "why do you not accept the other nine gifts?" "Because, 0 king," Apollonius replied, "I have made no other friends here."

After spending two years among the Persians, Apollonius grew impatient to continue his journey to India. Accepting camels and supplies from the Babylonian king, the pair began their long trek through the Caucasus to the Ganges.

Having encountered a variety of wonders on their journey, most of which were doubtless the creations of Damis' fertile imagination, the two Greeks arrived at the palace of the Indian King, Phraotes. The King welcomed Apollonius heartily, telling him that he had been expecting him. Apollonius was surprised, understandably enough, that the King spoke fluent Greek, but Phraotes cleared this up by explaining that he had learned his Greek from the Brahmins who, like Apollonius, understood all languages. Apollonius and Damis remained at the palace of Phraotes for three days during which time the philosopher engaged the King in debate, occasionally coming out a poor second. Apollonius was so impressed by this monarch that, some years later, he chastised his enemy Euphrates for not having any of the philosophic virtues of Phraotes.

Proceeding on their way with a guide provided by Phraotes, Apollonius and Damis at last reached the goal of their journey, the dwelling-place of the Brahmins. Rising as high above the plains as the Acropolis, according to Damis, the temple of the Brahmins was as well protected as any fortress even though the Brahmins, due to their marvelous powers, needed no protection. Leaving Damis behind in the village, Apollonius, who had been summoned to the temple by name, ascended the steep path to his destination passing, on his way, several statues of some of the older Greek gods. Upon reaching the temple, he was greeted by several of the Brahmins and led into the presence of Iarchas, the Master of the temple. When Apollonius expressed his desire to learn the wisdom of the Brahmins if, indeed, they had anything to teach him, Iarchus responded by describing in detail several events in the philosopher's life. Convinced of the sages' powers, Apollonius swore to remain at the temple until he had drunk his fill of their wisdom.

Damis, who was summoned from the village to join his master, was continually amazed at everything about the Brahmins. At night, he said, they cast herbs on the ground where they were planning to sleep and, tiring of the earth on occasion, slept suspended a few feet above the ground. By day they prayed to the sun and by night they prayed to the fire of the sun which, according to Damis, they had captured in some unknown way. Not surprisingly, they dressed after the fashion of the Pythagoreans and observed the same dietetic restraints. Apollonius had a habit of discovering Greece wherever he travelled.

One day, Apollonius asked Iarchus what the Brahmins thought themselves to be. With a characteristic lack of humility which probably only Apollonius could appreciate, Iarchus replied, "Gods!" When Apollonius asked why, Iarchus said: "Because we are good men!"

In addition to maintaining moral perfection, the Brahmins claimed to know everything, including the full details of their previous incarnations. Iarchus, for example, had once been the hero Achilles as well as the Indian demi-god Ganges, a huge giant who freed his native land from the Scythians and founded sixty cities. Apollonius, on hearing this, told Iarchas about one of his own prior lives as a humble steersman on an Egyptian ship. It is to his credit that he didn't try to outdo the Brahmin by providing a more colorful pedigree.

Once, while Apollonius was visiting the Brahmins, a king came to consult Iarchas. This king, unlike Phraotes, was an arrogant, bad tempered character, just the sort of person to arouse ire in Apollonius who had little respect for crowned heads if they also happened to be empty. The King began his conversation with Apollonius by making a few insulting remarks about the Greeks. Apollonius replied with such an eloquent speech on the virtues of the Greeks that the King was moved to tears and admitted that he had been misinformed on the subject by some Egyptians.

Eventually, both Damis and Apollonius were admitted into the Mysteries of the Brahmins, learning that their doctrines were based chiefly on a conception of the universe as a living thing, both male and female. Despite its size, some control can be exercised over this divine animal for, as Iarchus said, "it is tractable and easily guided." the wisdom of the Brahmins consisted in knowing the techniques by which this kind of control could be exercised. Unfortunately, no description is given of how the Brahmins learned these techniques other than through leading a pious life of meditation and prayer. Apollonius held lengthy colloquies with Iarchus during which they apparently discussed this subject but, as usual, Damis was left behind.

Whatever Apollonius learned from the Brahmins he learned rapidly for, after a stay of only four months, he bade them goodbye. His farewell was made without sadness, however, no doubt because, as Apollonius said, "Even among the Greeks I shall be mindful of your teachings, so that I will converse with you as if face to face. . ." And so, Apollonius and Damis departed, travelling back by the same route they had come, passing a few pleasant days with Phraotes and the king of Babylon. Upon their arrival in Greece, they were greeted by a curious and awestruck populace for during the philosopher's lengthy absence, the oracles of Colophon and Branchidae had uttered prophecies about him, saying that he was as wise as Apollo and a great healer.

While at Smyrna he predicted that Ephesus would soon be ravaged by a plague. When this occurred, Apollonius was summoned to aid the Ephesians and, to the amazement of the people of Smyrna, he vanished and appeared at Ephesus on the same day. Immediately, he ordered the entire population of the city to assemble in the amphitheatre. When this had been accomplished, Apollonius, standing before a statue of Hercules, the Averter of Evil, cast his gaze over the crowd. Spying an ancient and miserable beggar curled up in his rags against the far wall of the amphitheatre, Apollonius commanded the people of Ephesus to surround the creature and stone him until he died. Appalled at this savage request, the Ephesians refused to move, saying that the old man had done no one any harm. Summoning all the authority and majesty at his command, Apollonius prevailed upon the crowd to follow his order, which they did reluctantly until, finally, the old man's corpse was buried beneath a mound of stones. Apollonius ordered the stones removed, whereupon the Ephesians found, not the body of a beggar, but rather that of a giant mastiff, lips dripping with foam. Then they realized that the beggar had really been a demon in disguise and had been responsible for bringing the plague down upon the city.

Probably because of incidents such as this, Apollonius gained a reputation among his contemporaries as a sorcerer and he was refused admission into the Eleusinian Mysteries because the high priest claimed that he was unorthodox in his theology. Unperturbed, Apollonius replied that the real reason the high priest refused to initiate him was because the priest was jealous of his wisdom and wished to humble him before the crowd. When the assembled people applauded Apollonius' bold reply, the high priest swiftly reconsidered and said that the philosopher could be admitted into the Mysteries. To the consternation of the high priest, however, Apollonius refused to be initiated, saying that another priest, whom he named and described as a man of wisdom, would become high priest in four years and that he would initiate Apollonius into the Mysteries.

Apollonius gathered many disciples around him and, together, they visited most of the temples of Greece and Asia Minor. Many of these disciples were mere dilettantes while others, like Damis, were thoughtful and serious students of the doctrines which Apollonius preached. One of the most promising of these disciples was a young man named Menippus whom Apollonius often singled out for praise on account of his remarkable intelligence and unassuming manner. One day, on the road to Cenchreae, Menippus encountered a beautiful young woman who, after engaging the shy youth in a few moments' conversation, looked searchingly into his eyes and proclaimed that she had long been in love with him for he had appeared in her dreams since she was a child. Seduced by her charms, Menippus understandably enough forgot all about philosophy and went to live with her in the beautiful villa which she owned in Corinth.

After several months of drinking the best wine and feasting on the finest foods as well as enjoying the charms of so beautiful a woman, Menippus proclaimed to Apollonius that he was planning to be married and invited the philosopher to the wedding feast. When Apollonius arrived at the celebration, he saw that all of the guests were thoroughly enjoying themselves, drinking excellent wine and playing games in a setting of unparalleled magnificence and luxury. Ignoring all of the revelry, Apollonius approached Menippus and his bride and, gesturing at the luxury which surrounded them, he asked Menippus if all of this belonged to him or to his bride. "Why it all belongs to her," replied Menippus. Apollonius turned to the revelers. "You have all heard of the gardens of Tantalus which appear to travellers in Hades to be real but are, in fact, merely illusions. That is also true of everything which surrounds you here." "What are you saying, Apollonius?" cried Menippus. "That you have been seduced by an illusion as all men are," said Apollonius. "However, in your case it is a much more serious matter for the woman who has captured your soul is no woman at all; she is a vampire!" Aghast, Menippus clutched to his wife who, sobbing hysterically, commanded Apollonius to leave. The philosopher refused to move and with a wave of his hand caused the golden goblets, the silver plate and all the other luxurious appurtenances of the household to disappear. The vampire, realizing that she was in the presence of one far more powerful than she broke down completely and admitted that she had been plying Menippus with luxuries so that she could drink his blood on their wedding night for the blood of the young and innocent was especially beneficent because of its purity. No doubt Menippus was forever discouraged by this experience from neglecting his philosophic duties; as far as is known, he remained a disciple of Apollonius for the rest of his life.

Upon his return from the East, Apollonius was soon besieged by requests from cities all over the Roman Empire to discuss his philosophy and to minister to the sick. For the next several years he travelled from city to city lecturing on such diverse topics as efficient city government and the proper worship of the gods.

Nero was emperor of Rome at this time, a cruel and vain tyrant who believed himself to be a god; not only that, but a god skilled in music, poetry, and athletics. Not the least of his quirks was his hatred of philosophers whom he considered to be troublemakers. Philolaus of Cittium, a distinguished rhetorician and a very careful man, was alarmed by Nero's persecutions of those who wore the philosopher's cloak. Fleeing from Rome, he encountered Apollonius and his disciples travelling in the direction of the Eternal City. Philolaus paused just long enough to warn Apollonius of the dangers that awaited him in Rome if he should dare to flout the emperor's will. Overhearing Philolaus' warning, many of the disciples grew fearful and began making excuses for not continuing with the journey. One claimed to be out of money;

another suddenly began to feel homesick; still others maintained that they had been forewarned in dreams not to enter Rome. This continued until of the thirty-four disciples who had begun the trek to Rome, only eight remained, including the ever-faithful Damis and Menippus. Apollonius was not dismayed by this desertion, however, for he wanted as disciples only men of courage and character. The chance encounter with Philolaus had provided him with an opportunity to rid himself of all the dilettantes who had clustered around him.

When they arrived in Rome the travellers stopped at an inn near the city gate. As they were eating their supper a strolling player entered the inn and began singing some of Nero's songs. Seeing that Apollonius and his companions were ignoring him, the player began to accuse them of public contempt of the emperor. Apollonius merely laughed and threw the singer a few coins telling him to be on his way. The player, a blackmailer and informer, left the inn and went directly to Telesinus, one of the Roman consuls, whom he told of the strangely dressed group of men who seemed to lack respect for the emperor.

The next day Telesinus summoned Apollonius to the palace where he interrogated him about his philosophy. The replies which Apollonius made impressed Telesinus so much that he gave the philosopher written permission to visit all of the temples in Rome and discuss philosophy with whomever he pleased.

Several days later Apollonius, in a public address, made the prophecy that great things would take place and yet would not take place. The meaning of this cryptic pronouncement was not appreciated until, three days later, a cup from which Nero was drinking was struck by lightning. The emperor, shaken but unhurt, began to entertain the suspicion that Apollonius was trying to murder him by magic. In a fit of terror, Nero commanded his prefect, Tigellinus, to question Apollonius and determine whether or not he was a magician. Tigellinus, who was noted for his skill as an interrogator, made the mistake of trying to intimidate Apollonius with threats and abusive treatment. The angrier and more threatening Tigellinus became, the calmer became Apollonius until at last, Tigellinus, thoroughly confused, cried out: "Why do you not fear Nero?" "Because, " replied Apollonius, "the God who has made Nero a tyrant has made me unafraid of tyrants." "Go then," said Tigellinus resignedly, "for neither Nero nor I have any power over you."

Apollonius remained in Rome until he had visited all the temples in the city. Then one day shortly before his departure as he was returning to his lodgings, he happened upon a funeral procession. A young girl had died the day before she was to be married. A long line of mourners followed the bier, some weeping pitifully, others cursing the gods under their breath. Moved by this scene, Apollonius halted the funeral procession and approached the bier. Bending over the dead girl, he whispered a few words into her ear. As he straightened up, the girl's eyelids began to flutter and, in a few moments, she had totally regained consciousness. The girl's grateful family offered Apollonius a large sum of money for performing this marvelous feat which the philosopher duly accepted and gave to the girl to add to her dowry. According to Philostratus, Damis did not believe the girl was actually dead and that Apollonius had merely discerned signs of life in her which the physicians had missed. Apollonius did not take credit for having performed a miracle but the event made such an impression upon the citizens of Rome and the story was so often repeated that Apollonius was widely believed to have the power of bringing the dead back to life.

From Rome Apollonius travelled to Spain and from there to almost every part of the Roman Empire. The deeds which he performed and the philosophy which he taught were in keeping with everything that we already know of him. For that reason, we shall not follow him on his journeys to Africa and Egypt or observe the philosophical disputes in which he so frequently engaged. Before we leave him, however, there is one last scene which should be recorded: his duel with the emperor Domitian.

After Nero had been murdered by a member of his own bodyguard, Rome underwent a year of anarchy during which it was ruled by four different emperors. This period of political instability was brought to an end by the accession of the able general, Vespasian, to the imperial throne in 70 C.E. Vespasian, who consulted Apollonius frequently, was a just and reasonable man as was his eldest son, Titus, who succeeded him after his death in 82 C.E. Titus, however, died after a reign of only one year and Vespasian's third son, Domitian, became emperor. Unlike his father and elder brother, Domitian had little respect for Roman institutions. He declared himself to be the sole ruler of the Roman Empire, an absolute monarch whose commands must be carried out with unquestioning obedience. It was not long before it became evident that Domitian was as great a tyrant as Nero had been and intrigues were devised to have him removed from the imperial throne. In order to forestall these plots, Domitian banished the three men most likely to succeed him to the furthest reaches of the empire. Hearing of the emperor's act, Apollonius exclaimed, "Thou fool! The man who is destined to succeed you will live on, even if you try to kill him." These words were reported to Domitian by Euphrates, a philosopher jealous of Apollonius' fame. Domitian decided to have all three of the men he had banished put to death but, in order to give the whole affair the semblance of legality, he arranged to have Apollonius tried for treason, thinking he could force the philosopher to confess to having conspired with all three of Domitian's enemies to overthrow the emperor.

Apollonius was arrested and subjected to intensive interrogation. As he had done before Nero's prefect, Apollonius once again refused to be led into any false confessions. Finally, the day of his trial arrived and he was brought before Domitian. The emperor informed Apollonius that he was convinced of his guilt and that he planned to have him executed. When Apollonius protested that he had not been allowed to present a defense, Domitian had him bound and ordered his hair to be cut off. Amused, Apollonius remarked, "I did not know I was risking my life on account of my hair."

Proceeding with the trial, Domitian used every device he could think of to intimidate Apollonius. At one point the philosopher was commanded to look at the "god of all men," meaning the emperor. Instead, Apollonius stared at the ceiling, paying homage to Zeus rather than to Domitian. As the trial progressed, the philosopher so impressed the spectators with his wit and courage that they began to applaud him. Sensing potential danger, Domitian thought to clear the hall of spectators and said, "I absolve you of your crimes but I wish to question you further." "I thank you, Sire," replied Apollonius, "but you could not have taken my soul-nay, not even my body, for you cannot slay me, since I am not mortal."
With these words, Apollonius vanished from the court. That same night he was seen at Puteoli, several days travel from Rome, where Damis was waiting for him.

Never again did Domitian attempt to interfere with either

Apollonius or his disciples. The philosopher continued to deliver lectures before large crowds in both Italy and Greece. Then one day, some two years after the trial, Apollonius was speaking to an assembly of freemen in the sacred groves of Ephesus when he suddenly began to clutch at his throat, shouting "strike the tyrant, strike him." On that very day in distant Rome, Domitian was assassinated by a freedman named Stephanus.

Nerva, who succeeded Domitian to the throne, invited Apollonius to Rome but the philosopher was now a hundred years old and did not feel strong enough to make the trip. He replied to Nerva in the form of a letter the delivery of which he entrusted to Damis. It was one of the last kind acts in a life marked to an uncommon degree with kindliness, although not with sentimentality, for while Damis was in Rome Apollonius died. The circumstances of his death are not known but it is probable that he died of old age and was buried in an unmarked grave by his disciples. Thus ended the life of a man who was more than just the simple philosopher he claimed to be, a man who was a rebel, a mystic and, at least so far as many of his contemporaries were concerned, the greatest magician of the age.

Chapter 6:
Simon Magus and
Gnosticism

Apollonius was a leading figure in the revival of Pythagoreanism, representing a trend in Greek thought that owed its inspiration to the Orient. Pythagoras' travels in Egypt and Persia, his ascetic mode of life, and the organization of his esoteric school, all lent verisimilitude to this belief. Not only did Apollonius write an influential biography of Pythagoras, he attempted to repeat his pattern of life, even going Pythagoras one better by visiting India which then, as now, exerted a strong fascination for the Western mind. Of course, Apollonius' Indian journey is improbable. The details presented in Philostratus are not convincing. Still, this story, whether legend or fact, is indicative of the profound respect in which Eastern wisdom was held at this time. Curiously, the great ages of magic always involve romanticizing the past. Great antiquity is equated with great wisdom. This is one of the reasons why Egypt and India have traditionally been regarded by magicians as great centers of magic when, in fact, they were nothing of the kind. Part of the fascination with Egypt lay in its deserts. The puritanism that accompanies dualist thought is nowhere better illustrated than in the strange pilgrimage of holy men to the deserts of Egypt during the early centuries of the Christian era. The Greek word for desert (erimia) was associated with the Greek word for tranquility of the soul (iremia); in fact, the two were often confused in ancient writings. Thus hermits (erimitis), solitary citizens of the deserts, were considered by many to be exemplars of the spiritual life.

Figure 2
Gnostic Gem

Dualism, asceticism, puritanism, and romanticizing the past: these were the earmarks of magical religions in late antiquity. These characteristics are all strikingly evident in that curious assortment of beliefs and practices, so important to the history of magic, usually lumped under the rubric of Gnosticism.

Gnosticism is not easy to describe because it was not a single religion with well-developed beliefs held in common but, rather, a variety of separate cults, each with its own myths and dogmas, sharing, at best, only a certain attitude of mind.

Simon Magus, who appears briefly in the New Testament, is generally thought to be the first Gnostic. He was a travelling magician with pretensions to divinity. Simon's constant companion was a woman named Helen who, the magus maintained, was a reincarnation of the divine Helen for whom the Trojan War had been fought. Simon believed, in opposition to Christian doctrine, that the world had been created, not by God, but by a demiurge. According to a passage in the Pseudo-Clementines, Simon is reported to have said that "he who framed the world is not the highest God, but that the highest God is another who alone is good and who has remained unknown up to this time."

The Gnostic doctrine of the demiurge, as articulated by Simon, provided a satisfactory dualist answer to the problem of evil. If the world was the scene of suffering and evil, it was not the fault of God or the Nous, who remained above and beyond the material world; the demiurge, a powerful but spiritually inferior being, was the sole author of evil. Simon represented himself as a redeemer who descended through the higher spheres to the material world in order to show the way to the path of redemption. Proof of his divine origin lay in the miracles which he performed, miracles analogous to those of Jesus and Apollonius. It seems probable that Simon was slandered by Christian writers who took a dim view of his claims. The Christian account of his end is certainly entertaining but doubtless apocryphal: Converting briefly to Christianity in order to learn the magic of the apostles, Simon was disillusioned to discover that such magic could not be learned, for it was the result of the gift of grace from God. He grew jealous of the apostles, especially Peter, whom he challenged to a magical duel before Nero. In an attempt to prove his divinity, Simon claimed that he could fly. Leaping off a high tower, he was, at first, successful but

Peter, fearful that Simon's feat might seduce his own followers away from Christianity, prayed to God. Suddenly the magus faltered in his flight and plummeted to earth. Simon's tragic end has provided the inspiration for a host of legends concerning the fate of magicians who aspire to forbidden heights, including the legend of Faust.

The Gnostic sect founded by Simon, the Simonites, does not seem to have been very widespread. Hostile Christian sources maintained that it never exceeded thirty in number. Other Gnostic groups, perhaps springing up independently of one another, were more popular. Among these were the Ophites, the Basilideans and the Valentinians.

Some Gnostics borrowed at least part of their inspiration from the teachings of Jesus. The **Pistis-Sophia**, a Gnostic text of the third century C. E., is representative of this kind of borrowing, providing in addition a good summary of basic Gnostic tenets. Supposedly presenting the revelations of Jesus to his disciples after his ascent into heaven and his return, The **Pistis-Sophia** contains a lengthy description of the various spiritual spheres through which Jesus passed in the upward journey of his soul. Twenty-four spheres separate heaven from earth, each ruled over by an archon (or aeon). In order to pass through these spheres the traveler must know a variety of secret keys and passwords. These constitute the gnosis (knowledge) which alone guarantees entry into heaven. Allusions to secret mysteries contained in each of the twenty-four spheres as well as references to a whole host of signs, marks, keys, and talismans are to be found throughout the **Pistis-Sophia**. The most important concept contained in this work is that of gnosis. Gnosis constitutes knowledge of a special kind, revealed knowledge, which could only be obtained by concentrating on the faint spark of divinity contained in the soul of each man. Gnosis is spiritual knowledge that confers magical power on the worshipper, enabling him to control his own salvation.

This is the potent idea that Gnosticism bequeathed to the philosophy of magic. Knowledge begets power and the way to obtain knowledge is by exploring the unknown regions of the soul.

How, exactly, the Gnostics performed such explorations is not known but, according to hostile Christian writers, they employed various kinds of magical techniques, the goal of which was to achieve a state of altered consciousness in which they were enabled to penetrate the mysteries of the supernatural. Dualist Gnostics were pessimists. As Hans Jonas has pointed out, Gnostic dualism results in a view of the world as the "product, and even the embodiment, of the negative of knowledge... Power thus becomes the chief aspect of the cosmos, and its inner essence is ignorance (agnosia). To this, the positive complement is that the essence of man is knowledge--knowledge of self and of God: this determines his situation as that of the potentially knowing in the midst of the unknowing, of light in the midst of darkness, and this relation is at the bottom of his being alien, without companionship in the darkness of the universe." The dualism is thus complete. Not simply the body, but the entire material universe is seen by the Gnostics as a prison, a tomb.

It is not surprising that Gnostic magic was, according to many reports, unusually powerful for magic is a central element in all dualistic world-views and the greater the sense of dualism, the greater need there is for a magic of power capable of transcending it.

The discovery in 1947 of a treasure trove of Gnostic manuscripts near Nag Hammadi in Egypt and their subsequent translation into the major European languages in the mid-1970s has given rise to a scholarly dispute about the origins of Gnosticism. Did Gnosticism arise out of Judaeo-Christianity in the first century C.E. or did it have non-Christian, especially Hellenistic roots as well?

For our purposes, the question of origin is irrelevant. To view Gnosticism as simply an early Christian heresy is to overlook the richness of its contribution to Western thought. We know that Gnosticism was expressed in Hellenistic language. The Gnostic concept of the demiurge is based on Plato's Timaeus which, as we have seen, was itself derived from Pythagoras' dyad. But in Gnosticism the demiurge is a principle of evil, the creator of the universe with all of its attendant sufferings and misfortunes.

Still, as Dan Merkur has argued, too much can be made of Gnostic dualism and the Gnostics' rejection of the material world. The key Gnostic contribution to mysticism and magic, says Merkur, ". . .was not its anticosmic dualism but a distinctive type of visionary experience. The visions were not regarded as ['extrasensory'] perceptions of objectively existing eternal realities. . .Gnostics recognized their visions as subjective mental experiences whose contents varied from moment to moment and individual to individual."

Gnostics underwent a spiritual journey through seven heavens to the eighth heaven, the Ogdoad (or Nous). Each of the seven heavens was governed by an archon. The leader of the archons was the demiurge. Within this broad framework there were a variety of possible structures. Take, for example, the Gnostic text On the Origin of the World, which probably dates from the fourth century. The demiurge Yaldabaoth creates "seven evil heavens: 'Seven appeared in chaos, androgynous. . .They are the [seven] forces of the seven heavens [of chaos].' Repenting in response to a revelation by Pistis, Sophia, the feminine portion of the sixth power, leagued with Sabaoth, the masculine portion of the second power, to overthrow Yaldabaoth, their father and creator, who had the seventh heaven as his place of rule. The 'great war in the seven heavens' ended with the repentant Sabaoth ruling 'over everyone so that he might dwell above the twelve gods of chaos.' Sabaoth made his abode 'in the eighth heaven,' the Ogdoad, where he made himself "a mansion. . .huge, magnificent, seven times as great as all those that exist in the seven heavens.'"

Another important element of Gnosticism was the belief in a redeemer who descended from the Ogdoad to earth to transmit his teachings and then rose again to the Ogdoad. The redeemer was sometimes Jesus but many other names were used as well, including Seth, Adam, Enoch, Sophia, Nous, and Logos.

The visions that Gnostics experienced were quite various and, unfortunately, the surviving texts tell us little about their methods for inducing visions. One of the most remarkable records of such a vision comes from the Zostrianos:

"There stood before me the angel of the knowledge of eternal light, He said to me, 'Zostrianos. . .'

"When he had said this, I very quickly and very gladly went up with him to a great light-cloud. I cast my body upon the earth to be guarded by glories. I was rescued from the whole world and the thirteen aeons [archons] in it and their angelic beings. . .

"Then I knew that the power in me was set over the darkness because it contained the whole light. I was baptized there, and I received the image of the glories there. I became like one of them."

In their ascent through the heavens, Gnostics used talismans as keys to bypass the archons and amulets to protect themselves against evil influences present in each heaven or sphere of creation.

The influence of Gnosticism has been immense. Latin Christianity eradicated Gnosticism in the West. But in the East, it flourished in the form of Manicheism until that too was suppressed by Islam in the seventh century. Gnostic influences in the Middle Ages may be found in the Bogomils, the Albigensians (or Cathari) of northern Spain and southern France. More important for our purposes, Gnosticism influenced the development of Later Pythagoreanism, Hermetism, the Cabala, and Sufism, with their emphasis on achieving ecstatic states and merging with the Nous.

In the twentieth century, Karl Jung has emphasized Gnostic concepts in his depth psychology and Hans Jonas has explored the parallels between Gnosticism and existentialism. G.I. Gurdjieff introduced a cosmological and psychological system to the West, called the "Fourth Way, which owes much to Gnosticism and which Gurdjieff described as "esoteric Christianity." This ancient "heresy" still has much to teach us.

Chapter 7:
Neo-Pythagoreanism

Scholars have dubbed the school of thinkers represented by Plotinus, Proclus, Porphyry and Iamblichus as Neo-Platonists.* But they are better viewed as Pythagoreans, not Platonists. Porphyry and Iamblichus both wrote biographies of Pythagoras. Plotinus' teacher was a Pythagorean. In essence, the philosophical project of this school was to rescue Plato from the aridities of the surviving Platonic Academy and reintroduce the Pythagorean elements of Plato's thought into the mainstream of philosophy.

It is difficult to tell to what degree Gnosticism (itself to some extent a product of Pythagoreanism) influenced the neo-Pythagoreans. Certainly Plotinus, the greatest of the neo-Pythagoreans, inveighed against the Gnostics' contempt for the world and severely criticized Gnostic magic. On the other hand, Plotinus articulated an emanationist philosophy that is not far removed from Gnostic conceptions. The chief difference is that Plotinus believed in a fundamentally monist universe, rejecting the radical metaphysical dualism of the "pessimist" Gnostics.

According to Plotinus, reality is a series of emanations from the One, the source of all being. The first emanation is that of Nous, (intelligence, mind, the ground of being). The second emanation is that of Psyche (soul). Matter is to be found at the periphery of the Plotinian universe and is conceived to be that which participates least in the pure

---

*Peter Kingsley has reminded us that the terms neo-Pythagoreanism, neo-Platonism, and Middle Platonism are constructs created by modern scholars and have limited explanatory power for the philosophical and magical traditions they purport to describe. I have chosen to use the term neo-Platonist only to refer to the Renaissance Platonists. See Kingsley's instructive study of Empedocles and the Pythagorean tradition, **Ancient Philosophy, Mystery, and Magic** (Oxford, 1995).

being of the One. Man, part spirit and part matter, can attain to a knowledge of the One through concentrating on the inner, spiritual self. In essence, what Plotinus has done to Gnostic cosmogony is to eliminate the demiurge, the Gnostic Satanic principle. (He also seemingly eliminated the Pythagorean dyad, although Psyche could be interpreted as a benevolent version of the dyad.) At the human level, however, the dualism between body and soul, matter and spirit, usually found in magical philosophies, still obtains.

Plotinus has usually been regarded as an opponent of magic, largely on the basis of several passages in which he argues that the object of his philosophy is, at least in part, to free man from the influence of magic by adopting a life of reason and spiritual contemplation. It should be noted that the word Plotinus uses in this context is goetia, rendered better as "sorcery." In other words, Plotinus is opposed to the popular magic of his day, magic which acts on man's passive nature through the agencies of herb and incantation, transitive magic of the lowest kind.

Whether Plotinus was also opposed to the imaginative magic called theurgy advocated by such later neo-Pythagoreans as Iamblichus is difficult to tell. Theurgy has usually been considered to be an elaboration of the later, more decadent (in the eyes of modern scholars) followers of the Pythagorean/Platonic tradition.

But two incidents in Plotinus' life reported by Porphyry suggest Plotinus may have been a believer in magic. The first concerns the attempt by Olympius, a magician who was jealous of Plotinus, to harm the philosopher by directing star-rays against him. Plotinus was not only able to resist Olympius' spells but even turned them back on the magician. The second incident involves a séance at which Plotinus was present. According to Porphyry, Plotinus accepted the invitation of an Egyptian priest to attend the evocation of a (good) demon. When, instead of a demon, a god appeared, the priest was amazed. (He was attempting to evoke Plotinus' familiar, the demon or, in Christian terms, the guardian angel which was thought to oversee each individual's actions.) The priest congratulated Plotinus for having a god as his familiar spirit and the jealousy or fear of the other persons present soon caused the god to disappear.

On the basis of these two stories, coupled with an analysis of various aspects of Plotinus' philosophy, the scholar Philip Merlan came to the conclusion that Plotinus not only recognized the efficacy of magic (a fact recognized by most scholars) but was also not above practicing it on occasion. As Merlan says, "This reminds us that indeed Plotinus' universe is a magic universe. . . It is obvious for him that because of the principle. . .of universal sympathy. . . every part of the universe is in rapport with some other part. It is for this reason that the stars and powers can influence us. . .And precisely for the same reason we can influence them--or for that matter any of the occult powers permeating the universe."

Whether or not Plotinus practiced theurgy, there is no question that many of his followers did. Theurgy, however, was not an invention of the neo-Pythagorean school. According to Dodds, the first practitioner of theurgy of whom we have any knowledge was Julianus, who lived during the reign of Marcus Aurelius. In all probability, Julianus wished to distinguish between discussing the gods and his own practice of manipulating them or, as Dodds suggests, even creating them. He is thought to have been the author of the Chaldean Oracles, a work that profoundly influenced the magic of late antiquity and of the Renaissance. The Juliani, followers of Julianus, possessed a considerable reputation as magicians. Julianus' son was reputed to have caused the thunderstorm that saved the army of Marcus Aurelius from destruction in 173 A.D. Also Julianus is depicted in Christian legend as a more powerful magician than either Apollonius or Apuleius. Julianus' most important legacy was not his reputation as a magician but the techniques which he outlined in the Chaldean Oracles for achieving communion with and control of the gods. The theurgy of Julianus caught the imagination of Proclus and Iamblichus who elaborated upon and refined theurgic ritual and incorporated it into later neo-Pythagorean philosophy.

Theurgy, as developed by the neo-Pythagoreans, involved two fundamental procedures: telestiki, the incarnating of the spirit of a god in a material object such as a statue for purposes of divination and katokhos or dokheus, the temporary incarnation of a god in a particular human being.

Telestiki was accomplished through the magical use of talismans and invocations. Also known as the "understanding warmed by fire," telestiki was preceded by long periods of silence and fasting. Words as well as amulets were used to put the petitioner in contact with the god. In all likelihood, drugs, probably mild opium derivatives, were used to help induce the appropriate trance state.

Katokhus, on the other hand, was imaginative magic of the highest kind. The theurgist prepared himself for katokhos by donning a special garment and purifying himself with fire and water. He also wore a garland around his neck and a girdle with images engraven on it which corresponded to the deity being invoked. Then in a way which unfortunately is not clearly described, the theurgist induced in himself a trance state and commanded the god to appear. It is important to point out at this juncture that the theurgist did not merely request the god to enter his body but actually compelled him to do so. In this way theurgy differs from the mystical tradition which holds that illumination is the consequence of a spontaneous act of grace on the part of the divine and has nothing to do with the will of the subject. Theurgy should also be distinguished from modern spiritualism to which it bears a superficial resemblance. The theurgist aimed at invoking a particular supernatural presence and controlled the entire operation from first to last. The spiritualist, on the other hand, is at the mercy of whatever being (most of them decidedly inferior to judge from the transcripts of séances) who chooses to appear at a given time. The state of consciousness achieved by the theurgist, then, should not be confused with the passive trance state of the medium. The theurgist actively controls; he does not quiescently submit.

As Dodds remarks, "besides revealing past or future . . . the gods vouchsafed visible (or occasionally audible) signs of their presence. The medium's (theurgist's) person might be visibly elongated or dilated or even levitated. But the manifestations usually took the form of luminous apparitions. . ." The object of theurgy was, in general, to achieve an illuminated state of consciousness which enabled one to commune with the gods, even to be, temporarily, a god oneself. Of course the theurgist believed in the reality of the gods he invoked; that goes without saying. He did not aim, however, at transitive magic; nor was he merely content to achieve communion with the lesser spirits (daemons). The theurgist aimed at penetrating the highest spiritual realm which he believed existed, that of the gods.

Underlying the practice of theurgy, as Georg Luck has pointed out, are four principles: "(1) the principle of power. . .; (2) the principle of cosmic sympathy. . .; (3) the principle of sameness. . .; (4) the idea of the soul-vehicle.. ."

The principle of power simply means that power is available to those who know how to access it. Cosmic sympathy describes the intimate relationship of everything in the cosmos, regardless of how trivial it may seem. Sameness means that there is a similarity, however small, between man and the gods. And the soul-vehicle is "a kind of astral body that we have; the gods have one too." These four principles are the preconditions for theurgy, which aims at the achievement of visionary ecstasy.

By providing theurgy with a coherent philosophic rationale, the neo-Pythagorean theurgists raised the practice of magic to a much higher level than it had hitherto enjoyed. Its influence on the magical tradition is incalculable. Resurfacing in the Renaissance and again in the magic of the Golden Dawn and its offshoots in the late nineteenth and early twentieth centuries, theurgy has continued to evoke a profound vision of the most elevated form of transcendental magic.

It chanced once on a time my mind was meditating on the things that are, my thought was raised to a great height, the senses of my body being held back—just as men who are weighed down with sleep after a fill of food, or from fatigue of body.

Methought a Being more than vast, in size beyond all bounds, called out my name and saith: What wouldst thou hear and see, and what hast thou in mind to learn and know?

And I do say: Who art thou?

He saith: I am Man-Shepherd, mind of all-masterhood; I know what thou desirest and I'm with thee everywhere.

And I reply: I long to learn the things that are, and comprehend their nature, and know God. This is, I said, what I desire to hear.

He answered back to me: Hold in thy mind all thou wouldst know, and I will teach thee.

Even with these words His aspect changed, and straightway, in the twinkling of an eye, all things were opened to me, and I saw a Vision limitless, all things turned into Light—sweet, joyous Light. And I became transported as I gazed.

From the
Poimandres,*Hermetic*
treatise of the third century C.E.

Chapter 8:
Hermes Trismegistus

Arising from the same historical context as Gnosticism and neo-Pythagoreanism, the anonymous writings ascribed to Hermes Trismegistus have had a profound influence on the history of magic because of the eminence of their supposed author and the reputed antiquity of their origin. Hermes Trismegistus was no ordinary being; on the contrary, he was a god, the Egyptian god Thoth, who was later identified by Hellenic settlers in Egypt with the Greek Hermes. A cult devoted to the worship of Hermes apparently flourished in Egypt in the third century C.E., contemporary with Plotinus, producing a variety of devotional texts the authorship of which was ascribed, (whether out of piety or a conscious effort to deceive, it's impossible to say) to Hermes.

Hermes was believed to have lived in the remote past, perhaps contemporary with or even prior to Moses. No one knows for certain exactly how many books the original Hermetic corpus consisted of. Tradition maintained that they numbered 36,525 (an obviously mystical number based on the number of days in the year, 365 1/4). In any event, only fourteen have survived, along with a few short fragments of related material.

On the basis of these texts, Hermetism appears to have been a magical religion which bore a close resemblance to Gnosticism. Indeed, Hans Jonas regards Hermetism, or at least the Hermetic treatise, the Poimandres, as essentially Gnostic. The greatest modern authority on Hermetism, A. J. Festugière, also believed it to have been profoundly influenced by Gnosticism. Festugière has classified the Hermetic texts on the basis of whether they exhibit "optimist" or "pessimist" gnosis.

Optimist gnosis, in Festugière's view, is predicated on a belief in a divine principle suffusing the universe. In this respect it resembles the metaphysical monism of Plotinus. Pessimist gnosis, on the other hand, derives from a dualistic conception of the universe and is more directly related to the Gnostic tradition.

The "optimist gnosis" of the Hermetic corpus is reflected in such writings as The Mind to Hermes:

"All beings are in God but not as though they are placed in a place, for it is not thus that they are placed in the incorporeal faculty of representation. Judge of this from your own experience. Command your soul to be in India, to cross the ocean; in a moment it will be done. Command it to fly up to heaven. It will not need wings; nothing can prevent it. And if you wish to break through the vault of the universe and to contemplate what is beyond - if there is anything beyond the world - you may do it."

As Frances Yates comments, "The gnosis consists in reflecting the world within the mind, for so shall we know the God who made it."

The account of creation given in the Hermetic corpus corresponds to that of the Gnostics. The Nous appears to Hermes Trismegistus creating a vision of absolute light. "That light is I myself, Nous, thy God.. . .and the luminous Word issuing from the Nous is the Son of God "

The Nous brings forth the Demiurge which unites with the Word (Logos) creating the seven Governors of the material or sensible world.

"Now the Nous, father of all beings, being life and light, brought forth a Man similar to Himself, whom he loved as his own child. For the Man was beautiful, reproducing the image of his Father; for it was indeed with his own form that God fell in love and gave over to him all his works. Now, when he saw the creation which the Demiurge had fashioned in the fire, the Man wished also to produce a work, and permission to do this was given him by the Father. . ."

Man takes on a material body in order to unite with Nature and thus becomes, in all creation, the only being that is both mortal and divine. The union of Man and Nature produces out of the divine androgyny the separation of sexes into male and female and all the other manifestations of the material world. The Nous tells Hermes Trismegistus "You are light and life, like God the Father of whom Man was born. If therefore you learn to know yourself as made of light and life. . .you will return to life." The secret knowledge transmitted by the Nous inspires Hermes to convey the message to the world that Man can achieve divinity by ascending through the spheres of creation, shedding at each sphere a part of that which makes him mortal, until he reaches the Ogdoad and becomes intermingled with the Divine.

Hermetists practiced a kind of theurgy similar to that of neo-Pythagoreanism. Great emphasis is placed on the ability of man to communicate with the gods: "For it is possible, my son, that a man's soul should be made like to God, even while it is still in a body, if it doth contemplate the Beauty of the Good." Some of the texts describe the upward journey of the soul through the planetary spheres to the higher spiritual levels beyond. In all of the texts there is an atmosphere of intense piety and devotion and a powerful belief in the magical ability of man to assume any form he chooses:

"O Holy Thoth, the true sight of whose face none of the gods endures! Make me to be in every creature's name (or "true form")--wolf, dog, or lion, fire, tree, or vulture, wall, or water, or what thou will'st, for thou art able to do so."

And again:

"No darkness of the air obstructs the penetration of his mind. No density of earth impedes his work. No depth of water blunts his sight.

"Though still the same, yet he is all, and everywhere is he the same."

The Hermetists held a noble view of human spiritual potential, as witness this passage from the Hermetic corpus:

"Man is a divine being, to be compared not with the other earthly beings, but with those who are called gods, up in the heavens. Rather, if one must dare to speak the truth, the true Man is above even the gods, or at least fully their equal. . .We must presume then to say that earthly Man is a mortal god, and that the celestial God is an immortal man. And so it is through these two, the world and Man, that all things exist; but they were all created by the One."

One of the most remarkable and eloquent passages in the Hermetic literature is found in the Asclepius. Sometimes called The Lament, it prophesies the end of the Egyptian Hermetic religion:

"There will come a time when it will be seen that in vain have the Egyptians honoured the divinity with a pious mind and with assiduous

Figure 3
Hermes Trismegistus

service. All their holy worship will become inefficacious. The gods, leaving the earth, will go back to heaven; they will abandon Egypt; this land, once the home of religion, will be widowed of its gods and left destitute. . .Only the evil angels will remain who will mingle with men, and constrain them by violence. . .to all the excesses of criminal audacity. . .Such will be the old age of the world, irreligion, disorder, confusion of all goods. When all these things have come to pass, O Asclepius, then the Lord and Father, the god first in power and the demiurge of the One God . . .will annihilate all malice. . .Then he will bring back the world to its first beauty, so that this world may again be worthy of reverence and admiration. . .That is what the rebirth of the world will be; a renewal of all good things, a holy and most solemn restoration of Nature herself, imposed by force in the course of time. . .by the will of God."

Despite the elevated tone of much of the Hermetic corpus, it would not have been so influential had not so many respected authors believed firmly in its antiquity. Pagan writers like Iamblichus and Christians like Lactantius and Tertullian vouched for the age and authenticity of the Hermetic writings. During the Middle Ages Hermetism survived only in fragments and in the Latin translation of the Asclepius which was falsely attributed to Apuleius of Madaura. Even in such a dispersed form, it proved to be remarkably influential. It was in the Renaissance, however, when the texts of the Hermetic corpus which are known to us today were rediscovered and translated, that its influence reached unprecedented heights for the Renaissance neo-Platonists believed, on good authority, in the antiquity and even the divine inspiration of these magico-religious writings.

Conclusion

The magus was viewed by the classical world as virtually a superhuman being. Unlike the lowly sorcerer who commanded inferior demons and concocted love potions, the magus could communicate with gods, command them, even become a god himself. Although never widespread, the higher magic of the antique world was the product of a rich tradition combining, at different times, the legacies of Pythagoras and Plato, Gnosticism, neo-Pythagoreanism, Hermetism, and the mystery religions of the East.

It was a proud tradition, affirming human dignity without reducing respect and veneration for the gods. It was, of course, confined to a spiritual and intellectual elite and this, in the end, proved to be its downfall. A spiritual discipline which promised illumination to the few found itself unable to compete with a faith that promised salvation to the many.

Part Two:
The Magus as Heretic

Chapter 9:
Magic in the Middle Ages

During the early middle ages the Christian Church was successful in establishing a monopoly on magic. Official magic, the magic of church and saint was distinguished from unofficial magic which was indiscriminately labeled as sorcery. Miracles were wrought by the saints through the power of God but the same miracles when performed by a pagan or a heretic were clearly the work of the devil. The Ecumenical Council held at Laodicea in 364 C.E. forbade priests from dabbling in magic or astrology. Other church councils such as the one at Oxia in 525 and the Councils of Tours and Rome in the seventh and eighth centuries prohibited laymen from consulting diviners of any kind, ordered priests to teach that sorcery was ineffective as a method of healing, and provided excommunication as the punishment for violating these prohibitions. It is difficult to tell how effective the church was in rooting out magical practices. The Council of Leptines, meeting at Hainaut in the eighth century thought magic to be endemic throughout Europe and charged that far too many professed Christians were secret pagans. Nevertheless, it appears that ecclesiastical authority, reinforced by secular rulers such as Charlemagne, succeeded in keeping magical practices at the level of popular superstition.

There was nothing very sophisticated about early medieval magic; it perpetuated pagan practice while dispensing with pagan philosophy. The church, of course, maintained a monopoly on the magical texts of antiquity and used them to its own ends. Neo-Pythagoreanism, for example, formed the basis of a wholly respectable Christian mystical tradition while its magical implications were officially ignored.

Medieval magic did not come into its own until the twelfth and thirteenth centuries. During this period western Europe began to reestablish contacts with the East, partially through trade but primarily through warfare as Christendom embarked on its quixotic campaign to free the Holy Land from the clutches of the infidel. Valuable texts which had been lost to the West for centuries were discovered and translated into Latin. As well as preserving much of the magical lore of antiquity, the Arabs had done extensive work in magic themselves. Such Arab philosophers as Thebit ben Corat, Albumusar, and Avicenna soon began to exert a powerful influence on European intellectuals both within and without the church. The Arab philosophy of magic did not depend on the invocation of demons for it taught that all events were naturally caused even though the causes might be difficult to discern. Among the natural causes believed to be operative on mankind by the Arabs were the movements of the planets and the activities of the mind. It was precisely this "natural" magic which fascinated the medieval mind, reaching its highest development in the Renaissance.

One of the earliest medieval scholars to become interested in Arab magic was Michael Scotus (1175-1234). Little is known about Michael's early life, although it is generally assumed that he was born in Scotland and emigrated to England as a young man. We first hear of him as a student attending Oxford University. Apparently filled with that restless desire for knowledge which was characteristic of so many twelfth and thirteenth century intellectuals, Michael left Oxford to go to the Sorbonne where he studied for a few years, eventually attaining the title of mathematicus. During the next several years the young Scot wandered all over Europe tarrying for a while at Bologna and Palermo and, finally, in 1217, settling down at the great center of Arabic learning in the West, Toledo, in Spain. During his stay, Michael learned Arabic and began translating a number of important texts into Latin. He soon became so famous for his learning that he was invited to become court astrologer at the most brilliant and glittering court of the age, that of Frederick II at Palermo in Sicily.

Frederick was doubtless the most learned monarch who ever lived. He spoke at least nine languages, including Arabic, wrote poetry which was later to win the praise of Dante, and was fascinated enough by mathematics to cajole the Sultan of Egypt into sending his leading mathematician to his court. Michael Scotus was sufficiently impressed with the emperor's learning to exclaim, "I verily believe that if ever a man could escape death by his learning it would be you."

Frederick established the University of Naples during his reign in order to perpetuate the knowledge which had been gathered by the various scholars he had assembled at his court. It is recorded that Michael taught at this university for a time and then returned to England, bringing with him translations of several works by Aristotle (which, until that time, were unknown in England) as well as works on astrology and alchemy. After this his career becomes hazy once more and we have only legend to rely on to assert that he probably died in 1234 on a visit to Scotland. Naturally enough, since he made no efforts to conceal his interest in magic and astrology, a number of legends are attached to his name.

For example, when he was sent by the king of Scotland on a diplomatic mission to France, he used magic to cause the bells of Notre Dame to ring and so frightened the French king that he agreed to all the concessions which Michael asked of him.

A younger contemporary of Michael Scotus, much influenced by him, was Roger Bacon (1214-1294?). As a child, Bacon was said to have been unusually precocious, particularly in mathematics. Like Michael Scotus, Bacon studied at Oxford and Paris, specializing in mathematics and medicine. Throughout his long life, he displayed impatience with the elaborate and arid philosophizing of his time and argued for a philosophy built upon observation and experiment. He himself performed few experiments, although it is alleged that his alchemical work with nitre paved the way for the development of gunpowder.

His reputation as a precursor of modern science rests chiefly on his **Opus Maius, Opus Minus** and **Opus Tertium**. On the surface, these treatises appear to be essentially anti-magical in their intent for Bacon frequently railed against magicians and their ilk who pervert the true principles of nature. Nevertheless, it is evident that Bacon, as a good Franciscan Friar, was denouncing the kind of low magic which the church had always denounced. Natural magic, directed toward beneficent ends, met with his full approval.

Part of Bacon's reputation as a dabbler in the occult surely rests on his amazing prophecies of modern scientific achievements, prophecies which, although unusual, could still have been the product of a fertile imagination rather than the result of any peculiar precognitive abilities. Still, when one comes across some of these odd passages, it is difficult to believe that they were written in the thirteenth century:

"A fifth part of experimental science concerns the fabrication of instruments of wonderfully excellent usefulness, such as machines for flying, or for moving in vehicles without animals and yet with incomparable speed, or of navigating without oarsmen more swiftly than would be thought possible through the hands of men. . . Flying machines can be made, and a man sitting in the middle of the machine may revolve some ingenious device by which artificial wings may beat the air in the manner of a flying bird. . . Also machines can be made for walking in the sea and the rivers, even to the bottom, without danger."

Possibly as a result of publishing such wild imaginings as these, but more likely as a consequence of his criticisms of the Dominicans, Bacon was imprisoned by the church in 1277. His teachings were charged to have contained "some suspected novelties," a curious phrase which could refer to anything from a mild theological deviation to the practice of magic. It is not certain how long Bacon spent in prison but he was apparently free in 1292 for he published a book in that year. Not long after this he died, although the date and the place are uncertain.

Albertus Magnus, who was born in 1205, belonged to the rival Dominican order and seemed to take an even greater interest in magic than the Franciscan Bacon. Allusions to magic, alchemy and astrology are sprinkled throughout his works and he devoted an entire treatise to the occult properties of gems. Like a number of other medieval figures, including Robert Grosseteste and Pope Gregory VII, Albertus Magnus was alleged to have constructed a brass head which spoke perfect Latin and foretold the future. Another legend states that the philosopher devoted thirty years to building an entire man out of brass. Unfortunately, the brass man was something of a nuisance since it felt that its power to speak conferred an obligation to do so and it kept up such a constant stream of chatter that Thomas Aquinas (then a pupil of Albertus) flew into a rage and smashed it to pieces. On another occasion, while Albertus was lecturing at the University of Paris, he invited some friends to his home. When they arrived, he suggested that they all go out into the garden for luncheon. Since it was the dead of winter, the guests were extremely reluctant to comply with their host's request.

Eventually Albertus persuaded them that all would be well and, to their astonishment, when they entered the garden the sun beamed bright and warm upon them, the snow vanished and the birds began to sing.

Despite such apocryphal stories, most of which originated in the Renaissance, Albertus was not a sorcerer but a natural philosopher. Like many of the other philosophers of his age, he took an avid interest in the new magic as well as the new science of the Arabs. He was undoubtedly motivated by religious ideals but we begin to see in him, as in Michael Scotus and Roger Bacon, an impulse toward the acquisition of knowledge which could be described as secular. Each of them was careful to make their obeisances toward the church but each also seems to have realized that he was embarking on an odyssey of the intellect which the church might not sanction.

Chapter 10:
The Cabala

Jewish mysticism predates the development of the Cabala*. Even before the birth of Jesus, secret interpretations of the creation story and certain chapters of Ezekiel were circulated throughout the Jewish community. Marvelous powers were ascribed to the Tetragrammaton, the four letters comprising the Hebrew name for God, which could be written but never spoken. Jewish sects like the Essenes possessed secret writings which they showed to no one but the initiated.

The Jewish Hellenistic philosopher Philo, living in the first century C.E., expounded a mystical philosophy based on the Logos, the divine word of God. Many influences were brought to bear on Jewish mysticism, especially after the Diaspora. Zoroastrian dualism, neo-Pythagorean number mysticism and the theory of emanations, Gnosticism, even the mysticism of the medieval church have all left traces of their contacts with the Jews, especially in the most elaborate and complex of all mystical and magical systems, the Cabala.

Various theories have been adduced to explain the origins of the Cabala. The early Cabalists themselves believed that the Sefer-Yetzirah or Book of Creation had been composed by God and Abraham. Others have argued that it was a product of the first century C.E. when Judaism was beginning to feel the impact of Gnosticism and Christianity. Still others maintain that it was written by Babylonian Jews during the Geonim period, probably around the sixth century. None of these theories are entirely satisfactory for they depend largely on internal evidence, the kind of vocabulary employed in the **Sefer-Yetzirah**, its philo-

---

*The term Cabala has been subject to at least as many different spellings as the name of Libyan leader Mohamar Khadafi (Kabbala, Kabbalah, Qu'aballah, etc.) I have settled for the shortest.

sophical structure, and so on. It may be that the **Sefer-Yetzirah** was the written summary of a long and secret oral tradition, in which case internal evidence would only show when it was written and not necessarily when it originated. In any event, we first hear of the **Sefer-Yetzirah** in the ninth century when it was apparently introduced to the West from Babylon.

The **Sefer-Yetzirah** rapidly became popular among European Jews, inspiring a number of commentaries and new works along similar lines which, before long, were given the collective name of the Cabala, or "secret tradition." The most important of these later Cabalistic classics was the **Zohar**, or **Book of Splendor**, published in 1295, and probably written by the Jewish scholar Moses de Leon.

During most of the late middle ages the Cabala all but replaced the Talmud as the source of religious authority for the Jews. The Talmud, many Jews argued, was too cold, too austere, too remote, to serve as the holy book of the Hebrews. The Cabala, on the other hand, provided a comprehensive outline of the structure of the universe and, more important, demonstrated a method by which it was possible for the believer to transcend the mundane world and achieve knowledge of the divine. The Cabala, as we shall see, could also be used to achieve more immediately practical ends and practical Cabala, or in other words, sorcery, became extremely popular among European Jews.

The Cabala also had an impact upon Christian thinkers, especially during the Renaissance. Even earlier such Christians as the great Spanish mystic Ramon Lull (1235?-1315) believed much of the Cabala to be divinely inspired. Lull incorporated the number and letter mysticism which he had learned from studying the Cabala into his famous Ars Magna while other Christians claimed to have found everything in the Cabala from proof of Christ's divinity to the formula for the philosopher's stone.

We shall make no attempt to give anything like a complete interpretation of the Cabala in these pages. Such a task would be literally impossible. Most Cabalists study for years before they are able to attain even a glimmer of understanding of what the Cabala is all about. Because of its enormous influence, however, the broad outline of Cabalistic doctrine will be discussed. We will begin with the **Sefer-Yetzirah**.

The creation of the universe, according to the **Sefer-Yetzirah**, was accomplished through the ten sephiroth (numbers or principles), emanations from God. The doctrine of emanations was probably neo-Pythagorean in origin for, like the neo-Pythagoreans, the authors of the Sefer-Yetzirah wished to account for the existence of evil without blaming God for it. God had not willed the creation; His divine energy could simply not be contained and consequently radiated outward from Him in the form of sephiroth. That there were ten and not nine or seven sephiroth is again probably due to neo-Pythagoreanism which taught that the numbers from one to ten form the essence of all things. The sephiroth are usually arranged hierarchically in a diagram known as "The Tree of Life." The symbolism of the tree was probably used because it represented apparent multiplicity (the branches) linked together in an underlying unity. This arrangement of the sephiroth also represented Adam Kadmon, the primeval man, of which earthly men are only the insubstantial shadows

The first emanation, Kether, is the Spirit of God, the Divine One, absolute unity. Its symbol is the Crown.

The second emanation, Hokmah, is the principle of creation, the male principle. It is represented as Wisdom.

The third emanation, Hokmah's opposite on the Tree of Life, is Binah, the passive female principle, representing God's passive as opposed to His active intelligence.

These three form the first triangle on the Tree, the Briatic world of pure nature, inhabited by the angel Metatron who guides the planets and rules over the visible world.

The fourth emanation, Hesed, represents the active male principle of firmness, constructive energy.

The fifth emanation, Geburah, is the destructive female principle of punishment.

The sixth emanation, Tiphereth, is the creative life force completing the second triangle on the Tree, and serving as the mediating principle between Hesed and Geburah, construction and destruction. The second triangle constitutes the Yetziratic world, predominantly spiritual, yet containing some matter.

The seventh emanation, Netsah, is the male principle of instinct, a Dionysian principle of unreason, opposed to all that is unnatural.

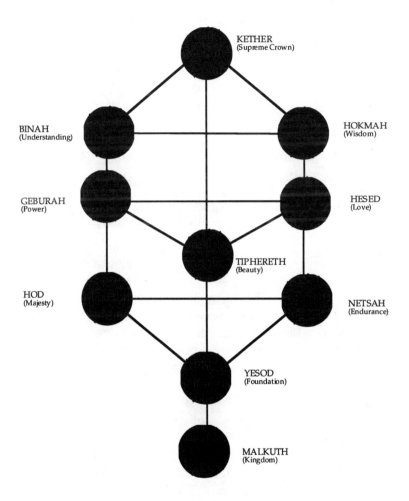

Figure 4
The Tree of Life

The eighth emanation, Hod, is the female principle of reason and restraint, the sphere of Apollonian calm.

Netsah and Hod are reconciled in the ninth emanation, Yesod, representing creativity, the proper union of instinct with reason.

The last emanation, Malkuth, represents the earth and while it is the least of the sephiroth still, as the tenth emanation, it contains elements of all the rest. It is this fact which permits man to recognize in himself the tiny spark of the divine which he contains and holds out the hope that with proper study he can ascend the Tree of Life and attain union with God. There are thirty-two paths on the Tree of Life, representing the ten sephiroth and the twenty-two letters of the Hebrew alphabet. Through meditating on the Tree and understanding what each of the paths symbolized, Cabalists believed that man could literally attain salvation while still on earth.

Because of the significance attached to the Hebrew letters in the Tree of Life, Cabalists began using the letters in different combinations to aid them in meditation. Several techniques were developed and applied to the divine words of God in the Old Testament. One of these was gematria which consisted of converting each letter in a word to its corresponding number, adding up the total and then finding another word with the same total. A famous example of gematria, drawn from a later time, is that the letters in the name Napoleon Buonaparte can be construed in such a way that they make three 6's or 666, the number of the Beast of the Apocalypse. Another method is notarikon by which it is possible to make new words by combining the first and last letters of a series of phrases. There is also temurah, treating all words in the Old Testament as anagrams. Each of these methods and many more were used by the Cabalists separately, or in combination, to make esoteric sense out of the words of the Hebrew Bible.

It was not a far cry from word and number mysticism to word and number sorcery and we soon find the Jews of the Middle Ages conjuring up demons and visiting curses upon their enemies with techniques based on the Cabala. This kind of "practical" Cabala exerted a fascination on Christian magicians and it was not long before Hebrew terms became commonplace in the incantations of sorcerers.

In the long run, however, the most compelling feature of the Cabala has been The Tree of Life. This is understandable for the Tree can easily be adapted to any mystical or magical schema. From Pico Della Mirandola to Aleister Crowley, the Tree of Life has been used in connection with every conceivable occult theory, black or white. The Tree, as W. E. Butler reminds us, is "a wonderful diagram of forces; not things... the whole universe in which we live is the theatre of an infinity of interweaving forces, and these forces are at work in both the objective and subjective levels of both the universe and the soul of .nan. The Qabalah declares that there is an enormous field of acting and reacting forces and lives..." The Tree of Life is surely, as some have termed it, an occult Rosetta Stone.

The Cabala was greatly influenced by Gnosticism. Both emphasize secret knowledge. And, as Shlomo Gioria Shoham has pointed out: "There are similarities between Kabalist and Gnostic cosmogonies. The Kabalist breaking of the vessels released profane shells intermingled with divine sparks to create the world and man; in Gnosis, light and darkness intermingled to set up this world. There is a marked similarity between the Gnostic aeons [archons] and the Kabalist sefirot, and the Gnostic Sophia is very much like the Kabalist Schechina. The major difference between the two, however, is that the Kabalist God is not evil but only accident-prone; the breaking of the vessels and the creation of the world were regrettable catastrophes that both man and God try to overcome. The Gnostic God, who created the world on the other hand, was vile ab initio. The Gnostics hate the created world and everything in it, including themselves."

In Cabalist terms, the "breaking of the vessels" is the original act of division, scattering sparks of divinity throughout the created world. The Cabalist Tikkun, or mending, seeks to reunite these sparks. In Tikkun is to be found the profound Cabalist doctrine that God is imperfect, i.e., not whole, missing the divine sparks set in motion by the breaking of the vessels. The task of Tikkun is then, not just to save man but also to save God. In Lurianic Cabala, Tikkun is even more transcendently important:

"The task of man in Lurianic Cabala is [infinitely] more formidable; the catastrophe that occurred within divinity can be mended by man and only by man. God seems to be entirely dependent on man for his redemption, while man's salvation will also follow with the successful mending of divinity."

Chapter 11:
Sufism

Islam is a religion much misunderstood in the West. Arising out of the same tradition of monotheism as Judaism and Christianity, Islam is more strictly monotheist than Christianity, with its doctrine of the Trinity. Viewed in the West as a harsh, desert religion, Islam has no church or clergy and worships a transcendent God that does not manifest itself in the material world. The Judaeo-Christian mystical and magical tradition of the *unio mystica*, the union of that divine spark in human beings with the godhead, is thus alien to Islam. Sufis, representing the principal tradition of Islamic mysticism and magic, seek to induce in themselves ecstatic states of consciousness that provide visions of God's uniqueness. As Julian Baldick puts it, "the Sufis are God's friends, perpetually engaged in remembrance (*dhikr*) of him. Sufism also constitutes a Path (*tariqa*), which begins with repentance and leads through a number of 'stations' (*maqamat*), representing virtues such as absolute trust in God, to a higher series of ecstatic 'states' (*ahwah*). These culminate in the 'passing away' (*fana'*) of the mystic (or perhaps just of his lower soul, or alternatively of his essence now adorned by the attributes of God)."

Sufism became a part of Islam as early as the eighth century. In the tenth century, Muslim mystics began to adapt the Pythagorean philosophy of Plotinus to Islam. Ahmad Al-Asafi integrated Plotinus' theory of emanations to the Islamic doctrine of creation. The twelfth century saw the founding of the so-called "theosophical" schools of Sufism in which the visions induced by the mystics were regarded as objectively real. A kind of self-hypnosis was prescribed for attaining such visions:

"When the inner eye is opened, the outer eye should be sealed to everything, the lips shut to everything; and the five external senses should cease to be used and the internal senses employed in their place such that when the patient wants to hold something, he should hold it with his inner hand, when he wants to see something, he should see it with his inner eye, when he wants to hear something, he should hear it with his inner ear, when he wants to smell something, he should smell it with his inner nose, and his sense of taste should come from the soul's palate. Once this is accomplished, he can regard the secret of the heavens continually and be informed at every moment from the world of the unseen."

The great Master of medieval Sufism was Ibn al-Arabi: "Ibn Al-Arabi conceived of the world of imagination as a phantasmagorical dimension of reality, an otherworld of unlimited variety, where the impossible was real and true. 'Many rational impossibilities, i.e. things which sound reason declares to be absurd exist there.' The world of imagination was limited only by its experience."

The Sufi Concept of Self

As the modern Sufi scholar A. Reza Arasteh has pointed out, "Unlike Western psychologists and psychoanalysts who have limited themselves in depth and dimension to the familial, social and occasionally to the historical self, the Sufis give an infinite and unlimited potential to self, which extends from the unknown point of creation (*aza*) to the unknown point of eternity (*abad*) . . ."

A significant element of traversing the Sufi path to selfhood is developing a true sense of both forgiveness and repentance. In this regard, the tale of Nasuh related by the Persian Sufi Rumi in his **Mathnawi** is instructive.

Nasuh was a masseur in a bath-house reserved for noble women, who had to disguise the fact that he was a man because, by law, men could not enter female bath-houses. But Nasuh was young and lustful and frequently satisfied his carnal desires with the many willing princesses who frequented the bath-house. Nasuh consulted a gnostic and asked him to pray for him. The gnostic, who guessed Nasuh's dilemma, prayed simply, "May God help you in your repentance."

A few days later, one of the princesses lost a valuable pearl earring in the bathhouse. A thorough search was instituted, requiring that all of the female masseurs be stripped naked and their orifices probed for the earring. Nasuh, nearly fainting from fright at his inevitable discovery and punishment, which was certain death, knelt and prayed, "Oh, Allah, thou hast the power to conceal man's sin. If you once more conceal my sin, I will repent of every sinful act that I have committed."

Nasuh was then summoned to be searched. He collapsed into unconsciousness and simultaneously experienced true repentance. The missing earring was miraculously found before the search of Nasuh's person was begun and Nasuh regained consciousness a transformed man.

From that point on, he firmly rejected the sexual advances of the princesses, at no small danger to himself, because to deny a princess any request was also to risk death. But he was not punished, Rumi implies because his repentance was sincere.

But repentance (*tawba)* is merely the first stage towards the attainment of true selfhood. The second is *wara*, the avoidance of doing wrong. In the third stage, "one becomes *zahid*, the seeker of *zuhd*," the state of total detachment from all things, which prepares the seeker for the fourth stage, *faq'r*, poverty, which Arasteh describes as a "state of irreducible simplicity, total detachment. . ." This prepares the seeker for achieving the state of *ilm al-yaquin*, "knowing certainty."

Arasteh states: "This knowledge is not like knowledge which is learned from instruction. It is experiential, vision-like, full of wisdom and occurs with total certainty where the speaker has a vision and its instrument is *intuition*.."

And this leads to what Arasteh calls, the "climax of Sufi being," the experience of *An*, or "moment of good fortune" which he defines as ". . .characterized by action for the sake of action, for the sake of the beloved, for the sake of someone, or some ideals outside of ourselves. It is self-explanatory, self-directing, self-forming, and self-expanding."

In terms of the history of noetic magic, *An* represents immersion in the **nous**. It is a state of consciousness that opens up an infinity of experiential realities:

"To the Sufis, the validity of the existence of multiple realities was based on the principle that each reality possesses its own language, its own values, and its own symbols; and furthermore, each is ruled by its own general law of detachment and unification. At each state the seeker must identify himself with the object of desire through experience of *An*. This psychological law is instrumental both within the sphere of a single reality and as a means of birth passing from one sphere of reality to another."

Ultimately the visions that the Sufi undergoes, the transformations of consciousness that he induces, culminate in a revelation of one's true self, not of the Reality which is God: "You will see your form in Him. Whoever imagines that he sees the Reality Himself has no gnosis; he has gnosis who knows that it is his own essential self that he sees."

Sufism contrasted gnosis with ecstasy: "Ecstasy is akin to passing-away while gnosis is stable and does not pass away."

As a poem by the Sufi Al-Junayd puts it:

> *In ecstasy delighteth he*
> > *Who finds in it his rest:*
> *But when Truth cometh, ecstasy*
> > *Itself is dispossessed.*

> *Once ecstasy was my delight;*
> > *But He Whom I did find*
> *In ecstasy claims all my sight*
> > *And to the rest I'm blind*

Theosophical Sufism is monist, not dualist. The created world is to be cherished, not despised. In theosophical Sufism we find optimist gnosis carried to its most philosophically attractive and ecstatic end.

Part Three:
The Magus as
Christian Humanist

Chapter 12:
Magic in the Renaissance

During the Renaissance magic once more emerged as a potent spiritual force. Writings which had lain hidden in remote monasteries were rediscovered and translated; attempts were made to assimilate the doctrines which they contained to Christian orthodoxy. Christian humanists, profoundly attracted by classical thought, found parallels between the philosophies of such pagan thinkers as Plato and Plotinus and the theology of Christianity. Such parallels, they believed, could not be accidental. God must have revealed the essential truths of Christianity to the best of the pagan philosophers who thus became, in the eyes of the humanists, not merely philosophers but pagan theologians or prisci theologi. The eminence of the prisci theologi was largely judged on the basis of their antiquity; thus Plato was more highly regarded than, say, Proclus. But the most highly revered (because oldest) of all the prisci theologi was Hermes Trismegistus, ancient contemporary of Moses.

The Renaissance humanists had good authority for believing in the antiquity of Hermes Trismegistus. Lactantius in his **Institutes** had maintained that Hermes was more ancient than Plato or Pythagoras. St. Augustine, while condemning Hermes, added the weight of his authority to the belief in the sage's ancient origins. But Hermes Trismegistus was not simply a religious thinker, he was also a magician whose magic was intimately connected with his religious beliefs. In addition, most of the other prisci theologi were magicians as well: Zoroaster, Orpheus, Pythagoras, and the neo-Pythagoreans. The prisci theologi were thus also prisci magi.

Magic was thus increasingly seen as an ancient and honorable discipline and the image of the magus was gradually transformed from that of the medieval sorcerer with his vile remedies and incomprehensible incantations to that of the Renaissance magician, benevolent practitioner of natural magic.

The problem which confronted the Renaissance humanist attracted to the study of magic was how to reconcile magic with Christian orthodoxy. The Florentine Platonists, Marsilius Ficino and Pico Della Mirandola, who were largely responsible for the revival of magic, were sincere and pious Christians. They did not attack Christianity; on the contrary, they hoped to shore it up, to support it by demonstrating that pagan wisdom was fully in accord with the wisdom of the Church. Yet the Church had always taken a firm stand against the practice of magic.

The Florentine Platonists solved the difficulty by maintaining that the magic which they practiced was not the kind of magic that had been traditionally condemned by the Church. The magic of Ficino and Pico was "natural" magic; it did not attempt to harness the powers of the supernatural, the demonic, to its purposes.

Ficino advocated a kind of "spiritual" magic, based on the notion of the "spiritus mundi." According to classical neo-Pythagoreanism, a series of emanations proceeded from the divine, incorporeal One. Various names were given to these emanations and, in the **Picatrix**, a work heavily influenced by Hermetism and neo-Pythagoreanism, we find the following triad:

Intellectus
Spiritus
Materia

The spiritus descends from the world of pure mind to the world of matter. "The whole art of magic," as Frances Yates points out, "thus consists in capturing and guiding the influx of spiritus into materia." Ficino, who was certainly familiar with the **Picatrix**, may have derived from it his conception of the spiritus mundi and identified it with the astral body of the neo-Pythagoreans. In any event, Ficino regarded the spiritus as part of the natural world (which included the planets) and made it the object of his magic to attract stellar influences into his own body by various means, the most important of which involved the use of talismans and the hymns of Orpheus. Ficino's magic was entirely subjective in nature. It was directed toward the transformation of the self rather than at influencing or acting upon minds or objects out-side the self. It operated through the vehicle of the vis imaginativa which transmitted the spiritus of the planets to the soul of the magus. What could be more spiritually edifying, less harmful to institutional-ized religion than this quiescent, imaginative magic?

Yet there were difficulties, as Ficino himself recognized. For one thing, if one substituted angels or demons for the planetary forces, that is to say, go one step further than Ficino into the world of the super-natural, the whole process became demonic magic, something which the church surely wouldn't countenance. And Ficino was not entirely successful in keeping his magic at the level of impersonal planetary influences. There were other difficulties as well. Natural magic of Ficino's variety produced spiritual illumination without the mediation of Christian institutions. It therefore could function as a substitute for rather than a bulwark of Christianity. Moreover, since natural magic claimed to produce spiritual illumination without any supernatural agency, it could be interpreted as a threat to belief in the supernatural itself. Whether all of these considerations occurred to Ficino is uncer-tain. But he was uncomfortable about the implications of his theory of natural magic and wanted its practice confined to a select circle of intellectuals who would refrain from vulgarizing it.

Ficino's younger contemporary, Pico Della Mirandola, was just as pious as Ficino, but more intellectually adventurous. Born in 1463 in Mirandola castle, not far from Modena, Pico was a child prodigy. He learned to speak several languages and, at the age of twenty-four, went to Rome where he offered to debate nine hundred separate theses, many of them having to do with magic. His theses were examined by an ecclesiastical commission appointed by Innocent VIII and a number were condemned as heretical. For this reason Pico never got a chance to defend his ideas in the public arena. His **Oration on the Dignity of Man**, which was written as a prologue to the projected debate, remains the most eloquent testament to the ideas and aims of the Renaissance magus:

"And so, 0 Asclepius, man is a magnum miraculum, a being worthy of reverence and honor." Thus did Pico begin his great oration with a quotation from the Asclepius, the Hermetic treatise. He went on to condemn evil magic and to extol the virtues of natural magic. Pico's version of natural magic, however, differed from Ficino's because Pico included not only gentile sources of ancient wisdom in his theory, but also the Hebrew Cabala.

To Pico, the Cabala was even more worthy of reverence than the Hermetic treatises because it belonged to the Judaeo-Christian sacred tradition. Moreover, Cabalism accords perfectly with Hermetism on all essential points. Both are based on a doctrine of emanation from the divine word of God; both therefore reflect the same spiritual universe. In uniting Hermetism with Cabalism, Pico took a daring step in the direction of demonic magic. No longer was the object of the magus to be merely the control of planetary influences. Cabalism opened up a higher celestial plane to the magician.

As Frances Yates says, "This was a spiritual magic, not spiritual in the sense of using only the natural spiritus mundi like natural magic, but in the sense that it attempted to tap the higher spiritual powers beyond the natural powers of the cosmos. Practical Cabala invokes angels, archangels, the ten sephiroth which are names or powers of God... It is thus a much more ambitious kind of magic than Ficino's natural magic, and one which it would be impossible to keep apart from religion."

Pico continued to run into difficulty with ecclesiastical authority. Prevented from debating his theses, he attempted to publish them only to be prevented from so doing by a papal bull. He then hurriedly left Rome and went to France where he was arrested and imprisoned at Vincennes. Powerful friends like Lorenzo de Medici obtained permission for him to return to Florence but he remained in the bad graces of the Church until the death of Innocent VIII. Innocent's successor, Alexander VI, was much more favorably disposed toward magic than the previous pope. In 1493, less than a year before Pico's death at the age of thirty-one, Alexander publicly affirmed Pico's orthodoxy. Privately, he wrote a letter in which he absolved Pico and all of his writings from any suspicion of heresy. This letter, which appeared in all subsequent editions of Pico's works, was profoundly influential in confirming the dignity and orthodoxy of natural magic. Now that magic was recognized by the Church itself, the most serious barrier to its acceptance had been overcome. The magus was free to practice his art as long as he did not venture into the forbidden realms of Black Magic.

As Renaissance magic developed, however, it moved further and further away from the elegant, subjective magic of Ficino and Pico. This is not to say that it ever became Black Magic in the medieval Christian sense. Most Renaissance magicians regarded themselves as exemplars of Christian piety. Whatever kind of magic they practiced they saw as good. Only other people practiced Black Magic. By and large this was true. Renaissance magicians were not interested in making pacts with Satan or in hurling demonic curses upon their enemies. If they sought to control higher spiritual powers, they dealt with angels or good demons (in neo-Pythagorean parlance) not with devils. Still, they were often regarded with suspicion by their less enlightened brethren and stories were circulated about their supposed dealings with infernal powers. Renaissance magic took a number of different directions. One of the most important was toward medicine and natural science. The magus, interested as he was in controlling the natural world, was often attracted to what we today would call scientific experimentation. A number of scholars, especially Lynn Thorndike, have emphasized the intimate link between the development of magic and that of experimental science during the Middle Ages and the Renaissance.

Another direction which Renaissance magic took, sometimes closely related to the first, was aimed not merely at the transformation and elevation of the self but also toward affecting objects in the outside world. D. P. Walker has called this "transitive" magic and has pointed out its significance in the occult philosophy of Cornelius Agrippa.

Agrippa, the author of **De Occulta Philosophia**, was one of the most influential of all Renaissance magicians. Although not particularly original, his treatise on magic is perhaps the most complete treatment of the subject to come out of the Renaissance. That Agrippa firmly believed in "transitive" magic is borne out by the following quotation from **De Occulta Philosophia**:

"The forms of things, although by their own nature they are conveyed to the senses of men and animals, can however, while they are in the air, receive a certain impression from the heavens, by means of which, as also by the fitness deriving from the recipient's disposition, they may be transmitted to the senses of one recipient rather than another. And hence it is possible, naturally, without any kind of superstition, and though the time in which this is done cannot be exactly measured, it will inevitably happen within twenty-four hours. And I know how to do this and have often done it. Abbot Trithemius also knows how to do it and used to do it."

Agrippa was a curious figure who waited to publish his **De Occulta** until after he had produced a skeptical work on the vanity of all the sciences, including magic. This has led some scholars to believe that he was afraid to publish the **De Occulta** until he disassociated himself from the conclusions which he had reached in that book. Others have argued that he sincerely had come to disbelieve in the power of man to know or control the natural world and felt that only faith was a sure guide to salvation.

Another important Renaissance magician, Paracelsus, is in the same tradition as Agrippa. He wrote of two different kinds of intelligence, the carnal and the spiritual. The spiritual kind, called Gabalis is responsible for prophecy and clairvoyance. Central to his conception of magic is his belief in the power of imagination. As one scholar points out, "All action is visualized by Paracelsus as flowing from an act of imagination--a process not connected with formal logical reasoning, but with the spirit-conscious or subconscious and in a broad sense embracing all strata of the personality." Paracelsus believed in transitive magic and, in his capacity as a physician, sought to cure illness by magical means. He also investigated the occult properties of herbs and developed a number of remedies which were achieved by natural scientific rather than magical means.

There is something impressive about these Renaissance magicians. They literally exude confidence in humanity's powers. They are curious about everything, pursuing the objects of their curiosity with energy and imagination.

It is time to look at the career of one such magus in greater detail, a man whose life displayed much that was best (and not a little of that which was worst) in the makeup of the Renaissance magician, for the life of Dr. John Dee epitomizes the development of Renaissance magic itself, beginning in exultation and ending in condemnation.

Chapter 13:
Tales of the Magi II:
John Dee, Renaissance
Magus and Royal Spy

In his own time Dr. Dee was suspected of Black Magic; his library was destroyed by superstitious neighbors, rumours circulated that he had made a pact with Satan; on two occasions he was involved in litigation over charges of sorcery. Nor has he fared much better since his death. Most biographers have portrayed him as either a charlatan or a fool, the master or the dupe of the mysterious and sinister Edward Kelley. The truth is that Dee was neither Black Magician, charlatan nor fool; he was a careful and responsible man, a faithful servant to his queen, a brilliant scholar and a clever spy. In addition, he was the very epitome of the Renaissance magus for, in his insatiable curiosity, Dee used every means at his disposal to attain an understanding of the universe, material and spiritual, which surrounded him.

John Dee was born on July 13, 1527 at Mortlake, not far from London, on the Thames. His father had been supervisor of the King's kitchen, a distinctly minor post, which may have aroused a certain amount of shame in Dee for he later devoted a great deal of effort to rehabilitating his pedigree, eventually claiming that he was, in fact, a cousin of Queen Elizabeth. The Dee family was Welsh in origin and it may have been this Welsh heritage which first stimulated young John's interest in the mysterious and the supernatural. It is known that he took a keen interest in everything Welsh, including Welsh legends and superstitions.

When Dee entered St. John's College, Cambridge in 1542, however, he as yet displayed no particular inclination toward the occult. In an age when university students were permitted almost total freedom and frequently abused it, Dee was unusual in his devotion to learning.

According to his own account, he reserved eighteen hours a day for reading and studying. Beneath the rather dull surface of the academic drudge, however, lay concealed a remarkably ingenious mind. Dee's ingenuity was first displayed in 1546 when he acted as stage-manager for a production of Pax by Aristophanes at Trinity College. For a scene requiring one of the characters to fly from the stage to the "Palace of Zeus" located above, Dee devised an elaborate machine which so successfully simulated actual flight that it gave rise to a rumor that he was a sorcerer.

It was not magic that interested Dee at this stage in his life but, rather, astronomy and navigation. In 1547, he journeyed to the Netherlands where he attended the University of Louvain. Mathematics, astronomy and navigation were strongly emphasized at Dutch universities for the Netherlands was beginning to come into its own as a maritime nation. Among the scholars Dee encountered at the University of Louvain was a certain Nicholas Biesius, an intellectual who took an active interest in the occult. Dee, who was pursuing a medical course of study, was attracted by Biesius' theories concerning the influence of celestial forces on the human body. Studying under Biesius, Dee first began to turn his inquiring intellect toward problems related to magic.

Upon his return to England in 1551, Dee was introduced to the court of the young Edward VI. The knowledge of astrology which he had received from Biesius and others at Louvain served him well and he soon attained the position of Astrologer-Royal under Queen Mary after Edward's death. Unfortunately Dee employed himself not only in casting the Queen's horoscope, but also provided the same service to Mary's younger sister Elizabeth. On one occasion Elizabeth asked to see her sister's chart and Dee made the mistake of complying. When knowledge of this leaked out, Dee was accused of conspiring with Elizabeth to murder the Queen by means of Black Magic. Fortunately the accusations were so flagrantly out of proportion to the offence that Dee was able to defend himself successfully before the dreaded Star Chamber. Nevertheless, although acquitted of all the charges against him, he was not freed, but instead remanded to the custody of the Bishop of London who was charged with determining Dee's religious orthodoxy. In 1555, Dee was finally released from prison.

During the final years of Mary's reign, Dee contented himself with leading an obscure and scholarly life, becoming an articulate exponent of the Copernican theory and publishing books on navigation, mechanics and optics. When Elizabeth became Queen in 1558, she first consulted Dee concerning the date that would be most favorable for her coronation. After consulting his star charts at some length, Dee settled on the fifteenth of January. Whether the stars had anything to do with it or not, the coronation carried out on that day was a brilliant success and Dee once more basked in the warmth of royal favor.

Precisely when Dee began acting as a secret agent for Elizabeth is uncertain, although it was probably not long after her coronation. His European-wide reputation as a scholar, his many influential contacts on the continent, and his subtle intelligence made him superbly qualified to undertake delicate espionage missions. Dee was one of three people whom the Queen referred to as her "eyes"; the other two were Sir Christopher Hatton and Robert Dudley, Earl of Leicester. In secret correspondence with the Queen, each of these men indicated their identity with marks symbolizing the eyes. Hatton used two triangles containing a dot in each one; Leicester followed the same pattern, substituting circles for the triangles; Dee, more inventive than the other two, signed himself 007, the elongated 7 presumably serving as a kind of stylized eyebrow as well as indicating Dee's determination to utilize not only his two eyes in the Queen's service but also his other four senses as well as his sixth, occult, sense. From this it can be seen that Dee never separated his interest in the occult from his other activities. This is borne out by what was surely the most remarkable event in Dee's espionage career, an event which required him to utilize his considerable knowledge of both espionage and the occult.

In 1585, one of his contacts on the continent, a scholar and suspected heretic named Francesco Pucci, told Dee he had learned that a group of French mercenaries had been hired by Spain to sabotage English shipbuilding. Arriving in England separately, they were to meet at an unknown place "before three years were ended and the nine men beginne their Perambulation."

Working with just this slender clue, Dee attempted to figure out the details of the plot. The first thing that attracted his attention was the use of the numbers three and nine. To Dee, steeped as he was in occult lore, the numbers had a special significance, for both had been sacred to the Druids. More aware than perhaps any other person in England of the extent to which many of the ancient Druid customs had survived into his own time, Dee remembered that the inspections of the Royal Forest of Dean were still conducted in accordance with the old Druid calendar. Every three years (a year was 360 days for the Druids) nine foresters, appointed by the Court of Verderers, made a regular inspection of the Royal Forest. Since Dee knew that the object of the Spanish mission was to deter the English from building up their fleet, he decided that their plan must be to set fire to the Forest of Dean, thus destroying a major source of English wood. He promptly dispatched these speculations to the Queen along with a suggestion that the saboteurs would probably attempt to signal their respective locations by building small fires in one or two of the squatters' chimneys scattered throughout the forest. Dee's calculations were proved correct down to the last detail. Agents were dispatched to the Forest of Dean and, before long, the saboteurs were rounded up. Dee, who had been in Prague throughout this entire episode, had good reason to be satisfied with his espionage techniques.

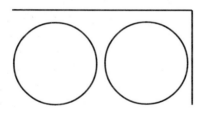

Figure 5
John Dee's Secret Signature

The Queen also had reason to be pleased with him, but her financial support of his activities was erratic and uncertain. Dee, who was a true patriot, did not expect to be paid large sums for his services; he merely wished to be reimbursed for the basic expenses incurred in travelling abroad on missions for the Queen. Occasionally, Elizabeth would respond to his requests for money but, more often than not, she simply ignored them. The consequence was that Dee became progressively poorer.

Despite the fact that he was increasingly called upon to serve the Queen, Dee maintained interest in an astonishing variety of subjects. His researches in the field of optics led him to investigate the possibilities of crystal-gazing or "skrying" as it was called. A "skryer" should possess all of the qualities of what we would call today a medium; above all, a good skryer must be sensitive to the occult world. Children were frequently employed as skryers during the Middle Ages and the Renaissance because it was thought that they were more sensitive than adults. Dee first tried skrying on his own but soon discovered that he didn't have the talent for it. It was in the fall of 1581 that he felt he had discovered someone with all the necessary qualifications to be a skryer in the person of a young man named Barnabas Saul. It turned out, however, that Saul was an extremely unreliable skryer and a petty criminal as well. Dee dismissed him after only two months and hired what appeared to be a far more promising person, a young man who displayed a real interest in the occult named Edward Talbott. Thus began Dee's association with one of the most enigmatic figures in the history of magic.

Little is known of Talbott's background. One theory is that he was the son of an apothecary who became attracted to the occult in hopes of discovering the secret of transmuting base metals into gold. Talbott was a man obsessed with a passion for wealth. When alchemy failed him, he turned to crime and when that became too dangerous, he entered Dee's service in the hope of obtaining clues to the whereabouts of buried treasure by communicating with the spirit world. Shortly after becoming Dee's skryer, Talbott (for what reason it is not known) changed his name to Kelley.

It is clear that, except perhaps in the beginning, Dee never fully trusted Kelley. On several occasions he noted in his diary that Kelley had attempted to deceive him. In some instances, references to Kelley have been erased, presumably by Kelley himself who also wrote comments along the margins, accusing Dee of dishonesty. If Dee suspected Kelley of fraud, why did he continue to employ him? Remember that Dee was not a naïve scholar, but a man of the world, versed in the arts of espionage and secret diplomacy. If he knew Kelley was trying to use him, why didn't he put a stop to it? One possible answer to this question is that Dee, recognizing Kelley's untrustworthiness, nevertheless believed him to be a skryer of considerable talent. To Dee's way of thinking, perhaps the benefits to be obtained from what he considered to be Kelley's genuine revelations far outweighed the disadvantages inherent in the skryer's occasional attempts at deception. Here he relied perhaps excessively on his own ingenuity in detecting fraud. Still, we should remember that Dee was in the tragic position of one who yearned for contact with the supernatural but lacked the ability himself to make such contact. He was thus forced to rely on others and he seems to have felt that while Kelley was certainly no prize, he was a better bet than Barnabas Saul.

Is there any substance to Dee's belief that Kelley possessed a genuine talent for the occult? Most authors have thought not, preferring to portray Kelley as the charlatan par excellence. There is, however, considerable evidence to the contrary. For one thing Kelley, after an initial show of enthusiasm, grew more and more reluctant to skry, complaining that he found the change of consciousness which skrying involved to be debilitating and unpleasant. Dee literally had to force Kelley to continue. Moreover, Kelley seems to have been afraid that his skrying might eventually result in the establishment of communication with the infernal rather than the celestial world, an indication that the visions which he described to Dee were, at least so far as he was concerned, frighteningly real. Another, more potent reason for believing that Kelley was not entirely a charlatan is that he dictated literally volumes of "spirit conversations" without apparent fraud, many of which give evidence of a command of language and an ingenuity far beyond Kelley's normal abilities. The best examples of this are the "conversations" relating to the discovery, or invention, of the language of Enoch.

The Enochian language has fascinated occultists since it first saw the light of print in 1659 in Meric Casaubon's A True Relation of what passed for Many Years between Doctor John Dee and Some Spirits. It was adopted by the Order of the Golden Dawn in the late nineteenth century and became one of the favorite magical devices of Aleister Crowley (who believed himself to be a reincarnation of Edward Kelley). The tendency of occultists to romanticize the past is nowhere more evident than in their attitude toward Enochian. While admitting that Dee and Kelley were the first to actually write the language down, the modern Satanist Anton Szandor LaVey, for example, points out that it is "thought to be older than Sanskrit," Despite such dubious speculations, there is good reason for the fascination with the Enochian language, for it possesses its own unique alphabet, grammatical structure and vocabulary. Nonetheless, it should be regarded as essentially a unique variation in the Renaissance tradition of word magic, a tradition that includes not only the Cabala but Trithemius' Steganographia, a work which, according to D. P. Walker, combined magic with cryptography and excited Dee's interest and admiration.

Did Dee rather than Kelley invent the language of Enoch? Some scholars have thought so, but this contradicts Dee's own description of himself as lacking mediumistic abilities. Probably Dee revised and improved upon Kelley's initial visions, incorporating techniques borrowed from Trithemius and others. The inspirational source, however, seems to have been Kelley himself. Not that Kelley greatly appreciated the magnitude of his discovery; the conversations with angels that he dictated to Dee in Enochian were largely beyond his comprehension. As Richard Deacon has remarked, despite the difficulty of translating Enochian, there is sense to the visions and, "more even than sense, colour and majesty of prose marching regally, flowingly and gracefully forward on occasions, flashes of imaginative genius such as one associates with the visions of William Blake..." This places Dee and Kelley squarely in the tradition of Renaissance magic inaugurated by Ficino, directed toward the imaginative elevation of the self to a vision of a higher spiritual reality.

The Enochian system of communicating with angels by means of crystallomancy had hardly been perfected when Dee and Kelley introduced a third person to their experiments: Prince Albert Laski of Poland.

Dee met Laski at a reception given by Queen Elizabeth and the two soon became fast friends. Laski was permitted to observe the "spirit conversations" and found them fascinating. Naturally curious about his own future, Laski requested Dee to ask the spirits what would become of him. After considerable circumlocution, he was rewarded with this reply:

"I say unto thee, his [Laski's] name is in the Book of Life: the Sun shall not passe his course before he be a King. His Counsel shall breed

Alteration of this State; yea of the whole world."

Laski was delighted with the idea that he was soon to become king of Poland and promptly invited Dee and Kelley to accompany him to his estate where he would supply them with whatever they needed on condition that they keep him informed about his prospects. It should he noted that for some time Kelley had been urging Dee to involve himself in alchemical experiments. Kelley was weary of skrying, especially since he had come to realize that the spirits weren't likely to provide him with the locations of buried treasure. His original passion, alchemy, now seemed to him the most likely way of acquiring riches. But alchemical experiments cost money, in which, unfortunately, both Dee and Kelley were notably deficient. It is therefore probable that Kelley, searching frantically for a rich patron, settled upon Laski as the most likely candidate. Laski was both rich and gullible; moreover, he had tremendous respect for Dee. Kelley saw that Dee would have to be included in any arrangements he made with Laski but this didn't bother him. Dee's reputation for scholarship and honesty provided the perfect cover for whatever illicit activities Kelley had in mind. Thus Dee embarked on a journey that was to result in the destruction of his reputation. In Poland, Kelley continued to feed Laski bits and scraps of prophecy and to pursue his alchemical researches. Laski soon tired of this rigamarole and withdrew his support. Hoping to get rid of the pair permanently, he provided them with letters of introduction to Emperor Rudolph II of Bohemia. Dee and Kelley, leaving their wives behind them in Cracow, set off for Prague. Rudolph, who had heard of Dee, received them kindly at first. But Dee used the occasion to tell the emperor in no uncertain terms that he was pursuing the paths of wickedness:

"The Angel of the Lord has appeared unto me," Dee informed Rudolph, "and rebuketh you for your sins. If you will not hear me, the Lord, the God that made Heaven and Earth (under whom you breathe and have your spirit) putteth down his foot against your breast and will throw you headlong down from your seat. Moreover the Lord has made this covenant with me (by oath) that He will do and perform. If you forsake your wickedness and turn unto Him, your seat shall be the greatest there ever was and the Devil shall become your prisoner."

Had Dee gone completely mad? Probably not, although there is some evidence that he was far from mentally stable at this time. No doubt he hoped to impress the emperor with this arrogant speech, operating on the mistaken assumption that monarchs, too often surrounded by flatterers, appreciate someone who speaks to them forthrightly. But Rudolph was distinctly unappreciative, although he succeeded in suppressing his anger for the moment and merely dismissed the pair from his court. After searching around for another wealthy patron, Dee and Kelley were finally expelled from Bohemia by the emperor. At this point the exact nature of their activities becomes uncertain but before long they were back in Bohemia, this time at the estate of Count Rosenberg at Trebona. Relations between Dee and Kelley were becoming increasingly strained. At one point Kelley claimed that it had been revealed to him in a vision that the two should exchange wives. Dee was no less shocked than his wife (who detested Kelley) and the projected exchange never took place. Moreover, Kelley now no longer needed the protection of Dee's reputation for now, it appears, Kelley's alchemical experiments were beginning to bear fruit:

"The transmutations of Kelley at this period are attested by several writers, including Gassendus. The most authenticated and remarkable, according to Figuier, is that which took place in the house of the imperial physician, Thaddeus de Hazek, when, by the mediation of a single drop of red oil, Kelley transmuted a pound of mercury into excellent gold, the superabundant virtue of the agent leaving in addition at the bottom of the crucible a small ruby!"

Such success was not to go unrewarded for Kelley was soon knighted by the once-hostile Rudolph. Since he no longer needed Dee, the inevitable break between them finally took place and Dee returned to England.

Kelley's success proved to be his undoing. In order to prevent him from disseminating his valuable secret to others, he was thrown into prison. There, in 1595, he died, reportedly from injuries sustained in a fall which occurred during a desperate effort to escape.

Doubtless the secret of Kelley's mysterious personality will never be uncovered. Was he seer or charlatan, alchemist or impostor? We shall never know. We do know that he was tormented by an unquenchable thirst for great wealth and that he directed all of his powers, real and assumed, toward the attainment of this end. That he died as a direct consequence of reportedly achieving the means to this goal seems somehow fitting.

Dee returned to England a broken man. He had spent all of his savings in wandering about the continent. His valuable library at Mortlake had been broken into by superstitious neighbors and destroyed. He no longer had the support of the Queen although she occasionally condescended to give him small gifts of money. He spent his declining years staving off poverty by casting horoscopes. In the early years of the reign of King James he made one last pitiful attempt to salvage his ruined reputation in the form of a plea to the monarch. He wished, he said, "to cause your Highness said servant to be tried and cleared of that horrible and damnable, and to him most grievous and damnageable sclaunder, generally, and for these many yeares last past, in this kingdom raysed and continued, by report and Print against him, namely that he is or hath bin a conjurer or caller or invocator of divels." The plea was ignored and shortly afterward, in December 1608, surrounded by his family at Mortlake, Dee died.

Thus ended one of the most remarkable magical careers ever recorded. Dee was a man of his age, insatiably curious about everything, willing to risk his fortune and reputation in the pursuit of knowledge. In other respects, his life points to the decline of the occult in the modern age for his spiritual conversations remind us of nothing so much as the séances of a spiritualist. As Richard Deacon has remarked, "With Dee one sees much of the present and not a little of the distant future in his own past. It is like looking at the whole of eternity through the shewstone of Elizabethan England."

We should not be led into overestimating the significance of magic in the Renaissance. At best it was the province of a tiny intellectual elite scattered across Europe. It never gained widespread acceptance and always lay in the shadow of suspicion. Still, for a time it flourished among at least a few enlightened minds and exercised an influence that was considerably out of proportion to the number of its adherents. Magic grew and developed for two centuries and then, as a potentially powerful intellectual force, it died out. Why was this? What were the factors that combined to spell the doom of Renaissance magic? There are no easy answers to this question. Some of the causes will likely remain forever unknown. Still, it is possible to venture a few tentative reasons for the remarkable decline of the Renaissance magus.

Renaissance magic had always heavily depended on the belief in the authenticity and antiquity of Hermes Trismegistus and of the Hermetic Corpus. Therefore, when Isaac Casaubon, in a work published in 1614, conclusively proved that the Corpus Hermetica was not the product of an ancient contemporary of Moses but was instead written in the early centuries C.E. by an unknown number of anonymous authors, the whole foundation upon which Renaissance magic had been built crumbled with one blow. Yet, as Frances Yates has pointed out, some Hermetists blithely refused to believe Casaubon and continued their pursuit of magic uninterrupted. By and large, however, Casaubon's argument had a profound effect on the intellectual position which magic had held. Another factor, more nebulous but perhaps more important, was the growing interest in natural science. Science was seen by many as potentially far more rewarding than magic. Careful observation and experimentation led to results that were more certain than any that could be obtained by means of magic. We should remember, however, that at the beginning of the seventeenth century modern science was still very much in its infancy. It had not yet attained the prestige which it was to achieve later in the century with the discoveries of Galileo and Newton. Nevertheless, the growing appeal of science must be reckoned as a factor in the decline of magic. Finally there was the witch-craze which reached unprecedented heights in the sixteenth and seventeenth centuries. Some of the enormous fear and suspicion which attached to the belief in witchcraft surely must have rubbed off on the once respectable Renaissance magus. Intelligent scholars who lent the weight of their erudition to the burning of witches, like Del Rio and Jean Bodin, often attacked magicians as well. Del Rio contemptuously dismissed the distinctions which had carefully been made between natural magic and Black Magic and claimed that all magic was heretical. Bodin accused Agrippa and other Renaissance magicians of being witches intent on overthrowing Christianity. Dee, as we have seen, was popularly supposed by his neighbors to be a Black Magician. As a consequence of such hysteria, many magicians became afraid to practice their art openly. Others gave it up altogether. Still others, who might have been attracted to magic but for the witch-craze, turned their attentions to other things. Whatever the case, it is certain that the witch-hysteria of the sixteenth and seventeenth centuries was influential in confusing magic with witchcraft. When Voltaire and other philosophers in the eighteenth century looked back on this extraordinary outburst of fanaticism and condemned magic, it was the popular magic of superstition and sorcery associated with witchcraft that they reviled. This confusion of magician with witch has persisted to the present and has contributed enormously to the decline of the magus in the modern age.

Chapter 14:
The Discovery of the
Impossible

What is missing from history as it is ordinarily written is a sense of the strangeness of the past. It is too often assumed that human nature is everywhere and in all times the same. Customs may come and go but the structure of the mind is forever constant. It should be noted that the constancy of human nature is the primary presupposition of all psychological theories. Psychoanalysis, behaviorism, humanistic psychology and associationism all maintain that behind the diversity of human thought and behavior there exists a mental structure which is essentially unchanging. But what if this assumption is incorrect? What if man's nature is itself a cultural artifact? If this is the case, if man has no nature but history, then the duty of the historian is to trace not only the political, cultural, and economic changes of the past but the psychological changes as well.

"Man," wrote Sir Thomas Browne, "is a great amphibian who lives in divers and distinguished worlds." One of the striking things about the mental attitudes of the seventeenth century is their apparently contradictory nature. Sir Thomas Browne himself was a scientific experimenter, a neo-Platonic mystic and a believer in witchcraft. Isaac Newton regarded his mystical commentaries on the Bible as possessing far greater significance than his scientific work. Peter Gay has called the seventeenth century the era of "Pagan Christianity" because it combined the rationalism of antiquity with the religiosity of the Christian Church. Such a distinction, however, obscures the psychological fact that in the seventeenth century even the most educated men and women perceived the world in a radically different way than they do today. To the seventeenth century mind the universe was fundamentally supernatural. The invisible and spiritual world was as real as the visible and material world. Skepticism about the existence of angels and devils was regarded as patently absurd. As John Locke put it in his **Essay Concerning Human Understanding:**

"If this notion of immaterial spirit may have, perhaps, some difficulties in it not easily to be explained, we have therefore no more reason to deny or doubt the existence of such spirits, than we have to deny or doubt the existence of body; because the notion of body is cumbered with some difficulties very hard, and perhaps impossible to be explained or understood by us."

Not only was it generally believed that the spiritual world was real but also that the inhabitants of that world could intrude on the material world. It was Robert Boyle who suggested that English miners be questioned about whether or not they ever encounter any "subterraneous demons; and if they do, in what shape and manner they appear; what they portend, and what they do."

Historians have too often regarded such statements as regrettable instances of the inability of even the greatest minds to transcend the common superstitions of their time. Why not concentrate on the valuable contributions of Locke, Boyle and Newton, the ideas they expressed which still have value? It ought to be obvious that the significant intellectual contributions of the seventeenth century were those which were oriented towards the future not those which were rooted in the past.

But to raise such objections is to defend a kind of historical amnesia. If we select from the past only those ideas which proved to be of significance to succeeding generations we are guilty of serious distortion. The fact that Newton, Boyle and Locke believed in spirits may not tell us anything about the rise of rationalism and the triumph of the scientific method but it does tell us something about Newton, Boyle and Locke and, by extension, about perceptions of reality in the seventeenth century.

Intellectual historians often write about ideas as if they were mere intellectual abstractions. But ideas which have their origins in a commonly shared culture shape and determine human experience and thus represent one of the most fundamental aspects of reality. What we experience as real, what we respond to and act upon as if it were real must, by any sensible standard, be real. The seventeenth century belief in a supernatural universe cannot be compared with the acceptance by a few intellectuals of the Cartesian cogito or Leibnizian monadology. It was a cultural presupposition, not an intellectual conclusion, one so powerful that not even the most brilliant minds of the time could escape from it.

For ordinary people the belief in the reality of the spiritual world led inescapably to belief in devils, in witchcraft, in magical cures, in the occult influence of the stars and in a variety of notions which we moderns prefer to dismiss as superstitions. But superstitions are beliefs that can be disproved or at least called into serious doubt. In the seventeenth century such ideas were not superstitions because they could not be refuted.

Seventeenth century skepticism regarding witchcraft and magic is instructive in this regard because it indicates the intellectual limitations to which skepticism was necessarily subjected by the contemporary climate of opinion. One of the best critiques of the belief in witchcraft in the early modern period was Reginald Scot's **The Discovery of Witchcraft** (1584). Scot admitted that witches exist but argued that witchcraft did not usually work. The Devil did not need witches to work evil on man for he was able to act directly on the material world without the need for human intermediaries. In Scot's view, witches ought to be tried for fraud rather than witchcraft because they pretended to powers they did not actually possess. Scot could not prove that witchcraft was impossible. He could not deny the reality of the Devil's influence on the material world. He could only provide an alternative explanation for the way in which demonic influence actually operated.

The first half of the seventeenth century, far from witnessing a decline in witchcraft persecution, actually experienced a significant increase. Historians have yet to provide a satisfactory explanation for this phenomenon but whatever social tensions led to the outbreak of widespread witchcraft persecutions, it can scarcely be argued that belief in witchcraft was declining in the seventeenth century. Moreover, belief in witches is only one symptom of a much broader set of shared cultural perceptions which, from the perspective of the twentieth century, have only one thing in common. They are impossible.

It is impossible to fly through the air without mechanical assistance. It is impossible to help or harm by imprecation. It is impossible to cure warts by rubbing them with a rind of bacon. Yet such beliefs were widely shared and rarely doubted in the seventeenth century. Law, medicine, and theology were grounded in the impossible.

In the seventeenth century, of course, these ideas were not regarded as impossible. On the contrary, it was true skepticism that was impossible. The pervasive belief in a supernatural universe rendered all things possible. Christianity, Catholic and Protestant alike, paid homage to the reality of the spiritual world and sustained its importance.

The metaphors of the spiritual world, angels and devils, witches and familiars are translated into human experience. Vague shadows are perceived as monstrous animals, ordinary dogs are transformed into the Devil incarnate, the village pauper becomes a minion of Satan. An example of the transformation of metaphor into reality (one of many that could be adduced) is provided by the Elizabethan writer William Fulke:

"More than sixteen years ago, on May-day when many young folk went abroad early in the morning, I remember by six of the clock in the forenoon there was news come to London that the Devil the same morning was seen flying over the Thames. Afterward came word that he lighted at Stratford, and there was taken and set in the stocks, and that though he would fain have dissembled the matter by turning himself into the likeness of a man, yet was he known well enough by his cloven feet.

"I know some yet alive that went to see him and, returning, affirmed that he was indeed flying in the air, but was not taken prisoner. I remember also that some wished he had been shoot at with guns or shafts as he flew over the Thames."

Although Fulke explains that the devil seen flying over the Thames was a cloud, he affirms that it was sent by God and took on the form of the Devil in order to strike fear in men and impress them with God's power. It is unlikely that Fulke's less learned contemporaries made even this simple distinction. What they saw was not a cloud transformed into a Devil; they saw only the Devil.

The decline of witchcraft persecutions and belief in the reality of the supernatural world has usually been explained by the gradual dissemination of the rationalism inaugurated by the Scientific Revolution. Yet, as we have seen, the great progenitors of the Scientific Revolution were not emancipated from beliefs in the supernatural world. The decline in witchcraft persecutions is first noticeable after 1650. As Robert Mandrou suggests, there was no diminution of belief in witchcraft in the second half of the seventeenth century; there was, rather, an increasing reluctance on the part of magistrates to bring witchcraft cases to trial. The reason for this lay in the fact that witchcraft was an extremely difficult crime to prove. The excesses of the first half of the century produced a reaction during the second half which, while it spared the lives of thousands of innocent people, left the popular belief in witchcraft and the supernatural relatively untouched.

The supernatural world did not die easily. The most serious outbreak of witchcraft persecution in America, the Salem witch-trials, took place in 1691-92. In 1712 a woman was convicted of witchcraft in England; in 1722 a woman was executed in Scotland for witchcraft. In Germany, the last recorded case of a witch trial occurred in 1793. Spontaneous outbursts of localized witch mania have taken place as recently as 1888.

At the level of popular superstition it cannot be said that the "cake of custom" has been altogether broken even in the twentieth century. In 1953 an official inquiry in France revealed that the popularity of magical and herbal cures was quite pronounced in certain regions of the French countryside.

What Lucien Febvre has termed the "discovery of the impossible" has indeed been a gradual process. By erecting an edifice of natural law in which immutable principles eternally operated, the seventeenth century leaders of the Scientific Revolution created a standard by which effects could be explained with reference to explicable causes. Yet they themselves did not realize the implications of their thought. It remained for the writers and publicists of the eighteenth and nineteenth centuries to relegate certain ideas to the realm of the impossible and the absurd. And yet the very triumph of the "discovery of the impossible" has created a paradox, especially for historians. Precisely because we think in terms of a rationalistic, scientific worldview with recognizable limitations of cause and effect we can neither fully understand nor appreciate the lost world of unquestioning belief in the supernatural. A realm of human experience has been closed off from us and we are the poorer for it. Only if historians learn not to project their own attitudes too dogmatically upon the past, only if they concentrate on those ideas which contemporaries scarcely questioned, which formed the basis of their mental and affective life, will something of this vanished world of the mind be restored to us.

The Renaissance was the last great age of magic. As science came to dominate Western thought, the widespread intellectual attraction of magic waned. Increasingly magic flourished only in the interstices between science and the supernatural. The seventeenth and eighteenth centuries saw the founding of esoteric occult societies, including the Rosicrucians and various branches of occultist Freemasonry like the Illuminati of Bavaria. But the occult societies inaugurated no new philosophical advances in magic; they looked to the past, not the future. The fifteen hundred year tradition of noetic magic became ossified, distorted, and increasingly linked with tendentious occult speculation, most of it grounded in little more than the childlike wish to believe. Not until the late nineteenth and early twentieth centuries did philosophy and psychology develop intersecting insights that pointed towards a new era in the development of noetic magic.

Part Four:
The Magus as Charlatan

Historians generally refer to the eighteenth century as the Age of Reason or the Era of Enlightenment and it is true that the diffuse and variegated movement known as the Enlightenment has traditionally occupied a dominant place in the intellectual history of the eighteenth century. Deservedly so, for that clever and sharp-tongued band of intellectuals and men of letters known as the *philosophes* succeeded in bringing about, in an astonishingly short period of time, a significant secularization of European thought. But the attention given by historians to the Enlightenment has served to obscure other intellectual movements whose significance may be as great or greater than the Enlightenment itself.

The eighteenth century was also an age of visions and visionaries. Christianity saw the rise of powerful new Protestant sects, most notably Methodism, which emphasized the internalized experience of union with God, the experience of spiritual rebirth. Millenarian prophetic movements emerged throughout Europe, especially in England. But perhaps the two most notable visionaries of the eighteenth century were the scientist, Emanuel Swedenborg and the poet, William Blake.

Born in Stockholm in 1688, Swedenborg was a scientific polymath who contributed to every field of science known in the eighteenth century. He was the first to advance the nebular hypothesis, invented the first fire extinguisher, and drew a design for a glider aircraft. But in the 1740s, Swedenborg abandoned science for theology and authored a series of anonymous works in which he advanced the principle that love and wisdom, emanating from God, form a series of corresponding levels of reality from the celestial to the material. His dream journals about the celestial world are among the most detailed and remarkable visionary experiences ever recorded. After his death in 1772, Swedenborgian societies sprang up all over Europe and two churches espousing Swedenborgian principles were established, the best known of which is the Church of the New Jerusalem.

Swedenborg greatly influenced William Blake as well as Baudelaire, Emerson, Yates and William James. But it is as a scientist who became a religious visionary that he is most representative of the intellectual and spiritual tensions that suffused eighteenth century life. Science, in the eighteenth century, was not yet the intellectual monolith that it later became. Swedenborg bridged the gap between science and religion with an intense mystical vision. Others, less gifted or perhaps just more cynical, preferred to bridge the gap with mumbo jumbo and fraud.

And so a century which has a reputation for studied thoughtfulness and an abhorrence for "enthusiasm" of any kind saw remarkable attention paid by men of prominent position to two individuals who made the most outrageous claims imaginable, men of doubtful origin who did not hesitate to accept the designation of magician when it was given them.

Of course, the fascination exerted by magic, indeed, by all things mysterious had never ceased to affect the poorer classes. The eminent French historian Albert Soboul has pointed out that books on magic were among the most popular of the street peddler's wares in pre-Revolutionary France. Intellectual movements (especially in an age lacking in immediate mass communication) cannot be expected to penetrate all ranks of society to an equal degree. Yet St. Germain and Cagliostro were the darlings, not of the laboring classes, but of the nobility. They moved in the highest circles, among men whose intelligence may perhaps be doubted but whose education was quite frequently the best that Europe had to offer. No convincing explanation of this seeming anomaly has yet been offered, although the place to start would no doubt be with an analysis of the appeal of Freemasonry to the elite of Europe, for St. Germain, Cagliostro, Mesmer, St. Martin and a variety of others with mystical and magical pretensions were leaders in the Freemason movement, which combined elaborate ritual with minimal religious belief and may have served as a kind of half-way house between Deism and Christianity. Indeed, a number of prominent men who were unquestionably sincere Christians were first attracted to the Freemason movement by the compelling personalities of St. Germain and Cagliostro and evidently joined for no other reason than to learn the amazing secrets which these men claimed to possess.

Chapter 15:
Tales of the Magi III:
The Comte de St. Germain:
Enigma of the Enlightenment

Who was the Comte de St. Germain? After nearly two hundred years we are not much closer to an answer to that question than was Frederick the Great when he pronounced St. Germain to be "one of the most enigmatic personages of the eighteenth century." Our chief knowledge of him is indirect and uncertain: letters and memoirs describing his activities, sometimes years after they were alleged to have taken place. The dates of his birth and his death are as uncertain as the events of his life. There is even a widespread belief among occult circles today that St. Germain is still alive, directing the activities of the Mystical Fraternity.

Our earliest record of him, one of the two surviving letters written in his own hand, is dated 22 November 1735 but reveals nothing other than the fact that he was then at the Hague. We next hear of him ten years later, on December 9, 1745, in a letter written by Horace Walpole to the British Envoy in Florence, Sir Horace Mann. Writes Walpole: "The other day they seized an odd man who goes by the name of Count St. Germain. He has been here these two years, and will not tell who he is or whence, but professes that he does not go by his right name. He sings and plays on the violin wonderfully, is mad, and not very sensible."

Considering the fact that St. Germain had been in London since 1743, it is surprising that more evidence has not turned up concerning his stay there especially since, as Walpole points out, he was such a remarkable character. Walpole's remarks, incidentally, are merely the first of a long series of double-edged tributes paid by eighteenth century memoirists to St. Germain's seemingly universal talents. The only other evidence we have relating to St. Germain's sojourn in England is an item from the **London Chronicle** dated 13-15 May 1760 which perhaps raises more questions than it answers:

"The author of the Brussels Gazette tells us that the person who styles himself Comte de St. Germain, who lately arrived here from Holland, was born in Italy in 1712. He speaks German and French as fluently as Italian, and expresses himself pretty well in English. He has a smattering of all the arts and sciences, is a good chemist, a virtuoso in musick, and a very agreeable companion. In 1746, he was on the point of being ruined in England. One who was jealous of him with a lady, slipt a letter into his pocket as from the young Pretender (thanking him for his services and desiring him to continue them), and immediately had him taken up by a messenger. His innocence being fully proved on his examination, he was discharged out of the custody of the messenger and asked to dinner by Lord H. Those who know him will he sorry to hear that he has incurred the Christian king's displeasure."

Although cleared of espionage, St. Germain, seeing that he had powerful enemies (it has been speculated that his accuser in this instance was the Prince of Wales, Frederick Louis) decided to leave England. Where he went is uncertain. St. Germain himself claims that he visited India for the second time in 1755 where, he says, he acquired his remarkable ability to transform jewels. In the same letter, he indicates that this was something he had been working on for a number of years.

At this stage in his life our picture of St. Germain is vague indeed. We know only that he is remarkably gifted in a variety of fields. His musical ability and command of languages indicates that he probably (though not necessarily) received the kind of education reserved primarily for the nobility. We know nothing of his physical appearance or his age (beyond the unsupported assertion that he was born in Italy in 1712). We do know, and this is sufficient to whet our curiosity, that he claimed to have the power of improving jewels. Fortunately, St. Germain was about to commence on the most fascinating (and best documented) period of his mysterious career.

In 1757, he was introduced to the Court at Versailles by the Comte de Belle-Isle, Louis XV's Minister of War, who had become acquainted with the magus in Vienna. St. Germain's rise to prominence in Court society was immediate and extraordinary. The King provided him with sumptuous quarters in the Chateau de Chambord where he established a laboratory for alchemical experiments. He soon attracted a devoted following of aristocratic admirers who pronounced him the most remarkable man in Europe. It was rumored that St. Germain had discovered the secret of eternal youth and was, in actuality, considerably older than he appeared to be. According to Madame de Hausset, lady-in-waiting to Madame de Pompadour:

"One day madame said to him in my presence, 'What was the personal appearance of Francis I? He was a king I should have liked.' 'He was, indeed, very captivating,' replied St. Germain; and he proceeded to describe his face and person, as that of a man whom he had accurately observed. 'It is a pity he was too ardent. I could have given him some good advice; which would have saved him from all his misfortunes: but he would not have followed it; for it seems a fatality attended princes, forcing them to shut their ears to the wisest counsel.' 'Was his court very brilliant?' inquired Madame de Pompadour. 'Very,' replied the count; but those of his grandsons surpassed it. In the time of Mary Stuart and Margaret of Valois, it was a land of enchantment--a temple sacred to pleasures of every kind.' Madame said, laughing, 'You seem to have seen all this.' 'I have an excellent memory, said he, and have read the history of France with great care. I sometimes amuse myself, not by making, but by letting it be believed that I lived in old times.'"

Madame de Hausset tells an interesting story which not only sheds further light on St. Germain's work with precious stones but also demonstrates his intimacy with Louis XV:

"The King ordered a middling-sized diamond which had a flaw in it, to be brought to him. After having it weighed, his majesty said to the Comte: 'The value of this diamond as it is, and with the flaw in it, is six thousand livres; without the flaw it would be worth at least ten thousand. Will you undertake to make me a gainer of four thousand livres?" St. Germain examined it very attentively, and said, 'It is possible; it may be done. I will bring it to you again in a month.' "At the time appointed the Comte de St. Germain brought back the diamond without a spot, and give it to the King. It was wrapped in a cloth of amianthos, which he took off. The King had it weighed immediately, and found it very little diminished. His Majesty then sent it to his jeweller by M. de

Gontaut, without telling him of anything that had passed. The jeweller gave him nine thousand six hundred livres for it. The King, however, sent for the diamond back again, and said he would keep it as a curiosity. He could not overcome his surprise and said M. de St. Germain must be worth millions, especially if he possessed the secret of making large diamonds out of small ones. The Comte neither said that he could or could not, but positively asserted that he knew how to make pearls grow, and give them the finest water. The King paid him great attention, and so did Madame de Pompadour. M. de Quesnoy once said that St. Germain was a quack, but the King reprimanded him. In fact, his Majesty appears infatuated with him, and sometimes talks as if his descent were illustrious."

It is difficult to know exactly what to make of this story. Obviously St. Germain could have substituted another diamond for the one given him by the King. But is it likely that he could have found a diamond exactly like the first except flawless, or that the substitute diamond would be able to fool not only the King but the King's jeweller? Moreover, what does the reference to "making pearls grow" signify? Is it possible that the Comte had stumbled upon the art of growing cultured pearls, a technique developed by the Japanese in the twentieth century?

During his stay in Paris, St. Germain gave every appearance of considerable wealth. He dressed simply but with considerable taste, his only concession to ornament the many diamonds with which he liked to adorn his fingers, his hat, even his shoes. He was a man of average size with intelligent and expressive, though not handsome, features. His rather dark complexion combined with his peculiar talent for recreating episodes from the distant past in a detailed and convincing manner, gave rise to the legend that he was the "Wandering Jew." Perhaps the strangest thing about him was that he gave no indication of the source of his obviously sizeable income. Those who have accused St. Germain of charlatanism should keep in mind that during his stay in Paris, indeed, during any part of his life of which we have any record, with only one exception, he made no apparent effort to extract money from anyone. His generosity was remarkable; he was always giving expensive gifts to ladies of the court; but, so far as is known, he never asked for anything in return---remarkable for a mere charlatan.

After three years of alternately titillating and dazzling the French court, St. Germain, who, by this time, had begun to wield a considerable amount of influence on French politics, was entrusted with a secret mission to the Hague by the King himself. France had become embroiled in the struggle later known as the Seven Year's War and was desperately looking for an honorable way out of it. St. Germain's assignment was to determine through cautious overtures to the English Ambassador at the Hague what terms England would accept should France sue for peace. Why Louis would entrust such a delicate mission to a man with no background in diplomacy rather than to an experienced member of his diplomatic staff can only be explained by the king's unfortunate predilection for secret diplomacy and by the remarkable sway which St. Germain had over him.

Inevitably, St. Germain aroused the jealousy of the regular French Ambassador to the Hague, the Marquis d'Affry, who entered into a correspondence with the Duc de Choiseul, an influential member of the French cabinet who, for reasons of his own, wanted the war prolonged. Meanwhile, St. Germain was making very little headway with the English Ambassador, General Yorke, who did little more than listen politely to the Comte's proposals. This intolerable situation came to a head when Choiseul managed to get hold of a letter which St. Germain had written to Madame de Pompadour. In high dudgeon, the Duc sent the following letter to d'Affry:

"Sir,

I send you a letter from M. de St. Germain to the Marquise de Pompadour which in itself will suffice to expose the absurdity of the personage; he is an adventurer of the first order, who is moreover, as far as I have seen, exceedingly foolish. I beg you immediately on receiving my letter to summon him to your house, and to tell him from me that . . . you are ordered to warn him that if I learn that far or near, in much or little, he chooses to meddle with Politics, I assure him that I shall obtain an order from the King that on his return to France he shall be placed for the rest of his life in an underground dungeon! After this declaration you will request him never again to set foot in your house, and it will be well for you to make public and known to all the Foreign Ministers, as well as to the Bankers of Amsterdam, the compliment you have been commanded to pay to this insufferable adventurer."

Not content with these measures, Choiseul extracted from the weak and vacillating Louis permission to have St. Germain arrested in Holland. Miraculously, the Comte escaped from the clutches of the police through the good offices of his friend and supporter, Count Bentinck van Rhoon, who has also provided us with perhaps the most incisive summation of this whole affair:

"If the Comte de St. Germain had shown as much prudence as he had shown zeal, he would have, I believe, much accelerated Peace; but he relied too much on his own intentions and had not a bad enough opinion of the men with whom he had to deal."

St. Germain's movements from this time until his death in 1784 are a matter of considerable dispute. It seems probable that from Holland he fled to England where he remained for a short while before returning to the continent. In 1763 we find him in the Austrian Netherlands, engaging in business activities of a rather questionable nature. Having overawed the Minister Plenipotentiary of this region, Cobenzl, with evidence of his alchemical virtuosity in improving metals and dyeing cloth, he proposed to set up factories throughout the land which would employ the cheap means of manufacture which he claimed to have designed. Cobenzl has left an interesting description of the Comte at this time:

"Although the story of his life and even his person are shrouded in mystery and obscurity, I discovered in him outstanding gifts in all the arts and sciences. He is a poet, a musician, a writer, doctor, physicist, chemist, mechanic, and a thorough connoisseur of painting. In a word he possesses a culture such as I have never yet found in any other human being, and he speaks all languages almost equally well, Italian, French and English particularly so. He has travelled over nearly the whole world, and as he was very entertaining in spite of all his learning, I passed my leisure hours very agreeably with him. The only thing I can reproach him with is frequent boasting about his talent and origins."

It was not long before Cobenzl had more than St. Germain's boasting to complain of, for the Comte disappeared with 100,000 gulden of the money which was to have been invested in the cloth and leather dyeing industries. This incident, contrasting so sharply with everything else that is known of St. Germain's character--his generosity, his refusal to exploit others for his own advantage when he could easily have done so--is the only documented instance of charlatanry in his entire career. It may well have been that straitened circumstances brought him to such questionable dealings. On the other hand, there is something incomplete and ambiguous about this entire affair, which is only increased by the fact that we don't know the Comte's side of the story. Whatever the case, his disappearance did not seem to have created much hardship, for Cobenzl himself stated that the factories which St. Germain had already established more than made up for the loss.

For the next twenty years he surfaced, in one guise or another, in almost every country in Europe, now as a Russian general, now as a Hungarian count. Each appearance added an additional coloring of mystery to his character. He seems to have participated in the founding of Masonic lodges, but the evidence is ambiguous. He was credited with miraculous feats, but we have no first hand proof. Even his death, well-documented as it is, is open to question. In 1779, St. Germain made the acquaintance of Prince Charles of Hesse-Cassell, a Freemason, who soon became his patron. Continuing with his alchemical experiments in a laboratory fitted out for him by the Prince, St. Germain spent the next several years in an atmosphere of scholarly simplicity far removed from the glittering court life to which he had become accustomed at Versailles. On the 27th of February 1784, he died, and the record of his death was duly entered in the parish register. Wrote Prince Charles in his memoirs:

"He was perhaps one of the greatest sages who ever lived. He loved humanity; he desired money only in order to give it to the poor. He even loved animals, and his heart was occupied only with the happiness of others. He believed he could make mankind happy by procuring for them new pleasures, lovelier cloths and colours; and his glorious colours cost almost nothing. I have never known a man with a clearer mind, and at the same time he was possessed of a learning, especially in history, that I have rarely found."

St. Germain's story does not, however, end with his death. In 1785, a year after he was said to have died, we find his name, along with that of Mesmer, Cagliostro and St. Martin, among those included in an invitation to a Masonic conference at Wilhelmsbad.

Did St. Germain really die in 1784? As one of his biographers puts it: "Evidence there is on both sides, and 'Church records' are not always infallible; how many a cause célèbre has arisen from a fictitious death. If the Comte de St. Germain wished to disappear from public life, this was the best way to accomplish his wish."

One of the most interesting pieces of "evidence" which purport to prove that St. Germain did not die is the story told by Madame d'Adhemar in her memoirs concerning the Comte's warnings to her of the catastrophe that would bring down the monarchy. This was in 1788, a year before the outbreak of the French Revolution and four years after St. Germain had supposedly been laid to rest at Eckernforde. The authenticity of these memoirs has been disputed and, as far as St. Germain is concerned, we should regard them as providing us with insight into the myth, not the man.

According to Mme d'Adhemar, several letters containing dire prophecies about the future of France were sent to her by an unknown correspondent. Fearing that there might be some truth to them, she passed the letters on to the Queen. Then, one day, she records, "On returning home, a note was given to me, thus worded:

"All is lost, Countess! This sun is the last which will set on the monarchy; tomorrow it will exist no more, chaos will prevail, anarchy unequalled. You know all I have tried to do to give affairs a different turn; I have been scorned; now it is too late. . . .Keep yourself in retirement, I will watch over you; be prudent, and you will survive the tempest that will have beaten down all. I resist the desire that I have to see you; what should we say to each other? You would ask of me the impossible; I can do nothing for the King, nothing for the Queen, nothing for the Royal Family, nothing even for the Duc d'Orleans, who will be triumphant tomorrow, and who, all in due course, will cross the Capitol to be thrown from the top of the Tarpeian rock. Nevertheless, if you would care very much to meet with an old friend, go to the eight o'clock Mass at the Récollets, and enter the second chapel on the right hand.

'I have the honour to be...

"'Comte de St. Germain.'

"At this name, already guessed, a cry of surprise escaped me; he is still living, he who was said to have died in 1784, and whom I had not heard spoken of for long years past--he had suddenly reappeared, and at what a moment, what an epoch! Why had he come to France? Was he then never to have done with life? For I knew some old people who had seen him bearing the stamp of forty or fifty years of age, and that at the beginning of the eighteenth century!"

Madame d'Adhemar, unable to resist so mysterious an invitation, kept the rendezvous. St. Germain appeared "with the same countenance as in 1760 and, in the course of a long conversation predicted in considerable detail the fate of the Bourbons. In a note appended to the original manuscript dated the 12th of May, 1821, a year before the Countess died, she wrote further: "I saw M. de St. Germain again, and always to my unspeakable surprise: at the assassination of the Queen; at the coming of the 18th Brumaire; the day following the death of the Duc d'Enghien; in the month of January, 1813; and on the eve of the murder of the Duc de Berri. I await the sixth visit when God wills.'" Nor was Madame d'Adhemar the last to see the enigmatic Comte. He has continued to turn up in as many different countries and in as many different guises dead as he did alive. One example, dating from the twentieth century, will suffice: "The other Adept whom I had the privilege of encountering physically was the Master the Comte de St. Germain, sometimes called the Prince Rakoczi. I met Him under quite ordinary circumstances (without any previous appointment, and as though by chance) walking down the Corso in Rome, dressed just as any Italian gentlemen might be. He took me up into the gardens on the Pincian Hill, and we sat for more than an hour talking about the Society and work."

It is pleasant to believe that the Comte is still alive, directing the activities of the Mystic Brotherhood, fated for the rest of eternity to be a Cassandra crying in the wilderness. Such a picture appeals to the romantic in us and does no one any obvious harm. On the other hand, has not the legend of St. Germain, along with other similar legends, tended to create the satisfying illusion that the future is in the hands of men whose wisdom surpasses human understanding and that, therefore, ordinary beings need do nothing about it? It is as dangerous as it is pleasant to believe in St. Germain, who is nothing more than a simple-minded substitute for that divine Providence which has for so long been singularly absent from the modern world.

Chapter 16:
Tales of the Magi IV:
Cagliostro: Friend of
Humanity or Quack of
Quacks?

In the winter of 1779 there appeared at Strasbourg a man of unusual powers, a clairvoyant and a healer. After staying with a noble acquaintance for a short time this man and his beautiful wife rented a house on the corner of the place d'Armes and the rue des Ecrivains where they began receiving visitors of all ranks and stations. The poor, especially, flocked to their door, were politely admitted and were, according to all reports, cured of a variety of diseases. Most extraordinary of all, the healer, who lived luxuriously, did not charge a single sou for his services.

Who was this "Friend of Humanity," as he liked to call himself? In Strasbourg he went under the name of the Count di Cagliostro but no one believed for a moment that this was his real name. As he later freely admitted, Cagliostro was only one of a series of pseudonyms that he had adopted in order to conceal his real identity. But what was the truth of his origins? The fanciful tale that he gave in his memoirs, possibly inspired by the legend of Christian Rozencreutz, about growing up in Egypt under the tutelage of the mysterious sage Althotas, can safely be discounted. It was the kind of story that Cagliostro hoped would charm his listeners and pique their imagination. He didn't really expect anyone to believe it. He had obviously learned a great deal from the Comte de St. Germain, if not personally (as seems unlikely) then certainly from the widely circulated stories about him. He knew how advantageous it could be to keep his past a mystery.

The problem of Cagliostro's true identity has not been satisfactorily solved to this day, despite the claims of his numerous biographers. Basing their arguments on unreliable contemporary sources, modern scholars have generally identified Cagliostro with the Sicilian rogue and counterfeiter Giuseppe Balsamo yet, as we shall see, such an identification raises as many problems as it solves.

Giuseppe Balsamo was born in Sicily in 1743, the son of a merchant who later went bankrupt. He was educated at the monastery of the Brothers of Charity at Caltagirone where he may have learned the rudiments of chemistry before being expelled for displaying an excessively bawdy imagination. After several brushes with the police in Palermo, Balsamo left Sicily and, after a time, appeared in Rome where he set about making his living as a forger. In 1768 he met the beautiful but probably illiterate daughter of a Roman copper smelter. Her name was Lorenza Feliciani and, within a few months, she became Balsamo's bride. Unable to support his new wife, Giuseppe went into partnership with two men, also forgers, who, after a quarrel, denounced him to the Roman police. The Balsamos fled Rome, travelled across Europe and, in the summer of 1771, arrived in London where they took a flat in Soho. It is alleged that Balsamo lived by trading on the charms of his simple-minded young wife during this period but this is uncertain. It seems likely that the young forger made an honest effort to change his ways and earn his living as a calligrapher. An unpaid bill forced him into unsuccessful litigation and, after various misadventures, he soon left England with Lorenza in tow, bound for parts unknown. Here ends the known story of Giuseppe Balsamo. The rest is undocumented legend.

In 1776, four years after the Balsamos left London, a man calling himself first the Marchese Pellegrini and then, shortly thereafter, the Count di Cagliostro, appeared in the English capital with his attractive wife Seraphina and took lodgings at Whitcomb Street. He devoted most of his time to esoteric studies and, before long, was initiated into the "Strict Observance" of English Masonry. What justification is there for linking the Sicilian adventurer Balsamo with the aspiring occultist Cagliostro?

The first person to make the connection between Balsamo and Cagliostro was the notorious Théveneau de Morande, a muckraking journalist in the pay of the French government at a time when the French monarchy had every reason to discredit Cagliostro. According to Morande, he obtained his information primarily from Cagliostro's wife,

Seraphina. At this time, however, Seraphina was in prison, charged with infidelity by her husband. If she really did confess, her motives for doing so are certainly open to question. Morande may have promised her clemency if she merely gave her assent to an identification which he thought up himself. Seraphina was never noted for either intelligence or loyalty. In any event, soon after she was reunited with her husband she completely abjured the confession.

The only other contemporary source that lends verisimilitude to the story that Cagliostro was really Balsamo is a biography of Cagliostro written by an anonymous Catholic priest based on the records of Cagliostro's trial before the Inquisition. However, as we know from the witch-trials of the sixteenth and seventeenth centuries, the "facts" which are elicited by Inquisitors tend to reflect their own often overheated imaginations more accurately than they do the actual beliefs and intentions of the accused.

Despite the obvious bias of these two sources, the circumstantial evidence remains fairly impressive. Cagliostro once gave his wife's maiden name as Feliciani which was the maiden name of Balsamo's "Lorenza." A man named Aylett alleged that he had known Balsamo in 1772 and that he was the same man who went under the name of Cagliostro in 1777. Moreover, Balsamo had an uncle named Giuseppe Cagliostro and Cagliostro once gave his own first name as Giuseppe. Finally, one of Balsamo's uncles claimed to have received a number of letters from his nephew signed "Cagliostro." The evidence is almost overwhelming--until one examines it more closely.

Feliciani is a common Italian name--no real proof here. Aylett was a convicted perjurer whose testimony cannot be relied on. The similarity in name with Balsamo's uncle is suggestive but inconclusive. The allegation by Balsamo's uncle was completely unsupported by any documentary evidence which, if he were telling the truth, should have been easy enough to produce.

What remains of this tissue of rumors, allegations, and uncertainties? Only a haunting suspicion that Balsamo and Cagliostro were one and the same. The evidence is clearly inconclusive. Yet scholars have not hesitated to jump on the Balsamo bandwagon. Why is this? Perhaps they prefer an inadequate solution to the mystery of Cagliostro's origin to no solution at all. In addition, nineteenth century biographers of the magus were anxious to discredit him; they were incapable of seeing Cagliostro as anything other than a charlatan. Witness this frenzied outburst on the part of Thomas Carlyle as he attempts to describe Cagliostro's appearance:

"Fittest of visages; worthy to be worn by the Quack of Quacks! A most portentous face of scoundrelism; a fat, snub, abominable face; dew-lipped, flat-nosed, greasy, full of greediness, sensuality, oxlike obstinacy; a forehead impudent, refusing to be ashamed; and then two eyes turned up seraphically languishing, as in divine contemplation and adoration. . . ; on the whole, perhaps the most perfect quack-face produced by the eighteenth century."

Anyone who has contemplated the bust of Cagliostro by Houdon on which this description is based, will not be able to summon up much confidence in historians like Carlyle.

Let us leave Balsamo or Balsamo-Cagliostro as a problem incapable of solution and direct our attention to the Cagliostro of Strasbourg as he prepares to enter onto the stage of European history.

Among the cures that Cagliostro is alleged to have made at Strasbourg, that of Mme. Sarrasin proved most advantageous to him. Sarrasin, a Swiss banker, implored Cagliostro to treat his wife who was suffering from a fever that had lasted for eight months. She appeared to be on the verge of dying. Cagliostro talked to her, gained her confidence and gave her his famous "elixir of Egypt," a harmless compound of herbs and water. Her rapid recovery brought Cagliostro Sarrazin's undying confidence and, more important, his financial support in times of need. No one knows for certain how many cures of this kind Cagliostro effected during his three-year stay in Strasbourg. Suffice it to say that there were enough to attract the attention of some of the most powerful men in France.

One of these was Cardinal Prince Rohan, Grand Almoner of France. The Cardinal, who was rumoured to have an income of 1,200,000 livres a year, was a member of one of the oldest and most distinguished families in the kingdom. He had been ordained a priest in 1760 and in 1771 was sent by Louis XV as a special envoy to the Court of the Austrian Empress Maria Theresa. There his dissolute habits and eccentric personality won him the enduring enmity of the Empress and of her daughter, Marie Antoinette, soon to become Queen of France. Rohan, who was nothing if not a fool, in the face of all this hostility nevertheless nurtured a secret passion for Marie Antoinette and used every means at his disposal to get into her good graces. All avenues failing, he turned to the miracle-man of Strasbourg for help.

At first Cagliostro ignored Rohan's entreaties for an audience, saying that unless the Cardinal was ill, he could do nothing for him. At last, Rohan, feigning an asthma attack, managed to persuade Cagliostro to see him. Before long the two were fawning over one another in mutual admiration. "Your soul is worthy of my own," Cagliostro is reported to have told Rohan, a remark which could be interpreted as an insult to them both.

With Rohan's help, Cagliostro obtained letters from the Foreign Minister, the Comte de Vergennes; the Keeper of the Seal, the Marquis de Miromesnil; and the War Minister, Marshal Ségur, all attesting to his genius and honesty and requesting provincial officials to treat him with the greatest respect. Armed with such irresistible recommendations, Cagliostro left Strasbourg for Bordeaux and Lyons where he continued to perform remarkable cures. In 1783 in Lyons he founded a Masonic Lodge devoted to the so-called "Egyptian Rite," a blend of farce and bad Rosicrucianism. Then in 1784 he arrived in Paris intending to take part in an international meeting of European Freemasons. Undoubtedly Cagliostro believed that he was now in a position to dominate European Masonry. The news of his cures had spread all across Europe; he enjoyed a reputation that eclipsed even that of Mesmer, who was also a Freemason. Cagliostro not only wanted his "Egyptian Rite" recognized by the established Masonic organizations; he demanded that it be installed as the highest form of Masonic ritual.

Cagliostro's messianic dreams were never realized. Although accepted at the Masonic convention with considerable initial enthusiasm, he soon alienated almost everyone there by adopting an attitude of regal superiority and autocratic rigidity that was laughable in light of his inadequate command of French and his proletarian ways. Moreover, he was soon to become embroiled in one of the most celebrated scandals of the century, the notorious "Affair of the Diamond Necklace."

In order to understand this affair and the furor that it produced, it is necessary first to appreciate the hostility with which Marie Antoinette was regarded by much of the French populace. Remote, unapproachable, the "Autrichienne" as she was popularly called, was widely believed to be an unfaithful wife. As a song of the period had it:

> Would you know
> A cuckold, a whore, a bastard?
> See the King, the Queen
> And Monsieur the Dauphin.

That there was no justification for doubting the Queen's fidelity is not important.   Overwhelming popular dislike of Marie Antoinette accounts for the alacrity with which people seized upon the details of the "Affair of the Diamond Necklace" and, believing the Queen to be guilty, inflated the whole incident out of all proportion to its true significance. Briefly what happened was this.

Two court jewelers had gone to a great deal of trouble to gather diamonds from all over Europe and make them into a necklace for Louis XV's mistress, Madame DuBarry. Unfortunately, Louis died before the sale could be effected. The jewellers were thus left with a bauble that no one but a monarch could afford. At this point Rohan entered the picture. His passion for the Queen and his eagerness to win her favor were well known, especially to the Cardinal's erstwhile mistress, the Comtesse de la Motte. The Comtesse, an adventurer who, like Cagliostro, forged her claim to nobility, saw a magnificent opportunity to make her fortune.

First she engaged a friend to imitate the Queen's handwriting in a series of letters which she then transmitted to the gullible Rohan. The upshot of this correspondence was that the Queen supposedly wanted Rohan secretly to buy the diamond necklace for her. As if this weren't enough, the Comtesse even arranged a clandestine meeting between Rohan and the "Queen" who was really the "Baroness" d'Oliva, a prostitute adept at impersonations. At this meeting, Rohan received numerous indications of the "Queen's" affection for him and soon resolved to carry out her wishes. He presented the letter authorizing him to buy the necklace to one of the jewelers who gave it to him in return for a promissory note for 1,600,000 francs. Rohan then turned the necklace over to the Comtesse de la Motte, his faithful go-between, and it was never (in its entirety, anyway) seen again. Presumably the Comtesse gave it to her husband who fled to England where he probably sold the diamonds piecemeal.

When Rohan was unable to meet the payments on the necklace, the whole affair was brought to light. Rohan was arrested and imprisoned in the Bastille. The Comtesse, who had fled into hiding, was located and arrested along with the "Baroness" d'Oliva and Retaux de Villette who was responsible for forging the letters. Also arrested was Cagliostro.

What role did the "Friend of Humanity" play in this sordid affair? Apparently none whatsoever. Cagliostro's only crime was his friendship with Rohan, which aroused the jealousy and hatred of the Comtesse de la Motte. Upon her arrest she violently denounced Cagliostro as the instigator of the crime. Despite his protests and the obvious lack of evidence, the magus was thrown into the Bastille on August 23, 1785 where he was to remain for nearly a year.

During this period Cagliostro was prevented from communicating with his wife who, unknown to him, was also incarcerated in the Bastille. He sent her several letters but they were intercepted by the Governor General of the prison and were never delivered. Months of agony and uncertainty followed. He engaged competent lawyers to defend him and together they drew up a remarkable document concerning his past and especially his relations with Cardinal de Rohan which is reminiscent of the **Confessions** of Rousseau:

"I am oppressed, I am accused, I am calumniated. Have I deserved this fate? I search in my conscience and I find there the peace which men deny me."

This memoir, which was widely circulated in Paris, made a good impression on a populace dissatisfied with the King's justice. Meanwhile Cagliostro was making progress in his efforts to clear his name. First the Comtesse de la Motte confessed that the magus had had nothing whatsoever to do with the fraud. Then Cagliostro had an opportunity to cross-examine her lover, the forger Villette, who broke down and confessed his role in the affair. Finally, on June 1, 1786, Cagliostro was released, completely exonerated. Also released (oddly enough) were the "Baroness" d'Oliva and Cardinal Rohan. Seraphina Cagliostro had been freed some weeks earlier. As for the rest of the principals, M. de la Motte was condemned to be beaten, branded and sent to the galleys;

Villette was banished and the Comtesse received a life sentence to the Salpetrière. This was by no means the last of the resourceful Comtesse, however. Within a year she escaped and went to London where she was reunited with her husband (who had been condemned in absentia). She had just enough time to write an autobiography full of calumnies against Cagliostro before she died in 1791.

Cagliostro's release was widely hailed by the citizens of Paris. But there were those at the palace, among them the King and Queen, who did not look so favorably on him. They believed him to be guilty and regarded his release as the judicial equivalent of a slap in the face. The day after he received his freedom, Cagliostro was ordered by the King to leave Paris within eight days and the kingdom within three weeks. Stunned by this fresh insult, Cagliostro complied. Traveling to Boulogne, he once again set sail for England.

A week after his arrival in London Cagliostro published his famous **Letter to the French People** protesting the injustice of his exile from France. One passage is worth quoting:

"Am I coming back to France? Only when the site of the Bastille has become an open square. . . You have everything you need for your happiness, you French, except one little thing: the certainty that if you are innocent, you will sleep safely in your beds. Let your parliaments work for this happy revolution. Then will reign over you a prince who will seek his glory in abolishing the royal warrants, and in convening your States-General. Realizing that abuse of power destroys, in the end, power itself, he will be the first among Frenchmen."

Counter-revolutionaries anxious to prove the complicity of the Freemasons in the French Revolution have often pointed to this statement as evidence of a Masonic conspiracy to overthrow the monarchy. Occultists hopeful of establishing proof of Cagliostro's alleged magical powers have argued that the statement is nothing less than the prophetic utterance of a clairvoyant. But a reasonable examination of the quotation reveals that there is virtually nothing prophetic about it. Beyond the mention of the destruction of the Bastille (clearly a wish, not a prophecy) and the convening of the Estates-General (a commonly expressed desire on the part of many Frenchmen at the time) there is nothing about these words that foretell the future. Who, for example, is the enlightened prince Cagliostro mentions? Napoleon? Even the most devoted Bonapartist would have difficulty in swallowing that.

Cagliostro had reached his apogee at Strasbourg and Lyons. From the time of his arrival in Paris, his career began to decline; it was not until he reached London, however, that his reputation was completely destroyed. The agent of destruction was Théveneau de Morande whose allegations against him have already been discussed. Whether these allegations were true, they were widely believed. Soon not even fellow Masons would be seen in Cagliostro's company. In vain did he try to strike back at the venomous Morande. At one point he even challenged him to a duel but Morande turned him down.

At last, utterly defeated, Cagliostro left England for Basel where the loyal Sarrasin and his wife promised to give him aid. Undoubtedly Cagliostro could have spent his declining years peacefully at Basel, reflecting on past glories. But his messianic dreams were not yet stilled; Basel did not offer him the kinds of opportunities that he still believed were part of his destiny. Restless, he soon left Switzerland. But where was he to go? France and England were closed to him. Morande's libels were being freely circulated throughout the continent. What country would have him? Running into opposition wherever he turned, he at last give in to Seraphina's importunings and returned to Italy. Arriving in Rome in May 1789, Cagliostro apparently tried to make his peace with the Catholic Church, hoping to get his Egyptian Rite recognized. When this failed, he began holding his Egyptian services, beginning in September and continuing sporadically into December. No one was very interested and he was forced to sell the healing services that he had once given away; but this didn't work either. His powers, like his luck, had deserted him; indeed, the two were probably closely related. On 27 December 1789 Cagliostro was arrested by the Inquisition and imprisoned in the fortress of San Angelo. After a trial lasting less than a month he was condemned to death as a heretic and a Freemason, a sentence which was commuted by the Pope to life imprisonment. Seraphina was treated less severely and placed in a convent for the rest of her life. After being transferred to the prison of San Leo, Cagliostro, on 26 August 1795, reportedly died of apoplexy. Two years later when the French armies under General Dumbrowski captured the fortress of San Leo, the first prisoner they asked about was Cagliostro whom they regarded as a victim of monarchical and papal injustice. He would have delighted in such a tribute.

Despite considerable documentation, the story of Cagliostro is as enigmatic and perplexing as that of St. Germain. At least with St. Germain, the spectre of Balsamo does not intrude at every turn in the road. Moreover, Balsamo is not the only mystery connected with Cagliostro. Where, for example, did his money come from? Until just before his trial by the Inquisition, there is no record of his ever having requested payment for his services. Indeed, from his first appearance he was well supplied with funds, certainly enough to live like a noble and to buy expensive jewelry for Seraphina. This was a problem that sorely vexed the Comtesse de la Motte: "In a word, without having ever inherited anything, bought anything, sold anything, acquired anything, Cagliostro has everything." The source of Cagliostro's wealth will likely remain a mystery. Conjectures there have been aplenty: that he was financed by the Illuminati in an attempt to overthrow the French monarchy; that he was an alchemist who manufactured his own gold; that he really did charge for his services despite all of the evidence to the contrary.

Despite whatever plausibility such statements may have (and they seem to have very little) they remain only conjectures. Another problem is Cagliostro's supposed spiritual transformation. Enthusiastic biographers have maintained that even if Cagliostro really were Balsamo, he was utterly changed by his initiation into the inner secrets of Freemasonry. E. M. Butler has even advanced the hypothesis that Cagliostro was a victim of a split personality: when things went well for him he was Cagliostro; when they grew sour, he became Balsamo again. All of these arguments rest on the assumption that Balsamo was sordid and Cagliostro was saintly. It is much more likely, even if the two were not one and the same, that both personalities contained elements of charlatanry and sainthood. When removed from the distorting lenses of calumny and hero-worship, Cagliostro may be seen as an ordinary man with extraordinary ambitions, a victim, in the last analysis of hubris. He was not, despite many good qualities, quite the "Friend of Humanity" that he claimed to be; nor was he, it should hastily be added, Carlyle's despicable "Quack of Quacks."

Part Five:
The Magus as Monster

Chapter 17:
Magic in the 19th Century

During the nineteenth century magic was increasingly regarded with contempt. Science proved itself competent to deal successfully with problems in a variety of new fields, especially geology and biology. Magic no longer seemed to have scientific potential. In the nineteenth century, scientific achievement kept pace with scientific theory and the gap could no longer be filled by the charlatan. Nineteenth century magic moved away from the transitive sorcery of Cagliostro toward the imaginative, largely subjective magic of Eliphas Lévi, the Theosophical Society and, at the end of the century, the Hermetic Order of the Golden Dawn.

The Romantic Movement was the last stronghold in the nineteenth century of the magical world view. Scholars have noted the prevalence of magical motifs in Romantic poetry, the abundance of charms, spells, love potions and prophetic dreams. The horror story and the Gothic novel, products of the late eighteenth and early nineteenth centuries, kept alive an attitude of wonder toward the unknown and the supernatural.

The mainstream of magical development in the nineteenth century can be regarded as a minor tributary of the Romantic Movement. The most famous magician of the first half of the century, Alphonse Louis Constant (c. 1810-75), better known as Eliphas Lévi, was hardly a practicing magician at all. His only known foray into practical magic was his attempted evocation of Apollonius of Tyana in London in 1854 which, even according to Lévi, was only partially successful. Despite his lack of practical experience, Lévi's writings influenced later occultists. His History of Magic is largely an exercise in imagination with little basis in fact. Lévi's other major work, Transcendental Magic, significantly influenced the trend toward ritual magic which reached its highest development in the Order of the Golden Dawn.

Among those impressed by Lévi's writings was Sir Edward Bulwer-Lytton whose novel, **Zanoni**, a romanticized version of the legend of St. Germain, reflects a number of Lévi's ideas. Lytton was also responsible for inaugurating a short-lived magical society in England around the middle of the century.

The Tarot

Of all the manifestations of the occult in modern culture, the Tarot card deck is the most widespread and the most misunderstood. Consisting of seventy-eight cards, fifty-six of which, the Minor Arcana, correspond roughly to the suits in an ordinary deck of cards and twenty-two Major Arcana, consisting of archetypal figures like the Fool, the Magician, and Death, the Tarot is, next to Astrology, the most popular form of divination in the Western world.

Occultists have blithely identified the Tarot as the precursor of the modern deck of cards, possibly Egyptian in origin, its twenty-two Major Arcana corresponding to the twenty-two letters of the Hebrew alphabet and thus linked to the Cabala, and originally used for purposes of divination and meditation. All of these claims are false.

Tarot cards first appeared in northern Italy in the early fifteenth century, several decades after the regular deck of playing cards was invented. They were not used for divination until the eighteenth century and the Major Arcana have no historical connection (except a recent one) with the Hebrew alphabet or the Cabala.

The modern, esoteric history of the Tarot begins in France in the eighteenth century with two obscure writers, Court de Gébelin and Jean-Baptiste Alliette (known under the pen name of Eteilla). Of Swiss origin, Court de Gébelin emigrated to France in 1760, became a Freemason and, in the 1770s and '80s, published a multivolume work called **Monde Primitif** in which appeared the first article on the occult use of the Tarot. It was Court de Gébelin who identified the origin of the Tarot with ancient Egypt and, in fact, argued that, properly understood, it was an Egyptian book:

"This Egyptian Book, the only remnant of their magnificent librar-ies, exists in our day: it is such a common thing that no scholar has deigned to concern himself with it; no one among us has ever sus-pected its illustrious origin."

A supplementary essay in **Monde Primitif**, probably written by the Comte de Mellet, states that the Tarot is actually the Egyptian Book of Thoth and that the word Tarot comes from the Egyptian TA-ROSH meaning the Doctrine of Thoth, ROSH being supposedly the Egyptian name for Hermes or Thoth.

The first professional cartomancer was Court de Gébelin's contem-porary Jean-Baptiste Alliette, who, under the pen name Eteilla, pub-lished a series of books and pamphlets on divination by cards, begin-ning as early as 1770. Eteilla subscribed to the Egyptian origin theory and, more than anyone else, was responsible for the wide dissemina-tion of cartomancy in France.

"It seems unlikely that, but for Court de Gébelin, Etteilla would never have thought of the Tarot pack as the 'Book of Thoth' or of using it for divination, let alone as the basis for elaborate occult theories. Conversely, had it not been for Etteilla, Court de Gébelin's speculation about the Tarot would most likely have been forgotten."

The next major figure in the history of the Tarot is Alphonse-Louis Constant who wrote under the pen name Eliphas Lévi. Both Court de Gébelin and the comte de Mellet had hinted at a possible correspon-dence between the Major Arcana and the twenty-two letters of the He-brew alphabet. But it was Lévi who turned their hints into a full-blown theory. Unfortunately, it had no basis in fact:

"Lévi's theory is historically untenable. The Tarot arose, around 1425, among Italian Christians who knew nothing of the Cabala. . .Nei-ther the Cabala nor the Tarot originated in remote antiquity. They did not originate together. They do not express the same doctrine or em-ploy the same symbolism."

Lévi's writings greatly influenced British occultists, especially the Order of the Golden Dawn and it was chiefly through a Golden Dawn member, the learned occultist A.E. Waite, that the Tarot has entered the occult iconography of the twentieth century. Waite supervised the cre-ation of his own Tarot deck, the so-called Rider-Waite deck, which has become the most familiar form in which the Tarot is used today.

The Proper Use of the Tarot

Although the Tarot may be enjoyable for fortune-telling, like all systems of divination, it is subjective, inaccurate, and potentially dangerous if taken too literally. Because of the archetypal nature of the iconography of the Major Arcana, however, it is useful as a device for aiding meditation and stimulating imagination. Chapter 30 contains suggestions for how to use the Tarot in a Jungian meditation.

Theosophy

Another occultist who looked favorably on Eliphas Lévi was the founder of the Theosophical Society, Helen Petrovna Blavatsky (1831-1891). Madame Blavatsky set the tone for all later occultism with her romantic mixture of traditional magic and eclectic orientalism, best articulated in **The Secret Doctrine**. It was Madame Blavatsky with her tales of the Secret Chiefs (who lived, if that is the word, in remote Tibet) and her belief in spiritualism and Hindu mysticism who, more than anyone, provided the impetus, both intellectual and organizational, to the proliferation of occult societies witnessed by the twentieth century.

Blavatsky's central insight, that ". . . there are hidden powers in man, which are capable of making a God of him on earth," was derived initially from her encounters with Western occultism, especially the writings of Paracelsus and Giordano Bruno. Only later did she decide to add elements of Eastern mysticism to the concoction of concepts that she termed theosophy.

A natural rebel and youthful iconoclast, Blavatsky (or HPB as she came universally to be known) claimed to have experienced psychic events from earliest childhood, including innumerable conversations with her toy stuffed animals. But her public life as an occultist began in 1873 when she met the venerable journalist Colonel Henry Steel Olcott, an American with a profound interest in spiritualism. By 1875, the two had created the Theosophical Society, an organization devoted to establishing universal brotherhood and investigating man's hidden godlike powers. HPB supplied the Society with its manifesto, the two-volume **Isis Unveiled**, reported to have been partially dictated to the hashish smoking Blavatsky by spirits knowledgeable in gnostic and cabalistic doctrines.

HPB enjoyed demonstrating her alleged psychic powers, which she claimed were performed through her by her secret masters in Tibet. She was merely their chela, or disciple. In 1884, after volunteering to have her powers investigated by the London-based Society for Psychical Research, HPB's former housekeeper in India, Emma Coulomb, informed the press that Blavatsky was a fake, and produced incriminating letters from her mistress that seemed to substantiate the charge. Worn out by the controversy that the charges of fakery created as well as by long hours devoted to writing her magnum opus, **The Secret Doctrine**, Blavatsky, who had Bright's disease, died in 1891 at the age of sixty.

Her creation, the Theosophical Society, thrived under the leadership of Olcott and the charismatic Annie Besant, spawning dozens of imitators, including Rudolf Steiner's Anthroposophical Society. What passes for the occult in the modern West is largely modeled after HPB's brand of higher nonsense.

The Order of the Golden Dawn

The Order of the Golden Dawn was strongly influenced by both Lévi and Blavatsky. Aleister Crowley, born the year of Lévi's death, believed himself to be a reincarnation of the French magus. Initiates into the Golden Dawn were strongly encouraged to read The Secret Doctrine, although they were certainly not enjoined to believe everything they found there. Despite such obvious intellectual antecedents, however, the Order of the Golden Dawn was essentially the product of a particular historical situation, the lineaments of which are only now beginning to be understood.

"First of all, you must never speak of anything by its name - - in that country. So, if you see a tree on a mountain, it will be better to say 'Look at the green on the high'; for that's how they talk--in that country. And whatever you do, you must find a false reason for doing it--in that country. If you rob a man, you must say it is to help and protect him: that's the ethics of that country. And everything of value has no value at all--in that country. You must be perfectly common-place if you want to be a genius--in that country. And everything you like you must pretend not to like; and anything that is there you must pretend is not there--in that country. And you must always say that you are sacrificing yourself in the cause of religion, and morality, and humanity and liberty, and progress, when you want to cheat your neighbour--in that country."

"Good heavens!" cried Iliel; "are we going to England?"

From **Moonchild** by Aleister Crowley

Chapter 18:
Tales of the Magi V:
The Anti-Victorians: Yeats, Crowley and the Golden Dawn

The origins of the Golden Dawn are connected with that somewhat disreputable branch of Freemasonry known as Rosicrucianism. In the 1850s there had flourished in England a Rosicrucian society headed by Sir Edward Bulwer-Lytton which dabbled desultorily in magic. Since almost nothing is known of this organization, it was safe enough for members of the Societas Rosicruciana in Anglia, a club which was founded sometime in the 1860s and allowed as members only Master Masons, to claim intimate connection with the older group. In any event, the Societas Rosicruciana was, at least initially, an antiquarian's club which devoted itself, more or less seriously, to the study of Pythagoreanism, Hermetism, the Cabala and other aspects of the occult in classical antiquity.

In 1888, three of the leading members of the Societas Rosicruciana, S. L. McGregor Mathers, Dr. William R. Woodman, and Dr. William Wynn Westcott, founded the Hermetic Society of the Golden Dawn in London. The inspiration for this new occult organization, which, unlike the previous Rosicrucian societies, was solemnly devoted to the practice of ceremonial magic, was a manuscript allegedly found by Dr. Woodman in a bookshop in Farringdon Road, London. Unable to decipher the manuscript, which was written in a mysterious code, Woodman showed it to one or two of his friends. To everyone's surprise, only one person, Mathers, was able to translate it. According to Mathers the manuscript contained instructions for performing ceremonial magic along with the address of a German adept named Anna Sprengler who lived in Nuremberg. Communication was soon established with Ms. Sprengler who provided further information on the ceremonies along with a charter for establishing a magical society in England.

The apocryphal nature of this tale is obvious; but it is clear that Mathers was the guiding force behind the founding of the Golden Dawn as well as its most important member. Mrs. Mathers who was, significantly, Henri Bergson's sister, described her husband's position in the Golden Dawn in this way:

"In 1888, after the publication of The Qabalah Unveiled, my husband started the working of his esoteric school... Dr. Woodman and Dr. Wynn-Westcott aided in the administrative side of this school and its teaching to a certain extent.

"As a pioneer movement, for the first ten or twelve years it encountered many of the difficulties that beset work that is given ahead of its time, but we had been told that the beginning would be in the nature of an experiment and that the students would be sifted. Dr. Woodman died in the year 1890, and in 1897 Dr. Wynn-Westcott resigned, after which my husband entirely reorganized the school under orders, and further teachings were given him."

All of this is murky enough, but it is evident that Mather's prominence was chiefly due to his ability to communicate with those mysterious beings known in occult circles as The Secret Chiefs, remote unapproachable shapers of humanity's destiny who conveniently provided Mathers with instructions whenever he ran into difficulty. Mathers, the son of an English clerk, never visited Scotland in his life. Nevertheless, he adopted the middle name of McGregor and frequently boasted of his non-existent Scottish ancestry. Before long he transposed his real and adopted names and became Mathers McGregor. This was unsatisfactory, so he ennobled himself with the title of Chevalier. Mathers ended his career of self-conferred nobility by becoming the Comte de Glenstrae.

Despite elements of farce and charlatanry in the makeup of the Golden Dawn and in its leadership, the appeal which it exerted should be taken seriously for it counted among its members such significant literary figures as W. B. Yeats, Arthur Machen and Algernon Blackwood, scholars like Westcott and A. E. Waite and, at one time, the Astronomer Royal of Scotland, Dr. James W. Brodie-Innes. In short, its membership was nothing less than brilliant.

What was the appeal of the Golden Dawn? In the first place, it had all of the alluring trappings of any secret society: complex initiation rites, secret passwords, bizarre dress and the like. More important, its rituals were better-written, more evocative, and more poetic than those of most occult societies. This was clearly a factor in the attraction which the Golden Dawn had for Yeats who would have been repelled by crude, unaesthetic language. Most significant, however, was the Order's insistence that it was possible to attain absolute perfection through the conscientious application of magic.

Magic, to the members of the Golden Dawn, was not the ability to perform unusual feats of mind-reading, clairvoyance or levitation. It was, rather, a severe form of mental and spiritual discipline which, if properly practised, would result in the ability to penetrate the "veil of illusion," the world of everyday life. Members were encouraged to work their way up through a complicated series of grades culminating in Ipsissimus, the tenth grade, in which one became virtually a god. No member of the Golden Dawn apparently achieved this exalted state, although several, including Mathers, rose to Grade Nine, the Magus. To Yeats (who joined the Order in 1890) magic was second in importance only to his poetry; indeed, it was the very stuff of which poetry is made. In his essay "Magic," written in 1901, Yeats pointed out the basic similarities: "I cannot now think symbols less than the greatest of all powers, whether they are used consciously by the masters of magic, or half unconsciously by their successors, the poet, the musician and the artist." But Yeats' belief in magic went far beyond this. He believed that it enabled human beings to manipulate their environment, to control their own destiny:

"The central principle of all the Magic of power is that everything we formulate in the imagination, if we formulate it strongly enough, realizes itself in the circumstances of life, acting either through our own souls, or through the spirits of Nature."

To Yeats, then, magic was essentially a philosophy of power, which located the source of power in the individual human will and there alone.

Why was Yeats attracted to magic? In his autobiography he portrays himself as an extremely shy and introverted young man. He felt like a cog in the great machine of industrial life. Yet, although he detested industrial society and Victorian social conformity, he continued to lead a respectable and circumspect life. His was chiefly a rebellion of the intellect, expressed in his poetry by a longing for an idealized Irish past and in his essays by visions of a spiritual utopia in the indefinite future:

"I cannot get it out of my mind that this age of criticism is about to pass, and an age of imagination, of emotion, of moods, of revelation, about to come in its place; for certainly belief in a supersensual world is at hand again."

Yeats was really not so very different from thousands of other Victorians who, caught up in the deadly routine of ordinary life, applauded the exploits of General Gordon and thrilled to the adventure novels of H. Rider Haggard. Romanticism was not alien to the Victorians, if kept within proper limits.

Another member of the Golden Dawn whose opinions on magic and the social order are well known was Aleister Crowley. Unlike Yeats, Crowley was an anti-Victorian in life as well as thought.

Crowley was born in Leamington, Warwickshire on October 12, 1875. Concerning his birthplace, he once characteristically observed: "It has been remarked a strange coincidence that one small county should have given England her two greatest poets--for one must not forget William Shakespeare (1550-1616)." His father was a Quaker who belonged to the particularly austere sect known as the Plymouth Brethren. Crowley's mother, who was mentally unbalanced, believed her child was the "great Beast" whose coming had been prophesied in Revelations. Crowley grew up in an atmosphere of Puritan fanaticism. Gradually he began to think of himself as the living embodiment of all the values which the Plymouth Brethren professed to despise. Accepting his mother's view of his debased character seriously, Crowley adopted an ethic of antinomianism. His early indoctrination by the Plymouth Brethren, however, had convinced him of the reality of the spirit world. He thus contained within himself two contradictory urges: an impulse toward skepticism, and an equally strong bent toward spirituality, tendencies which were also strikingly evident in the late Victorian society into which he was born, especially in the struggle between the spirit of scientific positivism and that of an Evangelically inspired Christianity. Crowley was to attempt a reconciliation of these two contradictory traditions in a way that proved to be equally shocking to the adherents of each, thus earning for himself the Sunday Supplement title of the "wickedest man in the world."

In his first year as an undergraduate at Trinity College, Cambridge, Crowley underwent a spiritual crisis. Rejecting Victorian respectability and its religious underpinnings, he began to move in the direction of magic:

"The forces of good were those which had constantly oppressed me. I saw them daily destroying the happiness of my fellow-men. Since, therefore, it was my business to explore the spiritual world, my first step must be to get into personal communication with the devil."

Crowley spent much of his remaining years at Cambridge (he never took a degree) looking for a method by which he could achieve this bizarre goal. In 1898, when he left Cambridge, he wrote: "I was whitehot on three points: climbing, poetry and Magick." Within the year, he had been initiated into the Golden Dawn.

It should be emphasized that he entered the order in a spirit very different from most initiates. Crowley was possessed of neither humility nor patience. He wanted to learn all he could about magic (or magick, as he spelled it) in as short a time as possible. He was disgusted with the somewhat seedy respectability of most members of the Golden Dawn and found it hard to believe that these dignified representatives of the upper middle class were the impassioned seekers of spiritual experience that he had been looking for.

Crowley did not get on well with most members of the order. On one occasion, he showed Yeats some of his poetry. Apparently Yeats attempted to be polite about it but was unable to carry it off very well. Crowley interpreted this incident in typical fashion: "What hurt [Yeats] was the knowledge of his own incomparable inferiority."

Despite personal difficulties, he made rapid progress in the order, rising to the Fourth Degree of Initiation in less than a year. He also became a close friend of Mathers who was then living in Paris, but still ruled the London lodge with a firm (and increasingly resented) hand. Meanwhile, rumors that Crowley was homosexual began circulating among the London group. Thus when he applied for initiation into the

Fifth Degree, he was refused on grounds of moral turpitude. He promptly rushed off to Paris where Mathers, disregarding the strenuous objections of his London subordinates, duly performed the required rites.

The upshot of this incident was that the London lodge disassociated itself from Mathers and declared its independence from his authority. A ludicrous series of events ensued, involving charges of Black Magic on both sides, culminating in the splintering of the Golden Dawn (for the rebels were unable to agree among themselves as to what course of action they should pursue) into several small groups, each claiming absolute authority.

Crowley continued to support Mathers until inevitably their two colossal egos collided and Crowley set up his own magical society, the Argentinum Astrum, in 1907. Meanwhile Yeats, who had aroused considerable opposition among many of the rebels against Mathers by conducting himself in a rather high-handed manner, continued as a member of the major Golden Dawn splinter group, the Stella Matutina, until 1919. Crowley distinguished himself by carrying on a variety of love affairs (with both sexes), writing execrable poetry, and becoming addicted to an astonishing variety of drugs. He died in 1947, in Hastings, at the age of seventy-two.

Although Crowley's bizarre career is unquestionably fascinating, it is his philosophy of magic which chiefly concerns us here, a philosophy which he developed while still a member of the Golden Dawn and continued to elaborate in a host of pamphlets, periodicals and books (many of them privately published) for the remainder of his life.

Unlike Yeats, Crowley regarded magic as a science. He frequently quoted with marked approval that monument to late Victorian industriousness, Sir James Frazier's The **Golden Bough**. One passage that especially attracted Crowley's attention contained an argument that the fundamental underlying conception of magic is identical with that of modern science: a belief in the orderliness of nature.:

"Indubitably," Crowley wrote, "Magick is one of the subtlest and most difficult of the sciences . . . There is more opportunity for errors ... than in any other branch of physics. It is above all needful for the student to be armed with scientific knowledge, sympathetic apprehension and common sense."

On another occasion he was even clearer: "In a certain sense Magick may be defined as the name given to Science by the vulgar." Although a science, magic deals with the realm of the spiritual, according to Crowley, and thus should not be expected to yield results comprehensible to the common man. Only those possessed of spiritual insight, like Crowley himself, can be expected to work magic. Trying to teach the average man to perform magic was, in his view, like trying to teach a savage the quantum theory.

It is instructive to compare Crowley with Yeats. Both were self proclaimed poets fascinated by magic. Yeats, however, was a true irrationalist as well as a true poet. Crowley was neither. Yeats was never interested in reconciling his pursuit of ineffable experience with the claims of modern science. Crowley, who counted T. H. Huxley among his few heroes, was never able to free himself from the restrictions which science imposed on his poetic (and magical) imagination. On the other hand, Yeats was outwardly respectable while Crowley was not. Crowley's life can only be interpreted as a conscious effort to outrage the English middle class by flagrantly violating every aspect of Victorian morality. In a curious sense both were restricted in their pursuit of the irrational by the Victorian milieu into which they were born, Yeats in action, Crowley in imagination.

As for the appeal of the Golden Dawn itself, it was founded at a time when doubts were strongly emerging about the value of crude scientific materialism on the one hand and evangelical Christianity on the other. The Golden Dawn offered a palatable alternative to these two extremes. Ultimately, however, it was barely indistinguishable from an ordinary London club: eminently respectable and (if we are to believe some of its former members) rather dull.

Chapter 19:
Tales of the Magi VI:
Rasputin, the Holy Devil

As Alan Moorehead writes: "Gregory Efimovitch Rasputin has been so blackened and discredited in the forty-odd years since his death that it is almost impossible to see him any more. Like Richard III of England or Italy's Cesare Borgia, he is all villain, the pure quintessence of wickedness, a monster with the cunning of Iago and the brutishness of Caliban." Yet we may well ask what foundation there is for Rasputin's evil reputation. He was not responsible for a single death. Although he had many enemies, he was rarely vindictive towards them. He seduced a wide variety of women (although the reports of his licentiousness are exaggerated) but his "victims" were surprisingly willing to surrender to his rough embraces.

The primary reason for Rasputin's reputation as a monster is the way in which he exercised his power over the Tsarina Alexandra. This supposedly malevolent influence has been regarded by aristocratic Russian émigrés (some of them, like Anna Vyrubov, former supporters of Rasputin) as one of the major causes of the 1917 Revolution. "Without Rasputin," wrote Alexander Kerensky, "there could have been no Lenin." It is understandable why Russian émigrés preferred to blame Rasputin for the fall of the Romanovs; it removed the onus of responsibility from their own shoulders. But in so doing, they created a legend so powerful that a critical evaluation of Rasputin's influence has become nearly impossible.

In Russian court society in the early years of the century, the nihilism of writers like Artsybashev and Andreyev was the intellectual fashion of the day. Among the court aristocracy nihilism was often combined with a kind of romantic decadence. Prince Felix Yussopov,

Rasputin's future assassin, was an ardent admirer of Oscar Wilde and he patterned his actions and attitudes after Dorian Gray. Mysticism (which, in its more superstitious forms, is closely akin to nihilism) was also widely popular. As a contemporary observed: "There is, perhaps, no country where spiritualism has so great a vogue. Several Russian princely houses have their familiar spirits; in some, the piano is always played by invisible hands whenever a member of the family, no matter where he or she may be, is dying." Another example of the popularity of mysticism can be found in the vogue for what the Russians called podvig, the voluntary acceptance of suffering in order to become close to God. It is not surprising that a society of wealthy, superstitious men and women who believed their lives to be devoid of purpose should prove easy prey to pseudo-religious confidence men and tricksters. Edmund A. Walsh, writing of this period, pointed out that "the possession of occult powers and the mysticism of charlatans never failed to exercise a fatal fascination for the intellectuals of Russia." Such men exercised an even greater fascination for Tsarina Alexandra .

The Tsarina, spiritually restless, melancholic, frantic in her desire to give birth to a male heir, was instrumental in establishing the power of several such charlatans. The first of these, the so-called Dr. Philippe, (who was, in reality, a butcher's apprentice from Lyons) claimed to have hypnotic powers. When introduced to the Tsarina, Philippe informed her that he could, through hypnosis, influence the sex of unborn children. Under Philippe's hypnotic ministrations, the Tsarina soon believed herself to be pregnant, a pregnancy which the good doctor assured her would result in a son. Unfortunately for Philippe, it was nothing but a hysterical pregnancy and he was soon deported from Russia loaded down with expensive gifts from the still faithful Tsarina.

Another charlatan on whom the Tsarina bestowed her favors was the mysterious Dr. Badmaiev, described by Maurice Paléologue, the French ambassador to Russia, as a Siberian adventurer without any medical training whatsoever. According to Walsh, Badmaiev claimed to effect cures by means of "exotic herbs, medicinal plants and magic formulae communicated secretly to him by sorcerers of the inaccessible Thibet" Badmaiev, after a brief vogue, soon fell into disfavor with the Tsarina and disappeared, never to be heard of again.

Only in this kind of a society, suffering from spiritual ennui and lack of purpose, could an illiterate peasant like Rasputin rise to power. He had neither the training nor the taste for rule. The claim that he was an incompetent administrator is both obvious and misleading. No one with a background like his could possibly be anything but incompetent. It is not he, but those who permitted him to come to power who should be blamed for contributing to the deterioration of monarchical authority in Russia.

His rise to power? It was once generally accepted that Rasputin was summoned to aid the Tsarevitch during one of the boy's more serious crises and, having succeeded in stemming the bleeding, (especially the internal bleeding which poses the greatest threat to the lives of haemophiliacs) won the Tsarina's admiration and trust. But, as Alan Moorehead points out, "it cannot have been only because of the illness of the Tsarevitch that Rasputin was first accepted at court; the child was only fifteen months old at the time." He had not yet undergone any serious crises in his health.

The explanation must lie elsewhere. Heinz Liepmann published a biography which he claimed was based on material from the Central Historical Archive in Moscow, maintaining that Rasputin came to the notice of Prince Pirakov, one of the leaders of the ultra-monarchist Union of True Russians who conceived the plan of introducing him to the court in order to counteract the influence of such foreign charlatans as Philippe.

By thus putting Rasputin in his debt, Pirakov supposedly felt sure that if Rasputin ever gained the ear of the Tsarina, the Union of True Russians would control the country. Liepmann's account is plausible but, unfortunately there is no way to check the accuracy of his statements. According to Colin Wilson, however, Liepmann's book is almost totally unreliable in those areas where it can be checked against other accounts. The most probable explanation for Rasputin's introduction to the Russian court is the one given by Sir Bernard Pares. According to Pares, the Grand Duchess Militsa, the daughter of King Nikita of Montenegro, saw Rasputin sawing wood in the courtyard of a monastery in Kiev, struck up a conversation with him and was so impressed with the air of religious intensity which he conveyed that she invited him to St. Petersburg.

This first visit occurred in 1903, a year before the birth of the Tsarevitch Alexis. Rasputin did not meet the Tsarina at this time, although he became acquainted with her spiritual adviser, Father John of Cronstadt. It was probably not until about two years later that Rasputin was finally introduced to the Tsarina, either through Father John or Bishop Theophan, another of the Tsarina's religious advisers. By that time, Rasputin had acquired something of a reputation as a holy man and a faith healer and was the favorite of a select group of St. Petersburg literati.

It is clear that the Tsarina was impressed with Rasputin even before he proved able to help her son. As Colin Wilson points out: "This pathologically shy woman felt herself to be a stranger in a hostile country. Then Rasputin appeared, a personification of the Russian peasantry, and assured her that she was loved by all simple Russians, that it was only at court that she was disliked and criticized." Romanticizing the peasantry was not simply a peculiarity of the Tsarina; it was shared by most of the aristocracy and the intelligentsia. Dostoevsky had prophesied that Russia would be saved by a peasant, a mouzhik; Tolstoy forsook rank and wealth to live as a peasant on his own estates. It is not difficult to understand why the peasantry should be regarded in this way by the upper classes. The simple, rough existence of the ordinary mouzhik was in stark contrast to the comfortable, purposeless life led by the aristocracy. Moreover, the Russian peasantry had traditionally been reactionary, a fact which induced in reactionary aristocrats the comfortable illusion that their policies expressed the will of the people. Naturally, glorifying peasant life did not lead to improving it. How improve on that which is already nearly perfect? This was surely the attitude of a great number of the court aristocracy, but, more important, it was also the attitude of the Tsarina and the Tsar.

A. A. Mosolov, one of Nicholas' ministers, once shrewdly remarked that the Tsar needed a peasant. Rasputin more than filled the bill. As Count Kokovtsev pointed out, Rasputin's importance lay in the fact that he reflected the autocratic attitudes of the Tsar and Tsarina, reinforcing their belief that the only real authority in Russia was the will of the sovereign. Rasputin played the part of the peasant to the hilt, addressing the Tsar as an equal, quoting Russian proverbs to him, amusing his children with folk-tales. There is no question that, at least initially, the Tsar was completely taken in. To a minister's criticism of Rasputin, Nicholas once replied: "He is just a good, religious, simpleminded Russian. When in trouble or assailed by doubts I like to have a talk with him, and invariably feel at peace with myself afterwards."

There were a number of factors, then, that contributed to Rasputin's rise to power. He was greatly admired by the aristocracy and the intelligentsia who introduced him to the court. He was a starets, a holy man, which pleased the Tsarina and he was a peasant, which pleased the Tsar. There is little doubt that he would have become influential even if he had not displayed the remarkable ability to save the Tsarevitch from death.

But the extent of Rasputin's power, even at its height, has been greatly exaggerated. He never interested himself in government administration beyond requesting that a few of his incompetent friends be given important ministerial posts. Rasputin's ethic was simple; if someone befriended you, you did him a favor. That capable, intelligent men like Stolypin and Rodzianko refused to befriend the starets out of a misplaced sense of pride, was not Rasputin's fault. Far from being the ruler of Russia, he was the tool of unscrupulous men like Beletsky, the chief of the secret police and Hvostov, the Minister of Justice. Potentially Rasputin's power was enormous; in practice, he used it infrequently, usually at the request of one of his sycophants. Clearly, if Rasputin had been the megalomaniac monster he has been painted, he would have used his power to far greater effect than he did. In fact, he was chiefly interested in ensuring himself a steady supply of complaisant women.

"Little need be said about Rasputin's political views," writes one historian, "for the simple reason that he had none. An illiterate and depraved peasant, he was incapable of discussing any subject of general interest, and world politics were entirely beyond his grasp." This was not altogether the case; there was one area of politics in which he took an active interest and in which his influence, far from hastening the decline of Imperial Russia, may have helped to postpone it, for Rasputin, far more than any other powerful individual in Russia, opposed the country's entry into war.

No doubt he sincerely believed that he was an emissary from the Russian people and that he had only their interests at heart, for he continually warned the Tsar that a war would mean the downfall of the Romanov dynasty. This attitude first became apparent in the Austrian crisis of 1908, when Russia seemed on the brink of war. As Colin Wilson says, "No one knows exactly what happened, for at this time Rasputin was not regarded as a man of political influence... But Rasputin stated on several occasions that he averted a war with Austria by telling the Tsar that such a war would be the end of Russia. In the light of his reaction to the prospect of war in 1914, this sounds more than plausible." Rasputin consistently opposed war with Austria and Germany in 1914, remarking that the Balkans were not worth the life of one Russian soldier. His enemies, however, had succeeded in temporarily discrediting him with the Tsar and he was banished to his native Siberian village of Pokrovskoe. On June 28, 1914 at almost the same instant that Archduke Ferdinand of Austria was assassinated at Sarajevo, Rasputin was stabbed and seriously wounded by a peasant woman who was clearly acting on someone else's orders.

As Colin Wilson remarks, "Ferdinand's death made war probable; Rasputin's injury made it certain, for he was the only man in Russia capable of averting it."

Rasputin swiftly recovered and, in a few months was back in St. Petersburg, once again in the good graces of the Tsar. Seeing that it was too late to stop the war, Rasputin concentrated on persuading the Tsar to take steps to reduce the suffering of the Russian people. He was especially concerned about rail transportation and made frequent efforts to cancel passenger train service so that ammunition and food could get to their prescribed destinations. While the war was going well for Russia, Rasputin's importunings for peace went unheeded by the Tsar. But when things began to take a turn for the worse, the Tsar gave Rasputin permission to attempt to negotiate a separate peace with Germany. How far these negotiations were underway at the time of Rasputin's assassination is not known, although Protopopov, the Minister of the Interior and a close friend of Rasputin had made at least one contact with the German government concerning this matter in the early summer of 1916.

Because of his opposition to the war, Rasputin was widely regarded as a traitor, possibly even a German agent. Thus Yussopov, Purishkevitch and the other conservatives who participated in Rasputin's assassination felt themselves to be doing only their patriotic duty. They could not have chosen a worse time. If Rasputin had been assassinated early in his career, before his intimacy with the Tsarina had led to a complete loss of respect for the authority of the crown or later, when a peace might have been negotiated with Germany, it is barely possible that the Russian Revolution might never have come about. As it was, the assassination of Rasputin at this crucial time made the fall of the Romanov dynasty a certainty.

Gregory Efimovitch Rasputin was not an admirable man, but he was no monster. His mysterious thaumaturgic and hypnotic abilities, like his political power, have been exaggerated. His enemies preferred to rationalize their inability to dislodge him from power by maintaining that they fought not against a man, but a magician. And so he has come down to us as a modern Svengali. It is not likely that the legend of Rasputin will be much affected by the reasoned words of the historian. Legends thrive because they appeal to something far more fundamental than reason.

Conclusion to Book One

It would be tempting to catalogue the similarities among the great ages of magic in order to arrive at a generalized theory about the historical conditions favorable to the magical world-view. Yet to do so would be to minimize the uniqueness of each particular historical situation. Thus it could be argued that magic flourishes during eras of extreme intellectual crisis and examples could be given from late antiquity and the nineteenth century.

But what a difference there was between the effects of the decline of Greek rationalism and the implications of the struggle between science and revealed religion! As for the Renaissance, magic was used, at least initially, to shore up the prevailing orthodoxy. If Ficino and Pico looked backward to late antiquity for their theories of magic they also looked back to such immediate intellectual ancestors as Thomas Aquinas for theoretical religious sanctions. If there was a crisis in Renaissance thought, as some scholars have argued, natural magic played little part in it.

It could also be argued that magic flourishes during ages of religious syncretism: witness the orientalism of late antiquity, the Neo-Platonist syncretism of the Renaissance and the romantic orientalism of the nineteenth and twentieth centuries among occult circles. Once again, important historical considerations are overlooked. The orientalism of late antiquity, unlike that of the modern age, was widespread, permeating all levels of Roman society. Furthermore, it was oriental only in a technical, relative sense; that is to say, classical syncretism received its inspiration from the religions of Egypt and Persia whereas modern occultism derives largely from India and Tibet. Renaissance magic, on the other hand, was syncretisic only in the sense that it tried to reconcile pagan philosophy with Christianity in a sincere effort to prove the essential unity of all truth. Arguments of this kind can usually only be sustained by ignoring everything that doesn't fit in and by playing irresponsibly with semantics. In the end, however, the irreducible uniqueness of historical events cannot be fitted to the Procrustean bed of preconceived theories.

But certain similarities should be noted so long as they are taken to be suggestive rather than definitive, tentative rather than final, including a tendency toward elitism and a romantic attitude with respect to the past. Transcendental magic has always attracted a very small number of adherents. The Pythagoreans, Hermetists and neo-Platonists of the ancient world never founded widespread, popular movements. They regarded themselves as members of a spiritual elite, clearly superior to the common run of humanity. Natural magicians during the Renaissance numbered only a handful of adherents scattered across the Continent. Like Ficino, many of them feared the vulgarization that would inevitably result if magic were allowed to spread to the naive and the uneducated. In the modern age, this tendency toward elitism is evidenced by the popularity of the secret society. Beginning in the seventeenth and eighteenth Centuries with Freemasonry and Rosicrucianism, continuing into the nineteenth and twentieth Centuries with Theosophy, Anthroposophy, and magical societies along the lines of the Golden Dawn, the secret society has become almost the only forum for the practice of magic.

Secrecy, rituals, complex initiations and the like have all become part of the ethos of modern magic. The secret society can be considered as an attempt to create a counter-universe, set apart from an increasingly rationalistic, technocratic society, refusing to share in the prevailing scientific world view. If such societies have their virtues (as far as their members are concerned) they also have their dangers. They can serve not only as the breeding grounds of enlightenment but of messianic delusions and distorted ideas as well.

Magicians have also generally tended to romanticize the past and the far away. Late antiquity saw the revival of the ancient religions of Egypt and Persia, the Renaissance, the revival of late antiquity. As Frances Yates has pointed out, Renaissance magicians, many of them accomplished classical scholars, possessed all of the critical equipment needed to disprove the antiquity of the Hermetic corpus. That they didn't do so can be explained, not as an act of conscious deception on their part, but simply as a refusal to question the credentials of something in which they sincerely believed.

Modern occultism has taken romanticizing the past to unprecedented extremes. Some occultists, not satisfied with the already exaggerated antiquity of their beliefs, have sought for the origin of the magical tradition in the fabled continents of Atlantis and Mu. Many occultists, it seems, have been unable to distinguish between a rejection of the scientific world-view and a passively uncritical acceptance of the improbable and the bizarre.

If there is much to criticize in traditional magic there is also much to admire. The magus refused to accept his assigned place in the accepted scheme of things. He strove to overcome, to dominate, to explore new reaches of the unknown. Even today, with all its bizarre trappings and its tendency toward credulity, magic remains one of the last outposts of the human spirit.

BOOK TWO: MAGIC FUTURE

All experience is magic and only magically explicable. It is only because of the feebleness of our perceptions and activity that we do not perceive ourselves to be in a fairy world.

-Novalis

Chapter 20:
Introduction to Book Two

Noetic magic has been largely forgotten in the twentieth century. The neo-Pythagorean, Gnostic, Hermetic, Cabalistic, Sufi tradition of inducing transformations in consciousness mediated through the **nous** has been merged into an incoherent modern occultism that ranges from the benign vagaries of Theosophy to the slightly sinister ritualism of Crowleyan "magick." The mechanistic science derived from Descartes and Newton has dominated Western thought for more than three hundred years, seemingly rendering magic obsolete and occultism ridiculous.

But science in the twentieth century has largely abandoned the mechanistic model. Relativity and quantum theory have transformed the limited Newtonian cosmos into an expanding universe, incomprehensible in vastness, unlimited in possibility. The impact of this revolution in physics and astronomy only began to be extended to the human sciences in the last third of the twentieth century. If, in Floyd W. Matson's dictum, psychology recapitulates cosmology, we stand on the threshold of a momentous change in human consciousness.

In Book Two, we explore the future of magic, beginning with an analysis of the life and thought of the most important modern magus, G.I. Gurdjieff, followed by an examination of two gurus of the media age, Carlos Castaneda and Deepak Chopra. The coming transformation in human consciousness is further explored in Chapter 23, while Chapter 24 develops the philosophical and theoretical basis of noetic magic. The concluding chapters develop further the principal themes articulated in Chapter 24, closing with suggested exercises in noetic magic and a brief discussion of future possibilities.

Most of us no doubt identify magic and the occult as aspects of the cultural phenomenon that the press has chosen to identify as the New Age. Although the sillier manifestations of the New Age are rightly an object of ridicule, the term covers a wide array of disparate beliefs and activities, some of which are worth further exploration. As David Spangler, a former co-director of the Findhorn Community in Scotland has observed, there are at least four levels at which the "New Age" operates:

"[The first level] is as a superficial label, usually in a commercial setting. A quick perusal of **New Age** magazine or **East West Journal**, both of which have national distribution, or any of the smaller new age oriented publications will demonstrate this application: one can acquire new age shoes, wear new age clothes, use new age toothpaste, shop at new age businesses, and eat at new age restaurants where new age music is played softly in the background.

"The second level is what I call the 'new age as glamour.' This is the context in which individuals and groups are living out their own fantasies of adventure and power, usually of an occult or millenarian form. Many UFO-oriented groups fall into this category. The principal characteristic of this level of attachment to a private world of ego fulfillment and a consequent (though not always apparent) withdrawal from the world. [On this level] the New Age has become populated with strange and exotic beings, such as extraterrestrials, with which channelers claim to communicate. It is a place of psychic powers and occult mysteries. It is in this context that one is most likely to find the words *New Age* used, unfortunately. . . .

"The third level is the new age as an image of change. Here the distinguishing characteristic is the idea of transformation itself, usually expressed as a paradigm shift. This image of the new age is the one most popularly presented to the public, in such books as Willis Harman's **An Incomplete Guide to the Future**, Marilyn Ferguson's **The Aquarian Conspiracy**, and physicist Fritjof Capra's **The Turning Point**. It is the level discussed in many international and regional conferences, debated by futurists and social theorists. . . .In this context the idea of an emerging new culture is usually seen in social, economic, and technological terms rather than spiritual ones. . . .

"On the fourth level, the new age is fundamentally a spiritual event, the birth of a new consciousness, a new awareness and experience of life. . . .It is the new age as a state of being, a mode of relationship with others that is mutually empowering and enriching. Rather than spiritual *experience*, which is the focus one is more apt to find in the second level - - that of psychic and spiritual glamour - - this level centers upon the spiritual *function*, which is service."

Although Spangler is too quick to discount the significance of spiritual *experience* on the fourth level, which surely includes modern Sufis, followers of Gurdjieff's Fourth Way, and other serious (but not solemn) students of alternate states of consciousness, his distinctions are useful. In this context, noetic magic should be situated on the fourth level, operating within the incomplete paradigms emerging from the third level.

The third level is the subject of Chapter 23 while succeeding chapters elucidate the fourth level.

But first to the astonishing life and thought of Gurdjieff, the greatest magus of the twentieth century.

Chapter 21:
Tales of the Magi VII:
Gurdjieff: the Magus as
Trickster

If Rasputin was the "holy devil," his contemporary, George Ivanovitch Gurdjieff, could well be called the "unholy saint." Rasputin's importance to the history of magic is in the realm of image; more than any other modern figure, including Aleister Crowley, Rasputin summons to mind the Black Magician incarnate, capable of bending great empires to his will. That the real Rasputin was nothing of the sort, merely a peasant starets who happened to catch the notice of the Tsarina Alexandra, has not affected the "holy devil's" legend.

But Gurdjieff has bequeathed to magic and the occult both a legend and an original philosophy of man and his relationship to the cosmos. That Gurdjieff was a trickster and inveterate liar seems indubitable. That he tricked and lied for a purpose, namely to keep potential followers on their toes and to inject his own brand of quirky humor into the excessively solemn search for spiritual awakening is equally true. And, although his extraordinary insights into the potential of human consciousness have been popularized in countless books and articles, he curiously remains one of the great unknown original thinkers of the twentieth century.

Born in Alexandropol in Russian Armenia, probably in 1866, the son of a moderately prosperous cattle rancher, Gurdjieff grew up amidst war between Turks and Armenians, abetted by Russia. Raised in Russian Orthodoxy, his parents wished him to become a priest. But he preferred a secular life and, in 1883, came to Tiflis where he became an overseer for the survey party of the Tiflis-Kars railway line and it was in Tiflis that he came to embark on the spiritual journey that consumed him for the rest of his life.

How exactly this came about is not altogether clear. But in the spiritual melting pot of Central Asia, where ideas and legends from a dozen ancient civilizations intermingled, Gurdjieff came to believe in an esoteric tradition transmitted orally through initiates of secret brotherhoods. Whether they be dervishes or monks, Pythagoreans or the mysterious Sarmoung Brotherhood, these initiates held the secrets of the meaning of life.

In fact, it was supposedly to find the remnants of the Sarmoung Brotherhood, an esoteric school of the sixth century C.E., that launched Gurdjieff on a twenty-four year spiritual quest (1887-1911), our knowledge of which comes exclusively from Gurdjieff himself as detailed in his autobiography **Meetings with Remarkable Men**. No independent source has ever been unearthed that confirms one iota of Gurdjieff's account, parts of which are so outlandish as to give rise to the suspicion that the trickster is hard at work.

And so, says Gurdjieff, he traveled. To Mecca and Medina, to Thebes, to Abyssinia and Babylon, to Tabriz, the Gobi Desert, the Pamirs, and India. In 1899, he claimed to have found "the chief Sarmoung Monastery," which lay twelve days travel from Bokhara (although Gurdjieff does not say exactly where). But what went on there, he does not bother to tell us: "The details of everything in this monastery, what it represented, what was done there and how, I shall perhaps recount at some time in a special book." The "special book" was, of course, never written.

After the discovery of the Sarmoung Monastery what greater challenge was left to him than to penetrate the inner mysteries of the remote spiritual stronghold of Tibet? During his perilous journey in Tibet, he was accidentally shot and taken to the oasis of Yangi Hissar, where he was treated by both European and Tibetan doctors. It was at Yangi Hissar that he experienced his fundamental insight:

"He is God and I am God! Whatever possibilities He has in relation to the presences of the universe, such possibilities and impossibilities I should also have in relation to the world subordinate to me. He is God of all the world and also of my outer world. I am God also, although only of my inner world."

Gurdjieff's adventures in Tibet, which he says included study of Tibetan magic and Tantrism, like all of his early adventures, have never

<u>Figure 6</u>
G. I. Gurdjieff

been independently corroborated. The Gurdjieff of history arrives on the scene only in 1911, where he is to be found in Petrograd and Moscow, married to the mysterious Julia Ostrowsky, whom he claimed to have been a former lady in waiting to the Tsarina, and forming a secret society, the most famous member of which was the Russian philosopher Piotr Demianovich Ouspensky.

Ouspensky, an inveterate seeker after transcendental truth, had published his **Tertium Organum** in 1912. It was a book that challenged the conventional notions of the limits of human consciousness. Enough to attract Gurdjieff's attention. In 1915, a meeting between the two men in a Moscow café was arranged. The fastidious Ouspensky, recently returned from the East, was initially taken aback by Gurdjieff's deliberately crude, peasant mannerisms but he was also deeply impressed:

"I saw a man of an oriental type, no longer young, with a black moustache and piercing eyes, who astonished me first of all because he seemed to be disguised and completely out of keeping with the place and its atmosphere. I was still full of impressions of the East. And this man with the face of an Indian raja or an Arab sheik whom I at once seemed to see in a white burnoose or a gilded turban, seated here in this little café, where small dealers and commission agents met together, in a black overcoat with a velvet collar and a black bowler hat, produced the strange, almost alarming impression of a man poorly disguised."

But the disguise intrigued Ouspensky precisely because it did not conceal, rather it revealed, Gurdjieff's true nature:

"To meet [Gurdjieff] was always a test. In his presence every attitude seemed artificial. Whether too deferential or, on the contrary, pretentious, from the first moment it was shattered; and nothing remained but a human creature stripped of his mask and revealed for an instant as he really was."

But Ouspensky never appreciated Gurdjieff's sense of humor. At the conclusion of a learned address to the Russian Imperial Geographical Society, Gurdjieff told the tale of his discovery of an inaccessible valley, the floor of which was strewn with diamonds. To retrieve the diamonds, the natives threw down chunks of raw meat, which trained vultures swooped down upon, bringing them back to their masters laden with diamonds. The Imperial Geographers were not amused and

Ouspensky was appalled.

Still, he could not deny Gurdjieff's powers. On one occasion, shortly after meeting him, Ouspensky took a walk in the forest: "A strange excitement. . .began in me, my pulse began to beat forcibly, and I . . .heard G's voice in my chest. On this occasion I not only heard but I replied mentally." Before long, Ouspensky says, he was conducting regular telepathic conversations with the Master.

There were other disciples, the alienist (psychiatrist) Dr. Leonid Stjoernval and his wife Elizabeta, Paul Dukes, then a music student, later a secret agent for the British; Vladimir Pohl, a brilliant young composer, and Andrei Zaharoff, a promising mathematician, among others. What did this eclectic group of middle class intellectuals find so intriguing in the teachings of an "illiterate Caucasian carpet dealer" (although Gurdjieff was far from illiterate)?

First, there was the man himself. Always deliberately acting a part, he nevertheless somehow seemed always natural, embodying his own dictum that "Truth can only come to people in the form of a lie." He never failed to impress others with the intensity of his personality, his extraordinary physical vigor, and his ruthless devotion to bringing about in his followers a heightened state of consciousness.

Second, there was the doctrine, curiously elaborate, oddly alien, yet somehow right, with its Laws, Rays, Tables, and Diagrams (see below for a discussion of Gurdjieff's doctrine).

Third, the times themselves added urgency to the disciples' quest. By 1916, Russia had lost millions of men in the Great War. Revolution was in the air. The longing for spiritual knowledge that transcended the carnage surrounding them was thus intensified for the members of the Gurdjieff group.

Enter in 1916 one of Gurdjieff's most distinguished and faithful disciples, Thomas Alexandrovitch de Hartmann, a brilliant composer, who was immediately taken with the Gurdjieff persona: "I realised that the eyes of Mr. Gurdjieff were of unusual depth and penetration. . .I had never seen such eyes or felt such a look." De Hartmann and his wife Olga became lifelong devotees of Gurdjieff and his teachings. Thomas de Hartmann composed the music for Gurdjieff's series of "sacred dances," while Olga was later to act as his amanuensis in the writing of his greatest book.

Figure 7
P. D. Ouspensky

While on the one hand, Gurdjieff professed disdain for magic ("There is neither red, green, nor yellow magic. . .Doing is magic") his first "sacred dance", developed for his students, was entitled "The Struggle of the Magicians", and there is little doubt that Gurdjieff saw himself as the embodiment of the White Magician in this enigmatic ballet.

By 1917, it was time for the Gurdjieff group to leave Russia. The Revolution was at hand. After brief sojourns in half a dozen cities, Gurdjieff and several of his followers came to Paris in 1922, eventually settling in a villa near Fontainebleu, some forty miles south of Paris.

By this time, a rift had developed between Ouspensky and Gurdjieff. Ouspensky was independently spreading the Gurdjieff gospel from his headquarters in London. But his own followers wished to hear from the master and so Gurdjieff was invited to speak at the Theosophical Hall in London, where he held forth on the subject "Man is a plural being." Among the listeners who came away convinced that Gurdjieff was the true master and Ouspensky but a pale, intellectualized imitation was the brilliant writer and editor of the **New Age**, Alfred Richard Orage.

Orage knew everyone in the British intellectual and literary world worth knowing. And he possessed an intellect at least as formidable as Ouspensky's. From 1922 onward he placed his considerable talents at Gurdjieff's service.

A rapprochement was worked out between Gurdjieff and Ouspensky. Ouspensky could remain in London, dispensing theory, while Gurdjieff would make his headquarters in France. And what headquarters they were! The Prieure des Basses Loges, a three story villa on two hundred forty-five acres of land, replete with fountains, a garden designed by Lenôtre, and a glass Orangerie, all for a 65,000 franc lease with an option to buy. The Gurdjieff group found it irresistible.

Where exactly Gurdjieff and his followers raised the money to lease this palatial estate has never been satisfactorily explained. Supposedly Gurdjieff's genius for business kept the enterprise going. He started two restaurants in Paris, then allegedly sold them to Russian émigrés for a hefty profit which he then invested in Azerbaijani oil shares and supposedly made a fortune. But is all this part of the Gurdjieff history or the Gurdjieff legend?

No matter, he founded at Fontainebleu the pretentiously named "Institute for the Harmonious Development of Man" where he attracted more distinguished followers, including the New Zealand writer Katherine Mansfield (who died of consumption at the estate), the wealthy and eccentric Lady Rothermere, and the Jungian therapist and writer Dr. Maurice Nicoll. As J.B. Priestley was later to observe, "The level of Gurdjieff's and Ouspensky's most devoted students was very high. In order to study this movement nobody will have to do any intellectual slumming."

Key to the early years of the Institute was Gurdjieff's emphasis on "Sacred Dancing," The Gurdjieff doctrine includes the simultaneous development of body, mind, and soul. The body is developed, he taught, through hard physical labor and the performance of sacred dances which, although Gurdjieff personally choreographed more than a dozen, were supposedly based on those he had encountered among remote tribes and in decaying monasteries during his forty year spiritual pilgrimage. De Hartmann composed the music for these and, on December 16, 1923 they received their first public performance at the Théatre des Champs Elysées to the bewilderment of critics and public alike. Nothing quite like these curious movements and mysterious melodies had ever been seen or heard by Europeans.

More public performances followed in the United States in 1924. But shortly after his return from America, Gurdjieff, a maniacal driver, crashed into a tree, nearly killing himself. Upon his partial recovery, he declared, "In principle, I had to die, but accidentally stayed alive. . . I died inside of me, everything is empty. . .I wish to live for myself. I don't wish to continue as before, and my new principle is - everything for myself. From today the Institute will be nothing."

His disciples, understandably shocked, resisted such a dramatic move and, in fact, most of them remained at the Prieure. But Gurdjieff, haunted by a new awareness of his mortality, set upon a different course, writing (or rather dictating to Olga de Hartmann) one of the most peculiar and challenging books of the twentieth century, **Beelzebub's Tales to His Grandson**, a curious mishmash of science fiction, the **Thousand and One Nights**, and cosmological concoction.

In 1926, Julia Ostrovksy, Mme Gurdjieff, died of cancer at the age of thirty-seven. Gurdjieff grieved and continued writing.

It was about this time that Aleister Crowley paid a surprise visit to the Prieure where he took tea and proceeded to lecture the Gurdjieffians on his philosophy of magic, remarking that he was raising his son to be a devil. Gurdjieff was not impressed and demanded that Crowley leave: "You filthy, you dirty inside! Never again you set foot in my house."

Gradually Gurdjieff drove away his followers, including Olga de Hartmann until by the early 1930s the only founding members of the Institute for the Harmonious Development of Man were Leonid Stjoernval and Jeanne de Salzmann, both disciples from pre-Revolutionary Russia.

Gurdjieff finished **Beelzebub's Tales** in 1929, though the book was not published until after his death. In the 1930s he also completed **Meetings With Remarkable Men**, the "autobiography" of his early years and **Life is Real Only Then When "I Am"**, both also published posthumously. The only work by Gurdjieff that appeared during his lifetime was **The Herald of the Coming Good: First Appeal to Contemporary Humanity,** privately published in 1933. Alas, it did not appeal. Written in a style so opaque that it makes **Beelzebub's Tales** seem a model of clarity by comparison, it won few converts to the Gurdjieff doctrine.

He made more trips to America but seemed intent on offending everyone. "Every person you see," he explained to the young son of one of his disciples, "including yourself, is shit." At a New York dinner party he complimented one woman on her appearance, noting that she must have dressed so well because she "wish to fuck."

But he also met Frank Lloyd Wright who was married to the former Olgivanna Hinzenberg, a Gurdjieff disciple. Wright, that most egocentric of modern geniuses, was immediately taken with Gurdjieff, calling him "the stuff. . .of which genuine prophets have been made."

Upon his return to France, Gurdjieff resumed the "Work", taking on new disciples and occupying a small apartment at 6 Rue des Colonels Rénard in Paris. He spent the war years quietly expanding his circle of initiates. After the war, his reputation came to eclipse Ouspensky's. Ouspensky had died in 1947. His masterpiece, **In Search of the Miraculous: Fragments of a Forgotten Teaching**, surely the most coherent account of Gurdjieffian philosophy, was published posthumously. Lacking a Master, Ouspensky's pupils flocked to Gurdjieff. And so a certain curious truth came to be conferred on Gurdjieff's statement "I am Gurdjieff. I not will die." For though die he did on October 29, 1949, his teachings were spread by dozens of articulate disciples, his books finally found a publisher, and a Gurdjieff cult of no small proportions has grown steadily throughout the past fifty years.

The Gurdjieff Teaching

Cosmology

One can only hope that Gurdjieff's cosmology was meant as a joke. God is identified with the "Most Holy Sun Absolute," originally sustained in equilibrium but forced into creating the universe by Time (in Gurdjieffian terms, "Heropass"). Time is God's shadow and, in order to protect Himself from its destructive force, He created the great universe ("Megalcosmos") which sustained itself forthwith without His direct intervention through the Law of Three and the Law of Seven.

The Law of Three governs every event and consists of the interaction of three sacred forces, Holy Affirming, Holy Denying, and Holy Neutralizing. The Law of Seven "governs successions of events. It states that whenever any manifestation evolves, it does so nonlinearly. There is a an orderly discontinuity in every progression of things, in every series. This lawful discontinuity is preserved in our musical scale which, as singing up and down any octave will show, is composed of unequal steps."

The most significant functioning of the Law of Seven is the "Ray of Creation", an octave descending from God (Do) through the universe, the Milky Way, the sun and its planets to the moon (Re) and the earth (Mi).

The "Terror of the Situation"

Gurdjieff derives man's existential predicament from made-up mythology. Supposedly the comet Kondoor struck the earth creating the moon and Anulios (a kind of counter-Earth). The Archangel Sakaki stabilized the moon, Anulios, and the earth by supplying them with "Askokin," a sacred substance that emanated from living organisms upon their death. The initial organisms evolved into man, a being which had the capacity to attain "objective reason." But Sakaki, afraid that acquiring "objective reason" and thus understanding the futility of existence, would cause humans to commit mass suicide and thus upset the equilibrium among the moon, earth, and Anulios, placed in man the "organ Kundabuffer." Located at the base of the spine, "Kundabuffer" caused man to experience life in a safe and highly suggestible state of "waking sleep." After a time, the crisis of equilibrium passed and Sakaki removed Kundabuffer. But alas, man had grown so accustomed to it that he continued functioning as if it were still an integral part of his organism. So Kundabuffer's influence lives on and continues to thwart our efforts to achieve "objective consciousness," keeping us perpetually in a state of "waking sleep" despite the positive influences generated by such messengers from God as Moses, Pythagoras, Buddha, Christ, and Mohammed. The "terror of the situation" is that man is capable of transcending ordinary consciousness but is so habituated to the lingering influences of Kundabuffer, that he rarely does so. He is like a free man who refuses to act upon his freedom and is thus no more than a slave.

As cosmologies go, Gurdjieff's effort is worth our interest. The joking part is, of course, the names that he gives to the players in his celestial drama. But even these had a serious purpose. Gurdjieff believed that our ordinary language amounted to a hypnotizing form of "word-prostitution" and he deliberately coined outlandish words to describe the cosmological progression. The net effect of his efforts, however, has been to dissuade most intelligent readers from taking him seriously.

One striking aspect of Gurdjieff's cosmology is that it is creatively dualistic. Unlike the Pythagoreans and their philosophical heirs, the

Gnostics and the Hermetists, Gurdjieff does not posit a principle of evil at war with good. Heropass (Time) is not the equivalent of the dyad or the demiurge. And mankind's existential plight is not the result of the actions of an evil force or malevolent archon. Sakaki is fundamentally benevolent, even going so far as to remove the "organ Kundabuffer" when it is no longer needed to assure cosmic stability. The cosmos, in Gurdjieff's view, is fundamentally good. Mankind's task is to transcend Kundabuffer and experience "objective consciousness."

Despite his rejection of absolute dualism, Pythagorean influences abound in Gurdjieff's teaching. The Law of Three and especially the Law of Seven with its emphasis on Pythagorean octave relationships are obvious examples. So too is the most widely influential of Gurdjieff's ideas, the enneagram.

The enneagram represents a fusion of the Law of Three and the Law of Seven. It is a circle divided into nine equal parts which was used by Gurdjieff to indicate the relationship among events and the sequences of events: "The days of the week can, for example, be laid out around the circumference. Now we see all sorts of intriguing possibilities. Sunday is the point where the trinity enters the week as is reflected in the Christian Sabbath. Shock points seem to occur on Tuesday and Thursday nights. And there seem to be two progressions in the week; the sequence of chronological time is represented on the outer circle while some other [non linear relationship] is represented by the inner connecting lines."

The enneagram is worthy of further contemplation and study. Unfortunately, it is largely used today as a kind of pop psychology prop, which delineates nine separate personality types and functions as a simplistic substitute for the Meyers-Briggs personality assessment test.

Gurdjieff's Psychology

If Gurdjieff's cosmology is not meant to be taken literally but merely as a convenient construct within which to re-view human reality, his psychology is an altogether different matter. At the same time that Husserl was developing phenomenology and Freud and Jung were creating modern so-called "depth psychology," Gurdjieff provided insights into the human mind that are only now beginning to appreciated by contemporary psychologists.

The Myth of the "I"

In opposition to the generally held notion that each of us possesses a stable, continuous personality, an "I" or ego, Gurdjieff held that we consist of many selves which are scarcely in touch with one another. This cluster of manifold selves creates a series of personae or, in Gurdjieff's term, "false personalities." which become the culturally prescribed "I" (or "I's"). These he contrasts with our "essence", that which makes us biologically and spiritually unique, our potential, which "false personality" channels, distorts, and suppresses in accordance with cultural norms.

Moreover, all of our "I's" are mechanistic reactions to our environment. In one of his most famous explications of Gurdjieff, Ouspensky asserts:

"Man is a machine. All his deeds, actions, words, thoughts, feelings, convictions, and habits are the result of external influences. Out of himself a man cannot produce a single thought, a single action. . . . Man is born, lives, dies, builds houses, writes books, not as he wants to, but as it happens. Everything happens. Man does not love, hate, desire---all this happens."

The Tripartite Brain

As Beelzebub tells his grandson, man has three brains incorporating five centers, the intellectual brain, the emotional brain, and the lower brain composed of the moving, instinctive, and sexual centers. In most people these five centers function mechanically and at cross purposes with one another. Human beings also possess two additional centers, the higher intellectual center and the higher emotional center. But rarely do human beings connect to these higher centers for they must do so intentionally. The language of the higher intellectual center is symbol and of the higher emotional center, myth.

Human Types and the Three Ways

Three human types correspond to the relative dominance of one of the three brains. Type One is Instinctive Man, Type Two, Emotional Man; and Type Three, Thinking Man. All three types are mired in mechanism but it has been possible for each to perfect his type by following one of three "ways": 1) The Way of the Fakir (Instinctive Man); 2) The Way of the Monk (Emotional Man) and 3) The Way of the Yogi (Thinking Man).

It is important to recognize that the three ways do not necessarily correspond to the religions with which they are traditionally associated. For example, the Way of the Yogi could very well be pursued by a Christian monk.

The Fakir controls and manipulates his body and instincts, The Monk his feelings, and the Yogi his intellect.

The Fourth Way and the Zoostat

Gurdjieff teaches a Fourth Way, the simultaneous development of body, emotion, and intellect. The Fourth Way avoids the inherent imbalance of each of the Three Ways and allows human beings to evolve into higher types of man: Type Four (Balanced Man), Type Five (Unified Man), Type Six (Conscious Man) and Type Seven (Perfected Man).

Gurdjieff's paradigm of consciousness, the Zoostat, consists of six levels: 1) the autonomic, or unconscious; 2) the subconscious; 3) sleep; 4) waking consciousness; 5) self consciousness; and 6) objective consciousness. The first three need no explication. But waking consciousness Gurdjieff identifies as "waking sleep." An even better term for it is psychologist Charles Tart's "consensus trance." We think we are awake, making decisions, working, making love but, in fact, we are only semi-comatose, reacting mechanically to outside stimuli.

How to awake from consensus trance is the essence of Gurdjieff's teaching. The first step is towards self consciousness for which the necessary preparation is "self-remembering," acknowledging the essential self (not false personality) in every moment of our lives.

Objective consciousness, the highest state of all, occurs sporadically in all people. It is a state of absolute oneness between the self and the cosmos and can be achieved by following any one of the four ways but to be in the state permanently or, at least at will, and thus achieve the seventh state, that of Perfected Man, one must follow the Fourth Way.

One of Gurdjieff's pupils, C.S. Nott, has provided a penetrating account of his experience of "objective consciousness":

"It was during this summer [at Taliesin] that I had the first deep and vivid experience of higher consciousness. The three previous experiences of this unexpected impact of higher forces were a taste of real consciousness of self. The present one was different. One hot day I was walking from the house across the fields to bathe in the Wisconsin River. About half way a strange and wonderful force began to enter into me and permeate my whole being, and filled me with light and power. I stopped and stood still and let the force flow. Although I was aware of my surroundings - the forest and fields and the hot sun, they were only a background to the inner experience; all anxieties and cares of ordinary life dropped away; at the same time I saw myself and my relations with people quite clearly; I saw the pattern of my life, my organism moving as it were along its appointed path. There was time no longer, and an understanding of the whole of life seemed possible for me. It was as if for a few moments I had entered into my real life; and the outer life, which had seemed so important and took up all my time, was not the real life but something ephemeral, a sort of cinema film with which I was identified. Only the inner something was eternal, the real self of me. I AM."

Development of the higher self requires a lifelong struggle against the maleficent, lingering influence of the organ Kundabuffer, a continuous process of self realization, of freeing one's self from the mechanical self. And for this one needs a teacher and a group.

The Teacher and the Group

Gurdjieff insisted on group work. "One man can do nothing, can attain nothing. A group with a real leader can do more." Individual members of a group reinforce one another. But the teacher must be ruthless and committed. The work, Gurdjieff wrote, is "To destroy, mercilessly, without any compromises whatsoever, in the mentation and feelings of the [disciple], the beliefs and views, by centuries rooted in him, about everything existing in the world."

The sacrifices that group work entails under a teacher like Gurdjieff are explained with Gurdjieffian irony: "I have already said before that sacrifice is necessary," said G. "Without sacrifice nothing can be attained. But if there is anything in the world that people do not understand it is the idea of sacrifice. They think they have to sacrifice something that they have. For example, I once said that they must sacrifice 'faith," 'tranquillity,' 'health.' They understand this literally. But then the point is they have not got either faith, or tranquillity, or health. All these words must be taken in quotation marks. In actual fact they have to sacrifice only what they imagine they have and which in reality they do not have. They must sacrifice their fantasies. But this is difficult for them, very difficult. It is much easier to sacrifice real things.

"Another thing people must sacrifice is their suffering."

The reward? "The whole point is to be able get pleasure and be able to keep it. Whoever can do this has nothing to learn."

Throughout one's life one encounters many teachers, each appropriate for a particular stage in one's development:

"Usually the [disciple] himself is not worth a brass farthing, but he must have as teacher no other than Jesus Christ. To less he will not agree. And it never enters his head that even if he were to meet such a teacher as Jesus Christ, taking him as he is described in the Gospels, he would never be able to follow him because it would be necessary to be on the level of an apostle in order to be a pupil of Jesus Christ. Here is a definite law. The higher the teacher, the more difficult for the pupil."

An Assessment of Gurdjieff's Teaching

Gurdjieff's fundamental insight, that *we are all asleep* has been described as "a social perception more subversive and revolutionary than anything remotely conceived by all the Trotskys and Kropotkins of history; an idea which, like death and the sun, cannot be looked at steadily - a world in trance!" His methods for transcending the state of "consensus trance" are equally revolutionary, the simultaneous cultivation of mind, emotion, and body, the way of the "sly man" as Gurdjieff termed it.

The foremost academic expert on altered states of consciousness, Charles Tart, regards Gurdjieff as unequivocally a genius. But Tart, like many others, makes the mistake of viewing Gurdjieff as "putting Eastern spiritual ideas and practices into useful forms." In fact, there is little evidence that Gurdjieff borrowed from Eastern thought. Like Madame Blavatsky he sought to clothe Western occult traditions in the exotic finery of the East. He frequently described his teaching as "esoteric Christianity" and there is indeed much to link it with Pythagoreanism and Gnosticism. Gurdjieff, in fact, stands in direct opposition to the Eastern mystical tradition of "lifting matter towards spirit." His approach was active, highly directed, and devoted to self-realization, not self-abnegation or self-extinction.

Gurdjieff's emphasis on group work and the role of the teacher is traditional esotericism and should be viewed with great caution. Psychologist Daniel Goleman puts it best:

"Spiritual groups . . . are susceptible to the full range of human foibles. Vanity, power-seeking, and looking out for number One are as likely to show up in a spiritual organization as any other. The very nature of such groups often makes it difficult to notice or acknowledge that something is awry. Group collusions such as 'It's all part of the Teaching' are invoked to alibi for meanness of spirit and pettiness."

And Goleman points out important warning signs that a group is close-minded and possibly dangerous:

"Taboo Topics: questions that can't be asked, doubts that can't be shared, misgivings that can't be voiced. . .

"Secrets: the suppression of information, usually tightly guarded by an inner circle.

"Spiritual Clones: in its minor form, stereotypic behavior, such as people who walk, talk, smoke, eat and dress just like their leader; in its much more sinister form, psychological stereotyping, such as an entire group of people who manifest only a narrow range of feeling in any and all situations: always happy, or pious, or reducing everything to a single explanation, or sardonic, etc.

"Groupthink: a party line that overrides how people actually feel.

"The Elect: a shared delusion of grandeur that there is no Way but this one. The corollary: you're lost if you leave the group.

"No Graduates: members are never weaned from the group. . .

"Assembly Lines: everyone is treated identically, no matter what their differences,

"Loyalty Tests: members are asked to prove loyalty to the group by doing something that violates their personal ethics. . .

"Duplicity: the group's public face misrepresents its true nature...

"Unifocal Understanding: a single world view is used to explain anything and everything; alternate explanations are verboten. . .

"Humorlessness: no irreverence allowed. Laughing at sacred cows is good for your health. Take, for example, Gurdjieff's one-liner, 'If you want to lose your faith, make friends with a priest."

Although Gurdjieff cannot fairly be accused of most of these faults of group work - he frequently "graduated" disciples by shooing them away, he encouraged individuality, and he possessed a wickedly subversive sense of humor - the same cannot be said for many of the Fourth Way groups that have flourished since his death. Also it's worth noting that none of these groups has produced a Gurdjieff, who is best described by his most incisive biographer, James Moore, as "a saint with balls."

Chapter 22:
The Magus as Media Maven: Carlos Castaneda and Deepak Chopra

In 1968, the University of California Press published an unassuming little book entitled **The Teachings of Don Juan: A Yaqui Way of Knowledge.** Its author was a UCLA graduate student in anthropology named Carlos Castaneda. Unlike the vast majority of university press publications, The **Teachings of Don Juan** was picked up by a commercial press and became a runaway best seller. Castaneda's style was simple and straightforward, occasionally rising to eloquence, and his subject matter was nothing short of spectacular. The book purported to relate the world-view of a Yaqui Indian sorcerer named Don Juan whose miraculous abilities Castaneda professed to have witnessed firsthand. Other best sellers followed, **A Separate Reality, Journey to Ixtlan, Tales of Power,** and **The Second Ring of Power.** In 1973, Castaneda received his Ph.D in anthropology. Also in 1973, he was the subject of a **Time Magazine** cover story, which explored the Don Juan phenomenon and raised questions about the authenticity of the books. Was Don Juan a real person or just a figment of Castaneda's imagination?

In the original book, Don Juan was unemotional and forbidding. In the later works he became progressively jollier, even though the time period covered was supposedly earlier. Why the inexplicable personality change? The first two books described a total of twenty-two drug trips that facilitated Carlos' exploration of the sorcerer's world. Beginning with the third book, drugs were no longer mentioned.

Journalist Richard de Mille, intrigued with the possibility that Castaneda is a fraud investigated the matter and wrote two exposés, **Castaneda's Journey** and **The Don Juan Papers.** According to de Mille, Don Juan never existed. Castaneda made him up, probably deriving his "teachings" from the UCLA library. De Mille demonstrated the parallels between passages in the Don Juan books and obscure works of European occultism. He also noted that no field worker familiar with the Yaqui Indians had ever encountered Don Juan's brand of sorcery, much less Don Juan, who appears to have been seen by only one person, Carlos Castaneda.

De Mille's books had no discernible effect on the Don Juan cult and even less on Castaneda who has totally ignored his critics and continues to produce best selling books, each a bit more fantastic than the others: **The Eagle's Gift, The Fire from Within, The Power of Silence**, and **The Art of Dreaming**. Book reviewers seem largely oblivious to the charges of fraud. "It is impossible to view the world in quite the same way after reading him," raved a critic for the Chicago Tribune. "If Castaneda is correct, there is another world, a sometimes beautiful and sometimes frightening world, right before our eyes at this moment - if only we could see." **Life Magazine** was even more fulsome in its praise: "Castaneda's sanity lends to even the most lurid experiences the force of data. It compels us to believe that don Juan is one of the most extraordinary figures in anthropological literature, a neolithic sage. It helps us to accept, from the continent we stole, a mysterious gift of wisdom."

Since his most recent book, **The Art of Dreaming**, was published in 1993, Castaneda has founded Cleargreen, a corporation that sponsors workshops and seminars on Castaneda's philosophy (now called Tensegrity) and publishes journals and videocassettes that further explore Castaneda- inspired concepts.

According to its World Wide Web page, "The name of Cleargreen stems from an idea that sorcerers who lived in Mexico in ancient times had about the configuration of our human energy. They believed that different kinds of energy had different hues, and that human energy has now an off-white coloration. but that at one time it was clear green."

As for Tensegrity, Castaneda has explained, "Tensegrity is the modernized version of some movements called 'magical passes' developed by Indian shamans who lived in Mexico prior to the Spanish Conquest. . . .The art of dreaming became for those sorcerers their most absorbing practice. In the course of that practice, they experienced unequaled states of physical prowess and well-being, and in their effort to replicate those states in their hours of vigil, they found that they were able to repeat them following certain movements of the body. Their efforts culminated in the discovery of a great number of such movements, which they called magical passes. . . .[Tensegrity] is a most appropriate name because it is a mixture of two terms: tension and integrity; terms which connote the two driving forces of the magical passes."

That Castaneda is an academic fraud who made don Juan up out of whole cloth seems likely. But are his teachings fraudulent as well? De Mille argues that the don Juan books are a mishmash of Gurdjieff, Aleister Crowley, and obscure works of European and Asian occultism dressed up in trendy New Age language and marketed to the credulous. And it does appear that Castaneda shrewdly chose as the vehicle for his philosophy an Indian from the Third World, thus appealing to the modern Western belief that great wisdom resides in the myths, legends, and folklore of indigenous peoples. The same message conveyed by a Western guru would not have resonated so profoundly with modern misconceptions of the noble and sage savage, blissfully unencumbered with rationalist presuppositions.

However Castaneda came to his occult teaching (so long as one doesn't seriously entertain the notion that there ever was a don Juan) much of it appears to have been the result of what Jung termed "active imagination," (see Chapter 29) the conscious induction, whether by drugs or meditation, of lucid hypnagogic states. And, despite the infelicity of Castaneda's terminology, the overall structure of the "don Juan teachings" possesses an impressive coherence.

Let's begin with the concept of "intent." Don Juan says, "The only way to know intent. . .is to know it directly through a living connection that exists between intent and all sentient beings. Sorcerers call intent the indescribable, the spirit, the nagual." And again, "All the possible feelings and beings and selves float in it like barges, peaceful, unaltered, forever." "Intent" or the "nagual" is quite clearly the equivalent of the **nous**.

To penetrate "intent," you must be able to alter your perceptions of the world at will, to shift your "assemblage point," (defined as "the point at which your awareness is focused on your luminous being") The techniques of shifting your assemblage point (or, in the terms of noetic magic, your perceptual paradigm) are many. Some techniques that Castaneda discusses are "stopping the internal dialog, i.e., stopping our description of the world; breaking the barrier of perception. Stopping the internal dialog is the key to the sorcerers' world. The rest of the activities are only props to accelerate the effect."

Don Juan says that there are seven gates of dreaming (although Castaneda discusses only four in **The Art of Dreaming**, perhaps leaving the remaining three for a subsequent book). The first gate is being able to sustain the visualization of anything that occurs in a dream; in the second, moving from dream to dream is achieved; at the third gate, the aspirant acquires the ability to "merge. . . dreaming reality with the reality of the daily world;" and "At the fourth gate, the energy body travels to specific, concrete places either in this world, out of this world, or places that exist only in the intent of others."

Although Castaneda veers away from the fantastic by consistently claiming that the magical events he describes consist entirely of altered perceptions rather than material changes in the "real" world, the underlying message of his books imply something else, that, in fact, to change one's perception of reality is to change reality itself.

In the end, the principal characters of the Castaneda books, don Juan and Carlos (who should be considered a character, the apprentice sorcerer, and not Castaneda himself, despite the author's protestations to the contrary) grow tiresome. Don Juan laughs too much, holding his belly and mocking the perpetually naïve Carlos, who is constantly forgetting key magical experiences until don Juan somehow reminds him. And the terminology becomes too cumbersome and complex, suggesting the operations of a mind that has far more in common with medieval scholasticism than with a New World tradition of tribal sorcery. It is devoutly to be wished that Castaneda never writes another book.

Deepak Chopra is a more recent New Age guru. His books, especially **Ageless Body, Timeless Mind** and **The Seven Spiritual Laws of Success** have been phenomenal best sellers, far surpassing even the sales of Castaneda's don Juan series. He has charmed American audiences with his appearance on PBS specials and he presides over a growing cottage industry that produces Chopra videotapes and audio cassettes and promotes Chopra seminars and workshops. His World Wide Web page is heavily trafficked and includes a forum in which Chopra devotees exchange banal insights based on the teachings of the master.

Although Deepak Chopra has never been accused of fraud, he has been criticized for over simplifying complex ideas and mixing Eastern and Western spiritual traditions into an unwholesome mélange of East meets West on Wall Street. The title of one of his books says it all: **Creating Affluence: Wealth Consciousness in the Field of All Possibilities**. Whether Chopra's methods have created wealth for anyone else is unknown. They certainly have worked for him.

Still, there is some evidence that Deepak Chopra is not just the pop guru of the moment. Trained in Western medicine, he appears to have a clear, though not particularly profound, knowledge of Eastern spiritual traditions and one of his objectives is to merge the Western magical tradition with Eastern thought. Hence his interest in Merlin and Western wizards in general. Much of Chopra's writing fits in well with the principles of noetic magic and it could be argued that he strives to express himself with simplicity, not simplification. In any event, his work so far is free of the kind of burdensome jargon that characterizes Castaneda's don Juan books.

Perhaps the best place to start with Chopra's work is with the seven spiritual laws of success, which are: 1) the Law of Pure Potentiality; 2) the Law of Giving; 3) the Law of "Karma" or Cause and Effect; 4) the Law of Least Effort; 5) the Law of Intention and Desire; 6) the Law of Detachment; and 7) the Law of "Dharma" or Purpose in Life.

The Law of Pure Potentiality postulates that human beings are pure consciousness: "Pure consciousness is pure potentiality; it is the field of all possibilities and infinite creativity." Chopra distinguishes between self-referral and object-referral. In self-referral, "our internal reference point is our own spirit, and not the objects of our experience." Object-referral, on the other hand, has as its internal reference point the ego, which points to circumstances outside the self, requiring human beings to be dependent on the approval of others.

The Law of Giving refers to the reciprocal nature of the universe, its inherent tendency towards "dynamic exchange." The more you give, suggests Chopra, the more you will receive.

The Law of "Karma" refers to the simultaneous operation of cause and effect. Every action instantly produces a reaction. This requires that the seeker become increasingly conscious of making decisions, keeping in mind that all decisions have consequences.

The Law of Least Effort is based on the notion that "Nature's intelligence functions effortlessly, frictionlessly, spontaneously. It is nonlinear; it is intuitive, holistic and nourishing." Chopra goes on to say that "Least effort is expended when your actions are motivated by love. . ." The three components of least effort are acceptance, responsibility, and defenselessness.

The Law of Intention and Desire allows seekers to utilize two qualities of consciousness: attention and intention. "Attention energizes, and intention transforms." Says Chopra: "The quality of intention on the object of attention will orchestrate an infinity of space-time events to bring about the outcome intended, provided one follows the other spiritual laws of success."

The Law of Detachment "says that in order to acquire anything in the physical universe, you have to relinquish your attachment to it." In short, in order to get what you want you must not want it.

The Law of "Dharma" or Purpose in Life "says that we have taken manifestation in physical form to fulfill a purpose. The field of pure potentiality is divinity in its essence, and the divine takes human form to fulfill a purpose." The three components to the Law of Dharma are 1) discovering our true Self; 2) expressing our unique talents; and 3) serving humanity.

Chopra's spiritual laws of success are anodyne and unlikely to do anyone significant harm. The key concepts are the unlimited potential of human consciousness and the opportunity for every human being to communicate with their true Selves and experience a sense of kinship with the divine. In this sense, Chopra's teaching has much in common with Sufism and, although much simplified with Gurdjieff's Fourth Way, especially the Gurdjieffian concept of self-remembering.

Perhaps the most useful contribution of pop gurus like Carlos Castaneda and Deepak Chopra is that they have thoroughly democratized the occult experience. No longer is spiritual transcendence limited to an esoteric elite. All human beings, with sufficient motivation and easily acquired insight can aspire to experiences available in the past only to the most skilled of theurgists.

Chapter 23:
The Coming Transformation
of Human Consciousness

To understand the magnitude of the coming transformation in human consciousness, we must recognize the extent to which our minds and imaginations have been shackled by the mechanistic world view of early modern science. Prior to the rise of rationalism and the triumph of technology, the organic unity of man and nature was regarded as a commonplace. In a psychological universe largely devoid of reason but irradiated with purpose and value, human beings felt themselves to be integral parts of a "system of which every part was meaningful, significant, valuable." This unitary structure was only briefly shaken by the rediscovery of the rationalistic writings of Aristotle, for St. Thomas Aquinas swiftly put Aristotle to work for theology and made the medieval synthesis complete. "Psychology," as Floyd W. Matson says, "recapitulates cosmology," and the psychology of the high middle ages "conveyed a new recognition of man, not as scientific object but as moral subject."

The irrational was well provided for in the Age of Faith but, despite the efforts of Aquinas and the Scholastics, man's rational impulses were neglected. Medieval irrationalism was as capable of the revolting excesses of the Inquisition as of the sublimities of a Dante or a Michelangelo.

The separation of man and nature, the dualism of subject and object, was brought about by a new way of looking at things, the way of science. Since the Renaissance science has reshaped man's conception of himself and, in so doing, has shattered the medieval synthesis into a thousand tiny and seemingly unrelated fragments.

Subject-object dualism was inaugurated by Descartes and rapidly assimilated by the growing tide of Western science. Thirty-seven years after Descartes' death, Isaac Newton published his **Principia Mathematica** which dealt the deathblow to the organic conception of the universe. In Newtonian physics the universe was a machine operating on absolute, exact, immutable laws. It was like a great clock, wound by God, but operating eternally without his intervention. This mechanistic conception left no room for the notion of freedom. All was predetermined. Cause and effect followed one another with mechanical regularity.

The impact of Newtonian thought was all-pervasive. "Newton's great mathematical system of the world struck the imagination of the educated class of his time, and spread with amazing swiftness, completing what Descartes had done." The degree of Newton's influence is demonstrated by Alexander Pope's couplet:

Nature and Nature's laws lay hid in night
God said, Let Newton be! and all was light.

Newton was irresistible and it was not long before philosophers were searching for absolute laws which would describe human actions with Newtonian mathematical precision. "Let us conclude boldly then," said the 18th century French scientist La Mettrie, "that man is a machine."

The reaction to this kind of 18th century rationalism, most vividly exemplified by the Romantic movement, tried to reassert man's independence. "I, for one," said Thomas Carlyle, "declare the world to be no machine!" But Romanticism, despite its profound influence on art, politics, literature and philosophy, affected science only in that its emphasis on nature contributed to a rising interest in Biology. "Biology may be seen as a factor in Romanticism and German philosophy, suggesting organic to replace mechanistic images." However, the greatest biological achievement of the century, Darwin's theory of evolution, was based on as mechanistic an idea as any that could be found in Newton, the idea of Natural Selection. Darwin drew a picture of a mindless and purposeless kind of evolution which favors only those organisms which happen to be more adaptable to a particular kind of environment. Thus, man himself was no more than an accident, a notion which bothered even Darwin. "Towards the end of his life he expressed strong misgivings about it (Natural Selection); for if mind was accidental, how could it make value judgments? How could one even rely on its opinions about natural selection?" If man was made to seem more a part of nature by the theory of evolution, it was a nature that was as blind, as accidental, as mechanical as the laws of chance.

The twentieth century has seen Cartesian dualism taken to its extreme by scientists in the field of psychology. The human being as subject was completely banished from the world to be replaced by the human being as object. The chief exponent of this mechanistic psychology was John B. Watson, who ushered in the aggressive movement known as Behaviorism. "The interest of the behaviourist is more than the interest of a spectator," declared Watson; "he wants to control man's reactions as physical scientists want to control and manipulate other natural phenomena." The most influential behaviorist, perhaps the most influential American psychologist of the past fifty years, was B. F. Skinner, who wrote: "The implication that man is not free is essential to the study of human behavior." He has also assserted as a "general principle that the issue of personal freedom must not he allowed to interfere with a scientific analysis of human behavior." What has been outlined above is the growth and spread of the mechanistic analogy from physics to the other sciences, a development that has resulted in the cult of scientism.

Scientism is the notion that the mechanistic analogy can be applied successfully to any field of human endeavor with uniform success. Nothing is immune from it. As we have seen, it came to dominate the field of psychology, but it is equally evident in such disciplines as sociology, political science, and economics. Even in philosophy, under the name of logical analysis, scientism has threatened to eliminate all opposition. It is guided solely by the canons of "impersonal objectivity and reductive analysis. It strives on the one hand to maximize its detachment from the thing observed and on the other hand to analyze it downward into its working parts and effective causes." The chief difficulty which scientism faces is that its chosen material is considerably more complex and intractable than the physical sciences and hence less capable of being reduced to neat, mathematical equations. This however doesn't seem to bother its proponents. Their attitude is summed up in Matson's phrase: Theirs not to reason why, theirs but to quantify.

Science and scientism are not identical, although it is sometimes hard to distinguish between them. The dim borderline between the two probably lies somewhere in the realm of biology or physiology, it is difficult to say. Science, however, is responsible for scientism. The tremendous prestige of science, the undeniable success of the mechanistic analogy, gave rise to the notion that such a concept would yield valid results in all fields of human activity.

Unfortunately, by Einstein's time, the mechanistic analogy had pervaded human thinking to such a degree that it could not easily be uprooted. In the physical sciences, the notion of a universal machine was helpful for a time. In the social sciences (witness the Orwellian pronouncements of B. F. Skinner, quoted above) it seems positively dangerous.

But late twentieth century psychology has witnessed a widespread revolt against behaviorism, exemplified by humanistic and transpersonal psychology which oppose reductive analysis and emphasize human understanding in wholes rather than in parts

Despite the remarkable advances made by science since the Renaissance, advances which no thinking person would want reversed, the whole approach of science has been, in a sense, destructive. In its indefatigable search for causes, science has eliminated purpose.

The Coming Transformation of Human Consciousness

Just as the Scientific Revolution of the sixteenth and seventeenth centuries led to the transformation of human consciousness from medieval to modern, so the Scientific Revolution of the twentieth century is moving towards an equally profound transformation. This can best be understood as the growing recognition that, in Willis Harman's formulation, consciousness is a causal reality.

This may seem like a commonplace. After all, don't human beings continually make decisions and act upon them? And don't these decisions arise out of our subjective thought processes? But mechanistic science succeeded until quite recently in banishing the entire realm of human subjective experience from serious scientific and intellectual consideration. Relativity and quantum theory have opened up an expanding physical universe that is also fundamentally unpredictable:

"The conception of the universe as an interconnected web of relations is one of two major themes that recur throughout modern physics. The other theme is the realization that the cosmic web is intrinsically dynamic. The dynamic aspect of matter arises in quantum theory as a consequence of the wave nature of subatomic particles, and is even more central in relativity theory, which has shown that the being of matter cannot be separated from its activity. The properties of its basic patterns, the subatomic particles, can be understood only in a dynamic context, in terms of movement, interaction, and transformation." And string theory, which posits vibrating strings as the source of all matter and energy in the universe, brings us full circle to Pythagoras' doctrine of harmonic vibrations and the music of the spheres.

If psychology does indeed recapitulate cosmology, the psychology of the future will resemble, not Freud's crude psychodynamics or behaviorism's mechanics but rather more Ken Wilber's spectrum psychology, which distinguishes four major levels of consciousness, the ego, the biosocial, the existential, and the transpersonal. At the ego level, the self is contained within the organism. The biosocial level extends the self outward to the interaction between the biological organism and the social environment. "The existential level is the level of the total organism, characterized by a sense of identity which involves an awareness of the entire mind/body system as an integrated, self-organizing whole." The transpersonal level approaches the experience of reality as mediated through the Jungian collective unconscious, merging ultimately with Mind or **nous**.

In brief, the move from the structured self-contained Newtonian universe to the open, expanding Einsteinian universe will increasingly be accompanied by a radical transformation in human perception and understanding.

Chapter 24:
Noetic Magic

Everyone creates the world they perceive, and we all perceive according to impressions fixed in the past.
Deepak Chopra
The Return of Merlin

As human consciousness undergoes its modern gradual but profound transformation, new modes of understanding and interacting with reality are emerging. As we become more aware of the profound implications of the fact that consciousness is a constituent of causal reality, we will come increasingly to explore our world by means of noetic magic.

"There are three main theories of the Universe," wrote Aleister Crowley in **Magick in Theory and Practice, "**Dualism, Monism and Nihilism.**"**

Like most of Crowley's statements, this is an oversimplification. Still, as a dictum concerning the metaphysical underpinnings of magic, it has some historical foundation. In the ancient world, magic received its inspiration chiefly from dualist conceptions of the world like those of Pythagoras and the Gnostics. With the advent of Neo-Pythagoreanism, the emphasis switched to monism, a trend which was reaffirmed by the practitioners of "Natural Magic" at the time of the Renaissance. Modern magic, heavily influenced by Hindu philosophy as interpreted by Mme. Blavatsky and her Theosophical confreres, has a decidedly monist orientation. As a distinguished modern magician asserts: "... the philosophy which underlies magic is the philosophy which appears in the Indian "Vedanta" the philosophy of 'Monism.' In this philosophy God and His Universe are seen to be one and the same. But this, it will be said, is Pantheism pure and simple. It would be if we were so foolish as to regard Nature as the whole of God. We do not only hold the idea of His being in and through His Universe, but we also believe He transcends it." And as Willis Harman has pointed out, the "global mind change" that is occurring in the late twentieth century is predicated on a shift from materialistic monism (matter giving rise to mind) to meta-physical monism (mind giving rise to matter). Magic and science are thus once again converging.

Still it is clear that magic, as it is practised today, under the aegis of a number of isolated Magical Fraternities, is sadly out of date. Consider the kind of mentality that prevails among members of modern magical societies. It is one oriented to the past, to past rituals, rites and customs which arose out of cultures far different from our own in response to situations that simply do not exist for us. Yet modern magicians are adamant in their refusal to change a single word or procedure in these antiquated ceremonies. They prefer the certainties of the old to the challenges of the new.

How is it possible to arrive at a coherent philosophy of magic which will liberate the magus from the artificial restraints of the magical tradition and, at the same time, not violate the modern distrust of the supernatural? Let us begin with an illuminating quotation from William Blake:

> *"The ancient Poets animated all sensible objects with Gods or Geniuses calling them by the names and adorning them with the properties of woods, rivers, mountains, lakes, cities, nations, and whatever their enlarged & numerous senses could perceive.*
> *"And particularly they studied the genius of each city & country, placing it under its mental deity;*
> *"Till a system was formed, which some took advantage of, and enslaved the vulgar by attempting to realize or abstract the mental deities from their objects: thus began Priesthood;*
> *"Choosing forms of worship from poetic tales.*
> *"And at length they pronounced that the Gods had ordered such things,*
> *"Thus men forgot that All deities reside in the human breast."*

With the breakdown of belief in the supernatural, we have substituted submission to the powers of impersonal forces for faith in the omnipotence of a personal god. But a world ruled by the iron laws of chance and circumstance has little place in it for man.

The turning away from religion that has characterized the twentieth century has not been the consequence of personal choice. Rather, the world of the supernatural has simply receded from view as the products of modern technology have blotted out the horizon. The few who are self-proclaimed atheists ordinarily justify their position with intellectualist arguments, obscuring the fact that they have ceased to believe in the supernatural because they no longer need to.

This rejection of the supernatural has been self-consciously proclaimed only by a few, the Romantics of the last century and the Existentialists of today. It was a Romantic who remarked, "It's a good thing God does not exist, for if he did, I would have to kill him." Not surprisingly, one of the chief deities of the Romantic movement was that great symbol of revolt against oppression, Satan:

"Satan is the grandest symbol of protest against tyranny, celestial or terrestrial, that the world can conceive. . . . Was not Satan the first of all rebels against constituted authority? Did he not first utter the words, 'Non serviam', which burn on the lips of all revolutionaries? . . .He was the leader of the great army of Human Freedom, as Heine called the lovers of liberty of his day. . . .Satan stood at the head of all the agitators and conspirators against political oppression of the past century, and as predicted by the Italian poet Rapisardi, Lucifer will also accomplish the social revolution which is now preparing in all European countries and bring a new era for mankind, in which social equity as well as political equality will be effected."

But existentialism (which is, as Colin Wilson points out, merely Romanticism with a more precise philosophic vocabulary) provides the foundation for a view of magic that can meet the challenges of the modern age.

The very picture of self-discovery that is painted for us in books on Hermetic philosophy and the Cabala can also be found in the writings of Heidegger and Sartre. The magus, like the existentialist, embarks upon a search for authenticity in a confused and troubled world. The obstacles which confront him on his journey are chiefly the temptations to participate in partial and, therefore, inauthentic existence. In the end, he arrives at an awareness of the absolute nature of his freedom. The journey is the same; only the landmarks differ.

There is much in the writings of the existentialists which illuminates new possibilities for magic. There is, for example, the existential analysis of human freedom. Freedom, for Sartre, means the actualizing of human possibilities. It is an active, rather than a passive phenomenon. Freedom is not something you have; it is something you do. Every human situation offers us far more possibilities of acting freely than we ever take advantage of. Freedom is also absolute. Everything in our world exists either because we passively permit it or actively will it. The existential analysis of freedom eliminates all excuses for our conduct; it eliminates the sociological excuse (society made me do it) as well as the psychological excuse (the Oedipus complex made me do it). If we are enslaved, it is we alone who are responsible.

The metaphysical foundation for Sartre's conception of freedom is his doctrine that "existence precedes essence." We are not born into the world with a nature fixed by heredity or supernatural forces; we make ourselves. The reason that we usually botch the job is that we have chosen to live passively, inauthentically.

Let us consider also the existentialist doctrine of the will. Unlike nineteenth and twentieth century positivists who regard the will as a mechanical instrumentality, Nietszche and Sartre saw the will as an integral part of our being-in-the-world. The will is the link between humanity and the world. Only through will can we actualize our freedom. Will is not a quality which can be understood apart from action; it is, in effect, freedom realized in action. Of course, the will can lie dormant or be realized in inauthentic activity. In such instances, it is again expressive of one's state of being. Existentialism encourages active willing because it encourages the authentic realization of one's freedom, something which cannot be accomplished without the participation of the will. There is in the writing of some existentialists an almost lyric glorification of the will. Witness Nietszche's "Ah, that ye would renounce all half-willing, and would decide for idleness as ye decide for action! Ah, that ye understood my word: 'Do ever what ye will-but first be such as can will."

The importance of the will in magic is equally profound. "Do what thou wilt shall be the whole of the law," was Aleister Crowley's magical motto. "What is a Magical operation?" asked Crowley. "It may be defined as any event in Nature which is brought to pass by Will. We must not exclude potato-growing or banking from our definition."

A common psychological universe, an emphasis on freedom and

will: these are among the things which link existentialism and noetic magic. It is interesting to look at that which most sharply divides them: the existentialist assumption that human consciousness is capable of operating only upon one plane.

Considering Sartre's brilliant analysis of consciousness in **Being and Nothingness**, it is surprising that he remains unaware of the possibilities of any kind of consciousness other than what Alfred Schutz calls "the consciousness of everyday life." Sartre appears to assume, moreover, that the consciousness of other human beings is very much like his own. Yet it is quite clear that despite his many virtues as a writer and philosopher, Sartre's consciousness was quite severely limited. Iris Murdoch and Maurice Cranston have pointed out in their excellent books on Sartre that he possessed a peculiar tendency toward rationalism, despite his avowedly non-rationalist philosophical stance, which was manifested in his passion to reduce exterior phenomena to a kind of logical order. It is also revealed by his anti-emotionalism, his stern devotion to the world of thought. The physical world, for Sartre, was almost always described as something which disgusted him, a universe of objects without beauty or other redeeming qualities. Clearly, such an attitude toward the physical world is not an attribute of consciousness in general; it was, rather, peculiar to Sartre, a projection of his own sense of despair onto the outside world. The only thing which was not free for Sartre was the freedom to choose his own consciousness. Yet it is precisely this freedom which is affirmed by the magus.

Magic is "the science and art of causing changes in consciousness to occur in conformity with will." The magus does not attempt to effect changes in the world; rather he attempts to effect changes in *his perception* of the world. The world does not exist except insofar as we are conscious of it. Such a position is in perfect agreement with that of existentialism. In our post-Kantian age it is impossible to talk of "things-in-themselves." The magus is not, however, a Kantian idealist; he does not deny the existence of matter. On the contrary, as W. E. Butler points out, "it is not matter which is unreal, only the appearances it presents to our consciousness..." As our consciousness is expanded, new aspects of reality are revealed. The forms of consciousness open to the traditional magician, while clearly far more varied than those of everyday life, are nevertheless surprisingly few. Books on mysticism and magic frequently contain descriptions of the "levels of consciousness" which it is possible to attain. The following table, taken from Gurdjieff disciple Robert S. De Ropp's **The Master Game**, can be considered fairly representative:

1) Deep sleep without dreams.	The First Level
2) Sleep with dreams.	The Second Level
3) Waking sleep (ordinary consciousness)	The Third Level
4) Self-transcendence (self-remembering)	The Fourth Level
5) Objective consciousness (cosmic consciousness)	The Fifth Level

The first three states of consciousness are self-explanatory, but let us hear what De Ropp has to say about the last two states: "Man in the fourth [state] really is his own master. He knows where he is going, what he is doing, why he is doing it. His secret is that he remains unattached to the results of his activity, measures his success and failure not in terms of outward achievement, but in terms of inner awareness ... A man [in the fourth state] knows what combination of forces can produce what sort of result." As for the fifth state, it is essentially the mystic vision of oneness with the universe which, in De Ropp's words "is impossible to sustain without long and special training."

Such are the traditional paths open to the magus.

If such a typology has its uses, it also has its dangers for, in the last analysis, it implies an ultimate state of consciousness which human beings can attain and beyond which we cannot go. From the perspective of noetic magic this is an unnecessary limitation. The problem is not, "How is it possible to go beyond cosmic consciousness?" Rather, the fault lies in the term itself. It is a catch-all label applied to every variety of ineffable experience. It covers not one, but many, perhaps even an infinite number of higher states of consciousness. Such states cannot be described, they can only be experienced. Nevertheless, there are methods for reaching them, ranging from Cabalistic magic to Zen Buddhism. But the problem with these methods is that they have grown too formalized. Emerging, in many cases, from the experience of a single individual, such techniques attempt to stereotype in advance the experience which is sought. Noetic magic breaks down these categories by suggesting, not a method, but an approach to higher states of consciousness. It is this approach which will be outlined in the following pages.

The philosopher Franklin Merrell-Wolf has advanced the noetic thesis, "that there is a third organ, faculty or function of cognition other than sense perception and conceptual cognition. . .that leads to metaphysical certainty." Merrell-Wolf calls this faculty "Gnostic Realization," a clear exposition of which can be found in Plotinus' letter to Flaccus:

"External objects present us only with appearances. Concerning them, therefore, we may be said to possess opinion rather than knowledge. The distinctions in the actual world of appearance are of import only to ordinary and practical men. Our question lies with the ideal reality that exists behind appearance. How does the mind perceive these ideas? Are they without us, and is the reason, like sensation, occupied with objects external to itself? What certainty could we have, what assurance that our perception was infallible? The object perceived would be something different from the mind perceiving it. We should then have an image instead of reality. It would be monstrous to believe for a moment that the mind was unable to perceive ideal truth exactly as it is, and that we had not certainty and real knowledge concerning the world of intelligence. It follows, therefore, that this region of truth is not to be investigated as a thing external to us, and only imperfectly known. *It is within us.* [italics mine] Here the objects we contemplate and that which contemplates are identical - both are thought. The subject cannot surely know an object different from itself. The world of ideas lies within our intelligence. Truth, therefore, is not the agreement of our apprehension of an external object with the object itself. It is the agreement of the mind with itself. Consciousness, therefore, is the sole basis of certainty. The mind is its own witness."

Throughout history we have grown accustomed to thinking of reality as an absolute. It is not merely that human beings have generally agreed that, indeed, "something exists out there," but if they consider themselves as belonging to a particular culture, within that culture they experience considerable agreement as to *what it is*, exactly, that exists. Reality consists of those perceptions which are universally shared by individuals within a particular culture. But this is only one aspect of reality, albeit the most commonly experienced one. It is the reality of everyday life. To a twentieth century American this is the reality of car payments and credit card transactions, of TV, pornography and potato chips. But there are other aspects of reality as well, not so commonly shared, perhaps not shared at all. Those aspects of reality which people share may be called "intersubjective." Those which are not shared, which are peculiar to a particular individual, may be called "subjective." These are the only two kinds of reality which human beings can experience for there is no such thing as "objective" reality. Those things which are termed "objectively" real are merely those aspects of intersubjective reality which are most widely shared. But why should this be so? Why should "reality" be a quality which depends on the agreement of others? There are a variety of answers to this question, but we will concern ourselves with only one. Clearly, unless we arrive at a mutual agreement about what things are real and what things are not, communication and, therefore, any kind of activity which involves more than a single individual is impossible. We can imagine a time in the early history of our race when cooperation (and therefore communication) were absolutely essential for survival. Those perceptions upon which our ancient ancestors were forced to agree in order to survive were no doubt initially few in number. The cry of an animal, a flash of lightning, the heavy tread of a mammoth's feet: all these (we may speculate) may have served to warn early humans of the possibility of imminent danger. Before long a whole variety of perceptions which we found useful to agree upon developed, so many, in fact, that the traditional means of communication soon proved inadequate. Slowly, in the course of time, we developed languages, systems of sounds, each one of which corresponded with a different object, emotion or idea. The invention of language thus facilitated communication beyond all comparison to what preceded it. At the same time, language imposed an artificial stereotyping on human experience. The only things that we regarded as real were henceforth those things which could be communicated, especially in the form of speech. Each separate language had its own rules, its own words, its own set of unstated presuppositions. The only way tribes could communicate with each other was through translation. But when they did this they discovered to their astonishment that other languages expressed concepts for which their own had no equivalent. In this way new concepts (and consequently new experiences) were gradually introduced into languages. Nevertheless each language, then and now, imposes certain restrictions upon individual perceptions. Those perceptions which had little or no survival value were soon dropped in favor of those that had. Each language, above all, constitutes a reference system, by means of which we perceive and communicate. Perceptions are, as it were, filtered through this reference system, and emerge as useful or meaningful only on its terms. Language, of course, isn't the only reference system which we use. Traditions, myths, customs, folkways and so one are some of the others. Within a given culture, however, all of these reference systems mutually support and reinforce one another. In this sense a culture can be said to be a reference system also, composed of a variety of other reference systems which combine to make a whole.

The peculiar thing about the meta-reference systems that we call cultures is that we take them for granted. We are born into them, raised in them, and die in them while rarely questioning the image of reality which they have imposed upon us.

The more perceptive of us may question an aspect of the culture; no one ever denies the culture as a whole. To do so would mean the destruction of the very reference system by which we perceive. We are hypnotized into accepting our culture's version of reality; few of us are aware of any alternative. Other cultures may differ from our own in many respects but the differences are rarely great or exciting enough to induce us to adopt another way of life.

It should be clear, then, on the basis of what has just been said that whenever we say that something is impossible, we really mean impossible in terms of whatever reference system we are currently employing. It is impossible for indigenous peoples to fly unless they participate in the reference system (i.e., get into the airplane) of "civilized" humanity. It is impossible to do algebra unless one understands the reference system upon which it is based. By its very nature, a reference system is limiting, constricting. Occasionally it will exclude a whole realm of human experience. It is in this way that the reference system by which most "civilized" people operate has excluded the experience of magic.

If you wish to practice magic you must first of all adopt a reference system in which magic is possible. This is much harder than it sounds. It involves a rigorous mental and physical process, a "dehypnotization" from concepts and modes of perception which have become almost second nature. But the end result, the ability to move at will from one reference system to another, to experience a much wider variety of perceptions than is presently possible, to become, in short, the sole shapers of our own destiny is well worth the effort.

To understand how the modern scientific world-view systematically excludes the possibility of magic, let's examine the arguments advanced against the occult by the scientist D. H. Rawcliffe in his **Illusions and Delusions of the Supernatural and the Occult.** Rawcliffe, in attacking psychical research, seems to feel that he need do no more to destroy the claims of that branch of science than to show its historical connection with the "dim underworld" of the occult:

"The majority of psychologists ... point out that the animus of Psychical research and parapsychology lies in the depths of the past, in myth and superstition, in magic, in the mysteries of ancient priestly cults; above all in the inherent psychological tendencies of the human mind to attribute to the agency of unseen powers those phenomena which it does not understand. They conclude from this that the great majority of the problems of Psychical research are raised by virtue of the peculiar bias or mental set of the investigator, who, believing for various reasons in the possibility of mysterious occult forces in nature, seeks to find practical instances of it in order to justify his beliefs; this approach generally tends to make him *ignore or disrespect other approaches which possess the merit of coherence within the normal scientific scheme of things."* (Italics mine) In other words, anything that is not explicable in purely scientific terms is to be dismissed, out of hand, as utter nonsense. Rawcliffe is so hypnotized by the reference system of modern science that he is not capable of admitting the possibility that anything existing outside of it could have any meaning whatsoever. This is made even clearer in the following passage, which surely equals, if it does not surpass in bigotry any religious denunciation of science:

"Psychical research represents a reversion towards occult beliefs which have had their origin in the earliest human cultures. Its claims to scientific status are confuted by the metaphysical, as opposed to the scientific, nature of its concepts and theories. These metaphysical concepts and theories are unmistakably derived from the supernatural beliefs and superstitions which have existed in various forms down through the ages to the present day. *Even if the accuracy of parapsychological experiments were to be fully substantiated the metaphysical theories and concepts upon which such experiments were based would not be scientifically established...* (italics mine) *Parapsychological theories of transcendental mental faculties would still remain speculative essays in metaphysics, possessing no relation to scientific theory.* (Italics Rawcliffe's) As such they possess no significance for the scientist, who recognizes that the sole justification of any scientific theory lies in its usefulness as a basis for empirical deduction."

In short, there is no way that psychical research, much less magic or any other form of occultism, can achieve scientific status. They are too metaphysical, argues Rawcliffe, forgetting, if he ever knew, that science has a metaphysical basis of its own.

We should keep in mind that the object here has not been to defend psychical research, but rather to show how closed the mind of a scientist can be toward anything that smacks even slightly of the occult. Rawcliffe clearly regards magic as impossible, but it is clear that the reason for this lies in his fanatical adherence to a scientific reference system. Thomas Kuhn, in his **The Structure of Scientific Revolutions**, has pointed out that science progresses by replacing old reference systems (or, in Kuhn's terminology, paradigms) with new ones which provide the possibility for more sophisticated scientific explanations as, for example, the Einsteinian paradigm of relativity replacing the old Newtonian reference system. Science, as Rawcliffe fails to recognize, is not an area of human thought which operates on immutable principles. Science has a history. To dismiss any avenue of research as unscientific is to demonstrate ignorance of that history.

Our immediate concern is not, however, with the history of science, but with the future of magic. In the modern world, we are immersed in a secular and scientific culture that controls and limits our existence. Its visible fruits are technology and the rational bureaucratic state. How can we transcend the limitations imposed upon us by such powerful impersonal forces?

In order to answer this question, we must examine the principles upon which noetic magic is based: the mind as an active force, the will as the link between man and the world, The necessary coupling of will and imagination, the doctrine of "anamnesis" or the "good unconscious" and the exploration of the antipodes of the mind by means of moments of visionary illumination, what Joyce called "epiphanies." Only when we have attained a clearer understanding of these principles, will we be able to embark on the long and arduous journey that leads to noetic magic.

In general, noetic magic possesses the following characteristics:

1) The **nous** is that part of the human mind that transcends consciousness.

2) The purpose of noetic magic is to explore the **nous**, bringing it more fully into our consciousness.

3) The means by which this is accomplished is the transformation of consciousness at will, using techniques drawn from both esoteric tradition and modern psychology.

A few additional observations. Noetic magic is skeptical. It does not posit the existence of a supernatural reality. Rather, it emphasizes the transcendental potential of imaginatively exploring the human psyche. Noetic magic is individualistic. It rejects groupthink and all forms of intellectual and spiritual conformity. And finally, noetic magic is communicative, oriented towards sharing insights and techniques with others in order that all who are interested can better appreciate the astonishing capacities of the human mind.

Chapter 25:
The Mind as an Active Force

Philosophical Sonnet

with

No Apologies to the Comte de St. Germain

Curious seekers of Nature sublime
I know its origin and its goal.
I see the shining gold at the bottom of its mine.
I have seized its body and surprised its soul.
I have showed by art the soul's terrestrial birth
in woman's womb, and its release, and how, with time,
a seed united with a grain of corn under the humid earth, one a plant,
the other a vine, are the bread and the wine.
All is nought, they say, purposeless and vain. This I deny, searching
in my soul's pain with no surcease and nothing to sustain.
At last, weary with the weight of praise and of blame, I found the
eternal, it called my name.
Yet listen! It was from my soul's void that this call came.

The belief in the mind as fundamentally passive is a relatively recent development. It was first explicitly articulated by John Locke in his **Essay Concerning Human Understanding**, published in 1689. In this work Locke argued that the mind, at birth, is a Tabula Rasa, a blank tablet. Knowledge comes to the mind in the form of sensations which impinge on human consciousness in such a way that they create lasting impressions. Such impressions, linked together, form simple concepts which, in association with other concepts, combine to form more and more complex ideas. However, no idea, no matter how complex or abstract, is derived from any source other than sensation. Locke's epistemology, called empiricism because it argued that all knowledge derived from experience, became popular in the eighteenth century, especially among scientists. In a modified form it is with us today and it remains the metaphysical foundation on which the entire edifice of modern science rests.

Locke's theory denies creative power to the mind. In empirical terms, the mind is nothing but the passive receptacle into which physical sensations of various kinds are poured. We are nothing more than the pawn of our environment, shaped and molded according to the nature of our experience. Science on the one hand gives us enormous power to effect creative change while on the other hand, it denies the existence of a creative faculty in us capable of effecting such change.

The "passive fallacy" (which is the term that we will use to refer to empiricism) has been subjected to considerable criticism by modern existentialist and humanist psychologists. The constitutive nature of human thinking, the creative manner in which thought affects and structures our experience, has come to be emphasized more and more. As one writer has very clearly put it:

"Experience is not simply something which happens to man; it is not a receptacle into which pure facts are poured that are then to be sorted out from subjective impressions. A human being is as actively engaged in experience as an artist in the moment of artistic experience; *every man structures the situation in which his perception will come to fruition..* (italics mine) Man is perhaps the only creature who senses that there is more in nature than meets the eye. Nature is filled with significance; but it is significance which is dependent upon man who encounters nature within the field of his perception. Man becomes human by being creative in experience."

Most of us go through life without being aware of the creative potential of the human mind. Experience, to us, exhibits a sameness, a uniformity from which we cannot escape. We are caught in the grip of the passive fallacy, regarding our minds as mere mechanisms which can respond but never create. We thus condemn ourselves to the meaningless existence which we profess to despise.

If the mind is an active, constitutive force, constantly shaping our experience, we must know how active, how creative it is.

The existentialists are remarkably unclear on this crucial point. Having emphasized the creative power of the mind, many of them shift to a discussion of the factors which limit this power: culture, technology, the historical situation. This does not help us and, indeed, we are right to be suspicious of the existentialists at this juncture. They have given us a glimpse of creative human potential and then have taken it from us. Moreover, they have done so without carefully exploring the possibilities of the problem they have raised.

The problem of the mind as an active force reduces itself to two clear possibilities (which are not mutually exclusive). Is the mind capable of subjectively altering the impressions it receives? And is it capable of objectively altering exterior phenomena? Both possibilities have formed the epistemological basis for magic.

Modern research in parapsychology is founded on the hypothesis that the mind possesses the independent ability to explore and/or alter events or objects in the outside world. Parapsychologists employ a variety of terms to describe such mental exploration: telepathy (mind reading), clairvoyance (the ability to see events or objects at a distance), precognition (the ability to foretell the future); the ability to actually manipulate objects with the mind is generally referred to as psychokinesis (PK). But even if one were to accept the most spectacular results which have been achieved in tests of ESP, they would provide a rather dismal picture of the mind's ability to affect the outside world. A series of scores slightly above chance in a test which involves five known alternatives (the Zener test), the occasional, highly unreliable ability to affect the roll of dice: this is the very best that parapsychological research has to offer us. One should not necessarily dismiss ESP research out of hand, however. New developments are occurring in the field everyday; perhaps the much longed-for "conclusive test" will soon be devised.

But noetic magic is not based on the assumption that mind can affect exterior phenomena. While it keeps an open mind on the subject of ESP, noetic magic emphasizes the subtler and potentially more rewarding ability of the mind to subjectively alter the sensations it receives from the outside world. ESP at its best offers us nothing more than rare and unpredictable abilities. It introduces no sense of new meaning into the world. One can quite easily imagine that if ESP were somehow made available to everyone, the world would be bored to death with it within a week. Noetic magic is more rewarding because it has the potential to infuse meaning into the subject's world.

To the noetic magus the world has meaning only insofar as we impart meaning to it. The world is neither hostile nor friendly; it is merely subjectively experienced as such. The problem is that most people are not aware of the degree to which their mental attitudes affect their experience. Consequently, they fail to exercise any control over their minds, allowing their consciousness to drift aimlessly, subject to the vagaries of external forces. This is the real problem of the passivity of human consciousness for it is precisely this kind of attitude which leads people to think of themselves as objects and to think of oneself as an object is to become an object. Yet this is the ordinary state of human consciousness. No wonder that Gurdjieff referred to it as the state of "waking sleep."

To what extent can we alter our subjective impressions of the outside world? To some extent we do it all the time although usually we are unaware of it. Let's listen to an example of this kind of mental activity which should be familiar to all of us:

"The shape in which things appear to us is remarkably variable. Not only do things have a tendency to meet us half way as far as our changing moods are concerned, but we can influence them, too; we are able, to a certain extent, to change things just by observing them differently. I can sit in my room and look at the furniture, at the curtains, at the assembled things of my existence, so unfavorably that they become hostile. They become my enemies, and after a while I wonder how in the world it has ever been possible for me to feel happy in this room with these things. If I change the intention of my observation, though; if, for instance, I resolve to draw from the things their favorable qualities, then, as a rule, it soon appears that the things which just a moment ago glared at me, start to smile and perhaps even entrust me with the sunniest aspect of their existence."

We have all experienced moments of the kind just described, yet few of us go on to explore further the ways in which such changes in attitude can be controlled. Any change in attitude comes about either because we permit it or because we will it. Usually it is because we permit it. We feel ourselves to be the victim of our moods. It rarely occurs to us that we should make our moods serve us rather than allow ourselves to serve our moods. Encapsulated as we are in a cultural reference system which denies our creative potential, most of us are content to play the approved role of victim. To become something more requires an effort of imagination and will which few of us care to make. It requires the imagination to deny the fundamental reality of ordinary consciousness and the will to break through the limitations which this consciousness imposes upon us.

The Unconscious, Personal and Collective and the Doctrine of Anamnesis

In the twentieth century, the Western world's conception of the mind's structure has been dominated by the psychoanalytic theories of Sigmund Freud and his followers, which divide the mind into three parts: the unconscious, the ego, and the superego. In Freudian terms, the unconscious is the repository of those impermissible impulses, primarily sexual, that the individual has repressed, the ego is our waking consciousness, and the superego represents our culture's mores and moral rules which the individual has internalized.

Freud's personal unconscious is a dark and dangerous place, a kind of basement of the mind wherein dwell grotesque creatures of great destructive power. The fact that there is no empirical evidence of the Freudian unconscious and that Freud himself conjured up his most famous case histories to fit a preconceived conception of the mind's structure has not prevented the West from incorporating the Freudian mental model into the deepest substructure of modern culture.

Psychoanalysis has invaded the popular mind to such an extent that millions of people who have never even heard of Freud speak glibly of such phenomena as repression and projection. But Freud was the greatest reductionist of all modern thinkers, diminishing the complexity of human experience to the suppression of the sexual instinct and the behavioral manifestations to which such suppression leads.*

Karl Jung rejected Freud's narrow emphasis on repressed sexuality and developed a broader interpretation, originating the concept of the collective unconscious, in which reside representations or archetypes of human cultural experience which manifest themselves in symbolic form. Jung himself was greatly interested in alchemy, which he interpreted as a gradual process of spiritual enlightenment akin to what he termed "individuation."

"Individuation" is the quest of individuals towards wholeness of being. For most of us individuation takes the form of natural cycles of growth, maturity, decay, and death. But Jung also believed that we can consciously direct our own psychological development, especially in the second half of life when we come to recognize the inevitability of death.

Contemplation of archetypal meanings through analysis of dreams and meditation on archetypal symbols allows us to progress towards psychological integration, facing up to the darker sides of our selves,

---

*Anyone who continues to believe in the Freudian model of the mind should read Richard Webster's devastating dismantling of Freudian theory **Why Freud Was Wrong: Sin, Science, and Psychoanalysis** Basic Books, 1995. For a critique of Freudian approaches to history see my "Psychomythology: A Phenomenological Critique of Psychohistory" **The Dalhousie Review** (Summer 1980).

our "shadow" selves and integrating our masculine and feminine sides (anima for men, animus for women).

Jungian psychology, while no more subject to empirical verification than Freudian psychoanalysis, depicts human development as mythoempirical and individuals, potentially at least, as heroes who embark on the quest for self-understanding, encountering perils, temptations and obstacles along the way, but ultimately, if they persist, successful in their journey. Jung's psychology is the Grail Myth made manifest in the human psyche.

In the Jungian schema, consciousness emerges out of the unconscious (the opposite of Freudian psychoanalysis). Jung's history of the psyche identifies four stages: primitives, ancients, moderns, and contemporaries. Primitives experience no distinction between the subjective and the objective. Ancients project their subjective selves onto the world as gods. Moderns withdraw their ego projections from the world and by denying the nonrational side of the self, dymythologize the world. Contemporaries, aware of their nonrational impulses, attempt to come to terms with them. Most people in the twentieth century, in Jung's view, are moderns. Only a minority are contemporaries. Whereas the moderns suffer from neurosis, contemporaries "suffer from emptiness or malaise." Jung identifies the spiritual problem of contemporaries as analogous to that of the Gnostics. Like Gnostics, contemporaries are alienated but "Where Gnostics feel cut off from the from the outer world, contemporaries feel cut off from the inner one." Where Jung parts company with the Gnostics is in his definition of the human quest for individuation. Gnostics sought to merge with the divine (the pure, undifferentiated unconscious). Contemporaries seek to bring that which is unconscious into consciousness. In the words of Jungian scholar Jolande Jacobi:

"Once the psyche reaches the midpoint of life, the process of development demands a return to the beginning, a descent into the dark, hot depths of the unconscious. To sojourn in these depths, to withstand their dangers, is a journey to hell and 'death.' But he who comes through safe and sound, who is 'reborn,' will return, full of knowledge and wisdom, equipped for the outward and inward demands of life."

As a flexible system of thought congenial to the quest of magicians past and present, Jung has opened up a rich world of symbolic interpretation than can be applied fruitfully to deeper study of Pythagorean-ism, Gnosticism, Hermetism, the Cabala, and the Tarot.

But a further concept proves useful here and that is Plato's *anamnesis*. Anamnesis, as Iris Murdoch has defined it, is the "good unconscious," that repository of ideal forms or ideas, which human beings possess whether they know it or not. In fact, we do strive towards an ideal of justice, perhaps without being able to define it clearly; we all have in our minds also ideals of truth, beauty, and love. And the "good unconscious" is something we can cultivate, providing us with ideals towards which we can strive. Anamnesis, speaking as it does to the "better angels of our nature" is far more powerful than the sinister impulses which Freud taught us to fear. The cultivation of *anamnesis* allows us to embrace the unknown splendors within each of us.

Chapter 26:
Will and Imagination

The theory that the will is the ultimate constituent of reality is a very old one. Christian theologians like Augustine argued that God is absolute will while skeptics like Hume have maintained that the will is the determining factor in human conduct. More recently, William James argued that the "will to believe" was the primary characteristic of all creative thinking. James was not talking of faith or indiscriminate belief in general; rather, he opposed the "will to believe" to the "will not-to-know," the passive will which refused to become involved in adventurous thought. In the twentieth century, books on how to increase your will power are as numerous as they are useless. Such books advance a theory of the will derived from our Victorian ancestors: will as cold hard determination to succeed, a kind of mental gritting of the teeth and mindless stick-to-it-iveness. This is not the kind of will involved in noetic magic.

Will, to the noetic magus, is that faculty in us which opens toward the future. It is the embodiment of our intentionality. Only when the future is open, filled with possibility, is will possible. We should all be familiar with this meaning of will from our own experience. When our lives seem constricted, when we experience a foreshortening of our mental horizons, we lose the ability to act. Action can only occur when we perceive the possibility of a future, however limited that future might be.

In noetic magic, we free our will by widening the horizons of our existence. We no longer sees the future as determined, closed, constricted. We view it rather as an immense arena in which we can act, an arena which is constantly opening up to us, revealing new potentialities. How does the noetic magus acquire such a vision of the future? Through imagination.

Imagination can be defined as the ability to perceive the new in the familiar, to suspect the unknown in the known. It is the creative power of the human mind in action. To the imaginative, the future as well as the present poses a constant challenge to our spirit of adventure. Yet imagination working alone is not sufficient. Imagination without will may degenerate into mere fantasizing just as will without imagination degenerates into mindless action. In noetic magic imagination and will are inseparable; each interacts with the other to keep us open to the future and to provide us with the ability to act.

It should be clear from this discussion that to will is not the same thing as to wish. Wishing implies a certain passivity, a divorce of thought from action. Willing, on the other hand, implies action; it is a self-imposed requirement to act. Noetic magic is not wish-fulfillment; it is will-fulfillment.

Imagination and will are familiar components of our everyday experience. The problem is that we exercise both infrequently and even then within the limited framework of our cultural paradigm. The man who pulls off a clever business deal surely employs imagination and will to some extent but the extent to which he has exercised these faculties is limited by the situation in which he sees himself acting.

Noetic magic is not concerned with limited imagination of this kind. Imagination, to be magically effective, must transcend the constricting parameters of one's cultural reference system and venture into the unknown.

We are confronted by the unknown everywhere we turn. Yet we avoid the confrontation. We fear the unknown as we fear freedom for they are two sides of the same coin. The unknown requires us to think and act in unaccustomed ways. Historically, we have propitiated our fear of the unknown in a number of ways, many of them involving the occult. The modern way of propitiating the unknown is to subject it to scientific scrutiny. Trends are projected into the future with a great show of scientific exactitude, yet we are all aware that such forecasts have little to do with what actually will actually happen. Almost invariably forecasts are wrong, but it is not really their function to predict the future, merely to give the illusion of doing so and thus relieve to some degree our fears in the present. The function of imagination in noetic magic is to overcome our fear of the unknown. Imagination prospects into the unknown. It reveals glimpses here and there of potential meaning. The unknown is not the unconscious, at least not in the Freudian sense. It is everything of which we are presently unaware. It is both inside and outside of us. Since it is not explicable in terms of our ordinary experience, we must approach it in a way that differs from our usual attitude toward knowledge, from the point of view of insight and intuition rather than rational awareness. Moreover, our insights result in an altered state of consciousness in which our imaginative faculties are given free rein. Needless to say the unknown may be pleasant or horrifying, a heaven or a hell. It is, however, within our power to choose which of these it will be . Imagination may provide us with a variety of alternatives but will determines which of these we shall choose.

"The variability of the things we observe is typical of our existence. This is what the tree of the knowledge of good and evil embodied: after man ate of it, he could see thousands of things in every object or incident. The apple tree was not just an apple tree, not just one diffuse fact which deserves but one ultimately undefined meaning. It was an infinite amount of facts; among many other things, it was a tree that gives understanding. The leap from the diffuse undefined observation to the observation of thousands of hard realities is full of dangers. For by seeing things in this manner, one can make this world a hell or a heaven... The leap toward the differentiated observation is the leap toward light and darkness, toward happiness and unhappiness, toward belief and unbelief; a promotion and a denigration, a becoming like God and a being infinitely far away from him."

These are among the alternatives that imagination provides us with in our ordinary conscious state. How many more could we perceive in a state of altered consciousness? There is obviously no way of knowing unless we summon up all the will and imagination at our command to transcend the conditioned limits of our consciousness. Only then will we be able, in Nietzsche's words, "to ride on every parable to every truth."

Chapter 27:
Exploring the Antipodes of the Mind

In **Heaven and Hell** Aldous Huxley coined the phrase "the antipodes of the mind," which refers to the unknown. As Huxley pointed out, the mind's antipodes are populated with a variety of strange flora and fauna. We know of the existence of this land as we know of the existence of any remote and exotic place: through traveller's reports. But unlike the reports of most travellers, the tales of those who have returned from these antipodes differ considerably in detail. Some speak of a heaven, others of a hell, but even the heavens and the hells which the travellers experience are by no means the same. We are right to suspect that the antipodes of the mind are not one place but many places and that the nature of the journey depends on the attitude and expectations of the traveller.

How do we get from where we are to a place in the mind's antipodes? Some, like Huxley, have advocated the use of drugs. Certainly drugs can transport us to some of the places we want to go. But the problem with drugs is that they require very little will and imagination on our part and they sometimes take us where we don't want to go.

Drugs can be useful in presenting alternatives which are open to us; they offer irrefutable proof that the world of everyday reality is merely an arbitrary perceptual construct, but they can take us little further than this.

We who wish to visit exotic places in the unknown at will can turn to a variety of other methods: Zen, Tarot, the Cabala: the list is long. The problem with each of these methods is that they are very difficult to learn so that if we are to achieve any real expertise in them we must choose one, two at the most, to the exclusion of all the rest. Moreover, each of these methods will take us to only one or two of the places we want to go. How can we choose? The problem is insoluble. Or is it?

Each of us as we make the rounds of our daily existence comes into fleeting contact with some place in the mind's antipodes. It is as if the unknown were continually beckoning us to come out of ourselves and only in rare moments when the constraints of our cultural reference system are weakest do we respond to this summons. *Usually this response is brief and we do not remember it.* The psychologists have a name for this kind of forgetfulness as they have for everything else; they call it retroactive inhibition. Retroactive inhibition works like this: The more original and illuminating our thought or insight, the more likely we are to forget it. Why should this be so? Quite simply because such illuminative moments directly contradict the nature of the reality in which we normally operate. They are dangerous forays of the unknown into our known and hence comfortable world. We have all experienced the frustration of trying to remember a particularly startling insight and being unable to do so, sometimes coming up with something that seems to us like utter nonsense. This is what Gurdjieff meant by "self-forgetfulness." Most of us are continually in this state because we choose not to disrupt the accepted version of reality.

I choose to call such epiphanic moments "illuminations." The rest of this chapter will be devoted to exploring ways in which we can make such illuminations serve as guideposts in our travels into the unknown. Shelley recognized the manner in which the unknown subtly makes its presence felt when he wrote the following lines:

The awful shadow of some unseen Power
Floats tho' unseen among us; visiting
This various world with as inconstant wing
As summer winds that creep from flower to flower;
Like moonbeams that behind some piny mountain shower,
It visits with inconstant glance.

We must first recognize that the unknown is all around us. We can infer its presence from a thousand things, from anything in fact. Knowing this we must make the most of our illuminations for only they can put us into touch with this as yet unseen world.

Once we are awakened to the fact that illuminations occur we must resolve not to let them pass unremembered.

We must seize each moment of illumination as it comes to us. if it denies our present sense of reality, all the better.

Illuminations are the poetry of the void. The void is in ourselves. The poetry is our own.

We must not try to capture illuminations in the net of rational thought. Insight is a frail thing, easily broken.

Each illumination has unsuspected implications. These we must explore.

We should not fear the consequences of our exploration. If our travels take us where we do not want to go it is a simple enough matter to break the journey off. Mundane reality is ever close at hand.

We should always keep in mind that the illumination is neither more real nor less real than what we are accustomed to call the real world. It is merely a reaching beyond ourselves.

Illuminations may be brief or they may last a lifetime. (Witness Blake) At first they will probably be infrequent. Later we will be able to stretch them out. We can play them as we do a musical instrument. Even if we play badly, we are still playing.

Each illumination leads to many others.

Each illumination is different.

Each illumination points the way to a higher form of experience.

There are no limits to these higher forms of experience for there are no limits to illumination.

Exploration of illuminations requires imagination and will.

As we explore, hesitantly at first, then with greater confidence we will find the future opening up before us.

The power of our will grows even stronger.

The limits of our imagination will recede from view.

Our self is transformed, not in one way but in a hundred.

Each illumination potentially leads to a new paradigm of existence if we explore it carefully enough.

Every new paradigm which we encounter vastly increases our power to act.

The greater our knowledge of other worlds the greater our power to act in this one.

We can help to transform this world by transforming ourselves and by pointing out the path of transformation to others.

The goal is not merely to achieve changes in consciousness at will; it is also to hold out the hope to others of doing so.

When more than one person experiences a change in consciousness, the improvement in this world is both quantitative and qualitative.

The goal is power.

Power over ourselves.

The goal for others is power over themselves.

Let's not get the goals confused.

Chapter 28:
Noetic Magic and the Other

Noetic magic, no less than traditional magic, is directed toward self-realization. The problem with any discipline having self realization as its end is that it is always in danger of degenerating into solipsism. The magus, preoccupied with exploring the self, is especially vulnerable to this danger. The self may be seen as the only reality and power over the self confused with power over the whole of creation. Crowley (a notable solipsist, most would say) sums up the consequences of solipsism admirably:

"Such a being is gradually disintegrated from lack of nourishment and the slow but certain action of the attraction of the universe, despite his now desperate efforts to insulate and protect himself, and to aggrandize himself by predatory practices. He may indeed prosper for a while, but in the end he must perish."

That mere awareness of this danger is not, by itself, sufficient to combat it is amply demonstrated by Crowley's own career. His arrogance, insensitivity and megalomania were the inevitable results of an increasing solipsism.

Philosophers have despaired at refuting the claims of the solipsist. Descartes, Leibniz, and Schopenhauer found no logical way out of the solipsist trap. The solution of the Cabala may perhaps be the best. We become aware of the reality of the existence of others through empathy with their suffering: "The suffering of the other, as internalized by the self, brings one first to recognize his existence as a separate entity, and enables one to sympathize and empathize with him."

How can noetic magic avoid this difficulty? Only through awareness of the reality of the Other. All experience is partial and incomplete and subjective experience particularly so. The magus whose goal it is to widen the limits of his experience cannot remain content with a merely subjective reality no matter how illuminating it may be. The subjective must enter into the intersubjective, the reality of which is dependent on the reality of the Other. To deny the reality of the Other is necessarily to close off entire realms of experience and, in the process, become not more, but less human.

The experience of Otherness is proof of the absurdity of solipsism. The Other is not an extension of ourselves any more than the self is an extension of the Other. Both exist independently, yet there is the possibility of communication between them. As Martin Buber points out, true communication is only possible when the Other is regarded, not as a thing, as an It, but as a person, possessing a mind and will of his own, as a Thou. We cannot impose our will on the Other for to do so would mean reducing the Other to the status of an object. We can only communicate the results of our illuminative experiences, either indirectly through a transformed self, or directly through interaction with others. Moreover, we should not see ourselves as teachers or guides, opening up the Other the road to wisdom. If we adopt this attitude we will be unresponsive to the Other. Dialogue will become dreary monologue.

There is a magic of the interpersonal in which the most profound experiences are shared. This is what the magus must aim for. Insights obtained in solitary exploration acquire, not only a new meaning, but literally a new life of their own when they are communicated to others. Transformation of the self can only be accomplished to a limited extent in solitude. It is in a constantly changing interaction with other people on the most profound level possible that the magus attains authentic selfhood, a selfhood that joyously affirms the reality of others.

Traditional magicians have often sought seclusion from society. As magic has become more subjective, less transitive in nature, the tendency toward self-exclusion has increased. Modern magicians have found safety in the bosom of secret societies in which the "secrets" of magic are shared by a limited number of members. It is true that the magus needs solitude. Some experiences are only born out of the isolated self in its confrontation with an inexplicable universe. But the magus must be wary of solitude; we must not let it become a way of life, only a necessary part of life. The noetic magus is committed to a life of action; our entire outlook is active rather than passive. We must therefore participate in the only world in which action has any meaning: the social world, the world of other people. If magic is to have any effect other than a purely individual one, the magus must seek out others. Values are not created in isolation, although the inspiration for the creation of new values may be partially the result of the solitary imagination. Self-realization, then, is only an aspect of the magical endeavor, not its final goal. As Maurice Friedman has pointed out:

"Self-realization cannot be made the goal without vitiating its very meaning as the attainment of authentic existence. Such an existence cannot be measured in terms of the self alone, but in terms of the meaning that the self attains through giving itself in relation to what is not itself to other selves and other beings. If one means by self realization no more than realizing the empirical self that one is, then one is already at one's goal. If one means, on the other hand, a self that has not yet become but can become, then one must still discover which of the many selves one can become is one's 'real' self. 'Potentiality' is essentially neutral. Only the direction of 'potentiality' makes it good or bad. Values cannot be based on self-realization or the realization of man's powers. On the contrary, we cannot define ourselves or our potentialities apart from the direction we give them, apart from what we become in relation to others. This direction, this becoming, implies a movement toward the authentic, toward values, toward the image of man."

Noetic magi differ from others principally in the power which they have attained over themselves and in their conscious effort to direct their imagination to new insights and experiences. They do not impose these insights and experiences on others; they merely offer them, as a gift of themselves, in the hope that, in the process of transformation by human dialogue, they will help to point the way to new values. In this sense the noetic magus does not want to become more godlike but more truly human.

Chapter 29:
Exercises in Noetic Magic

The aspirant to noetic magic should undertake a variety of mental and meditative exercises designed to increase access to heightened states of consciousness. The exercises listed here are in approximate order of difficulty and should be practised more or less in sequence. I say more or less because some of the later exercises, Jungian meditations on the Tarot, for example, represent choices that the aspirant can make, one of which could very well be to skip the exercise altogether in favor of others that, for whatever reason, seem more appealing. Also, the exercises suggested here are not intended to be exhaustive, merely suggestive. You should feel free to challenge your imagination in designing your own exercises. Results are the only criteria for success.

Self-Observation

Most of us rarely observe ourselves. We go through life responding to events mechanically. At times of great crisis we may achieve glimpses of self-knowledge, often surprising ourselves with unexpected reservoirs of strength and resourcefulness. The common excuse for leading an unexamined life is lack of time. Our days are too busy and full. In fact, recent surveys have shown that the amount of leisure time available to Americans has actually increased over the past twenty years. The problem is that we spend that time in passive, mindless activities like watching television. But, as Gurdjieff pointed out, self-observation is something that should be an integral part of daily life, not separate from it. Key to successful self-observation is ignoring the blandishments of false personality and willing **objective** self-observation. The commitment must be to emotional and physical awareness, not just intellectual attention. As psychologist Charles Tart has said, "The practice of self-observation . . .is the practice of being curious, along with a commitment to do your best to observe whatever is there, regardless of your preferences or fears." Tart recommends the Buddhist practice of **vipassana** or "mindfulness meditation." In **vipassana** you choose a designated time of fifteen or twenty minutes during which you sit with eyes closed and "try to observe **every** thought, feeling or sensation that comes along." Do not attempt to censor out any experiences. Pay attention to every experience that comes to mind.

Remember that self-observation is not self-analysis. Its purpose is to increase knowledge of your thoughts, feelings, and sensations, not to understand why you have them. Self-analysis is a separate and valuable process but one that should succeed periods of self-observation, not be intermingled with them.

Self-observation sounds simple. It's not.

Self-Remembering

Self-remembering is one of the fundamental Gurdjieffian exercises. It begins with a morning session designed to alert you to practice self-remembering throughout the day. Sit in a chair with your eyes closed and spend a couple of minutes relaxing your body. Then concentrate on the sensations your body experiences beginning with the right foot, moving up the right leg, shifting to the right hand, right forearm, upper right arm, then moving down the left hand side of your body to your left foot. The important thing to remember in this stage of the exercise is that you focus your attention on the actual sensations your body is experiencing, devoting about thirty seconds to each part and not permitting your mind to wander to any other matters.

The second part of the exercise involves integrating the sensations your entire body is experiencing and then opening up your senses to the sounds around you, then open your eyes and experience the sights around you. At this point you are "simultaneously sensing, looking, and listening," that is, you are engaging all three parts of the tripartite brain that Gurdjieff has described.

The morning exercise is intended to teach you how self-remembering works so that you can practice it throughout the rest of your day.

Again, the process sounds deceptively simple. In fact, it must be practiced regularly over a long period of time, usually several months, before the aspirant can even begin to be proficient at it.

Self-observation and self-remembering are two different processes. But self-observation begins at the level of false personality with your ordinary "I" observing the self. After sufficient practice, self-observation should become self-remembering in which the transcendental "I" is experienced, which becomes, in time, an overwhelming experience of "true" selfhood.

Conscious Prayer

Gurdjieff's concept of conscious prayer differs significantly from the customary religious practice of prayer as supplication: "These prayers are, so to speak, *recapitulations*; by repeating them aloud or to himself a man endeavors to experience what is in them, their whole new content, with his mind and feelings. And a man can always make new prayers for himself. For example a man says -- 'I want to be serious.' But the whole point is in how he says it. If he repeats it even ten thousand times a day and is thinking of how soon he will finish and what will there be for dinner and the like, then it is not prayer but simply self-deceit. But it become a prayer if a man recites the prayer in this way: He says 'I' and tries at the same time to think of everything he knows about 'I.' It does not exist, there is no single 'I,' there is a multitude of petty, clamorous, quarrelsome 'I's. But he wants to be one 'I' -- the master; he recalls the carriage, the horse, the driver, and the master. 'I' is master. 'Want' -- he thinks of the meaning of 'I want.' Is he able to want? With him 'it wants' or 'it does not want' all the time. But to this 'it wants' and 'does not want' he strives to oppose his own 'I want' which is connected with the aims of work on himself. . .'To be' -- the man thinks of what to be, what 'being' means. The being of a mechanical man with whom everything happens. The being of a man who can do. It is possible 'to be' in different ways. He wants 'to be' not merely in the sense of existence but in the sense of greatness of power. The words 'to be' acquire weight, a new meaning for him. 'Serious' -- the man thinks what it means to be serious. How he answers himself is very important. If he understands what this means, if he defines correctly for himself what it means to be serious and feels that he truly desires it, then his prayer can give a result in the sense that strength can be added to him, that he will notice when he is not serious, that he will overcome himself more easily, make himself be serious."

This process of recapitulation can, of course, be applied to any topic. But note that Gurdjieff's "conscious prayer" is not addressed to a supernatural being but rather to the transcendental self, the nous.

Tong Len

In his book **Waking Up**, Charles Tart describes the Tibetan practice of Tong Leng for dealing with unpleasant events. This is designed to "open your mind to compassionate options for future events." Tart recommends doing Tong Len after a successful practice of self-remembering:

" 1. Recall the specific problem or unpleasant situation that this Tong Len practice is to focus on.

2. Reflect on the various aspects of the problem situation, its atmosphere, as well as its specifics. Accept the problem, don't deny any aspect of its reality. See the multiple sides of the situation, the positive as well as the negative aspects.

 3. As you reflect on these positive and negative aspects of thesituation and the people involved, as you 'breathe them in,' also keep track of the equanimity, happiness and compassion you experienced in some degree in your [session of self-remembering], and give these positive feelings to the problemsituation and people. 'Breathe out' your happiness as an *unconditional* gift to them. You are not denying the negative, you are simply loving everything and everyone in the problem situation anyway.

4. Reflect on yourself with regard to this situation. We are all wondrously complex, many-sided beings, so reflect on howdifferent parts of you are responding to the situation. Don't deny anything you see about yourself, even if it's fearful or shameful. Accept all these different aspects of yourself, the 'good' sides and the 'bad' sides, and give your happiness as an unconditional gift to them.

5. Don't force changes, but if aspects of your self changes as a result of putting the positive and the negative together, giving your love to all sides, accept the change."

As Tart remarks, Tong Len "can significantly restructure your mind. Instead of having a steadily growing store of totally negative memories, of situations in which you were not compassionate -- which will, of course, increase your convictions that life is unpleasant and that you are not and cannot be a compassionate person -- you have processed memories to allow for compassion."

The Phenomenological Reduction

The philosopher Edmond Husserl developed a method for experiencing the transcendental self that underlies being, in our terminology, the **nous**. Although intended as a method of philosophical investigation, not as a meditational exercise, the phenomenological reduction is an excellent tool for the aspirant to noetic magic.

Husserl's method involves the progressive "bracketing out" of dimensions of human experience, neutralizing them perceptually. Each bracketing out (say, of the color that we perceive in our immediate surroundings) brings us to a new epoche, or level of perception. By bracketing out dimensionality, space, and time in all their aspects we progress to deeper *epochées* of consciousness until we reach the pure, transcendental self. Unlike similar exercises of mystics such as St. John of the Cross, bracketing out does not deny the reality of the phenomenal world, it suspends our perception of it. As Shomo Giora Shoham observes, "This is more than a Cartesian *cogito* or a Euclidean axiom. It is both an assumption and a hypothesis proved by the irreducible fact of our being, independent of perception and object relationship. . .If the objects, flora, fauna, and others,. . .are 'out there' performing a command performance for the [transcendental self] as participant observer, there must be a [transcendental self]. . .The phenomenological reduction makes the [transcendental self] 'shine forth and show itself,' which is the original meaning of the Greek *phainestai* and the root of the word phenomenon."

Active Imagination

Karl Jung originated the term "active imagination," which refers to the deliberate inducement of hypnagogic states that result in waking dreams. In Jung's analysis, active imagination was probably used by the Gnostics, the Hermetists and mystics such as St. Ignatius Loyola, author of **The Spiritual Exercises**. Other scholars have argued that active imagination was employed by the theosophical Sufis and the Renaissance neo-Platonists. Recently, historian of religion Dan Merkur has published a path-breaking history of the use of active imagination in esoteric spiritual traditions from the Gnostics to the Renaissance, **Gnosis: An Esoteric Tradition of Mystical Visions and Unions**.

In his autobiography, Jung described how he first experienced active imagination. Around Christmas 1912, he had an inexplicable dream that "led to a recurring fantasy of something dead that was also still alive." After several attempts to understand the dream, in which he encountered resistance to giving up control of his conscious mind, Jung experienced a breakthrough:

"I was sitting at my desk once more, thinking over my fears. Then I let myself drop. Suddenly it was as though the ground literally gave way beneath my feet, and I plunged down into dark depths. I could not fend off a feeling of panic. But then, abruptly, at not too great a depth, I landed on my feet in a soft, sticky mass. I felt great relief, although I was apparently in complete darkness. After a while my eyes grew accustomed to the gloom, which was rather like a deep twilight. Before me was the entrance to a dark cave, in which stood a dwarf with leathery skin, as if he were mummified. I squeezed past him through the narrow entrance of the cave where, on a projecting rock, I saw a glowing of red crystal. I grasped the stone, lifted it, and discovered a hollow underneath. At first I could make out nothing, but then I saw that there was running water. In it a corpse floated by, a youth with blond hair and a wound in the head. He was followed by a gigantic black scarab and then by a red, newborn sun, rising up out of the depths of the water. Dazzled by the light, I wanted to replace the stone upon the opening, but then a fluid welled out. It was blood. A thick jet of it leaped up, and I felt nauseated. It seemed to me that the blood continued to spurt for an unendurably long time. At last it ceased, and the vision came to an end."

In the months that followed, Jung had several dreams that related to his vision. These were so intense that he feared he might be going insane. The unconscious, having been released into consciousness, appeared to be running amok. Eventually, he was able to exercise some control over these "assaults" as he "abandoned . . .restraint on his emotions and allowed the images and inner voices to speak afresh. . . .To the extent that I managed to translate the emotions into images -- that is to say, to find the images which were concealed in the emotions - - I was inwardly calmed and reassured. Had I left those images hidden in the emotions, I might have been torn to pieces by them."

According to Jung, the technique of active imagination consists of "systematic exercises for eliminating critical attention, thus producing a vacuum in consciousness." Although this sounds similar to the phenomenological reduction, it is quite different. In active imagination, the subject releases unconscious fantasies into consciousness by relaxing the critical attention normally exercised as a restraint on the unconscious. As Jung says, "The whole procedure is a kind of enrichment and clarification of the affect, whereby the affect and its contents are brought nearer to consciousness, becoming at the same time more impressive and more understandable. . . . The previously unrelated affect has become a more or less clear and articulate idea, thanks to the assistance and co-operation of the conscious mind." Jung goes on to describe how to guide and direct these unconscious fantasies to areas of interest to the subject: "Critical attention must be eliminated. Visual types should concentrate on the expectation that an inner image will be produced. As a rule such a fantasy-picture will actually appear - - perhaps hypnagogically - - and should be carefully observed and noted down in writing. Audio-verbal types usually hear inner words, perhaps mere fragments of apparently meaningless sentences to begin with, which however should be carefully noted down too. Others at such times simply hear their 'other' voice. . .

"There are others again who neither see nor hear anything inside themselves, but whose hands have the knack of giving expression to the contents of the unconscious."

Active imagination can be a hazardous exercise. As Jung wrote in 1958, "A. . . danger -- and this may in certain circumstances be a very serious matter -- is that the subliminal contents already possess such a high energy charge that, when afforded an outlet by active imagination, they may overpower the conscious mind and take possession of the personality. This gives rise to a condition which -- temporarily, at least - - cannot easily be distinguished from schizophrenia, and may even lead to a genuine 'psychotic interval.' The method of active imagination, therefore, is not a plaything for children."

Jungian Meditations on the Tarot

Although Jung did not write about the Tarot and Tarot cards were not used for divination or meditation until the late eighteenth century, the images of the Major Arcana are evocative of Jungian archetypes. Whether it be The Fool, The Hanged Man, The Empress, The Hierophant, or any of the other Major Arcana, the images summon to mind important elements of Western myth.

Meditation on the Tarot need not involve entering a trance nor does it require the exercise of Jungian active imagination. There are several recommended ways of going about it: meditating on one card, meditating on all twenty-two of the Major Arcana beginning with the unnumbered Fool and ending with XXI, the World, meditating for a few minutes or up to an hour.

As with all of these exercises, sit in a chair, breathe deeply and relax your body before beginning.

Let's say you begin with one card. You should contemplate the card, accustoming yourself to its colors and design, without trying to understand intellectually what they might signify. After a time, close your eyes and visualize the card in your mind. Begin to add elements to it in your mind - three-dimensionality, more vivid colors, even movement so that the image takes on all of the characteristics of a real scene. The next step is move into the scene. Look at it from the perspective of one who is in the midst of the image. Move around within the scene, experiencing your surroundings. Then let your concentration relax and allow the scene to "speak" to you. As it does so, you may experience a variety of sensations. The characters in the scene might move and speak, certain aspects of the scene might change, becoming more detailed, for example.

Once you have completed your meditation (it should take several sessions before you are able to experience a fully visualized scene), you should write down what has occurred, thus beginning a record of the results of your meditations, allowing you to build on your previous perceptions each time you undertake a meditation session.

Because the Tarot provides such a wide variety of striking visual imagery, you can continue these meditations literally throughout your life, always experiencing something new and constantly acquiring new insights into the symbolic and affective meanings of the cards.

The Tarot, of course, is not the only possible source of such image meditation. But because the cards are easily available, portable and provide such a wide array of striking images, they are perhaps the most convenient "library" of images to use on a regular basis.

Reflecting on Anamnesis, the Good Unconscious

Plato recommended contemplating the divine forms, even though we could never access them in our mind directly. As the source of the ideals of all good things: beauty, truth, justice, compassion, love, anamnesis reflects the "good" unconscious. Rarely do we attempt to communicate with that part of ourselves that reflects in Lincoln's poetic phrase, the "better angels of our nature." But to do so is to remind ourselves that human beings and we, ourselves, are the repositories of great and noble feelings and perceptions. We dwell too much on the baseness of human nature and not enough on its grandeur.

As with other forms of meditation, you should sit relaxed, with your eyes closed. You should meditate upon a single quality, undeniable in its goodness. For example, you might choose kindness. Recall examples of when you were moved by acts of human kindness. Above all, remember specific instances in which you yourself acted kindly, generously, unselfishly. Recall how that made you feel at the time and experience how it makes you feel now. Allow yourself to acquire a sense of what kindness signifies without intellectualizing what that is. Do not try to define kindness. Concentrate on its universality, the fact that kindness is a human characteristic that transcends religion, race, and personal circumstance. Your meditation should conclude with a sense of having been cleansed, of having put yourself in touch with all of humanity, past, present, and future, who share this remarkable ability to be kind.

Do not stray from the object of your meditation by thinking of negative examples, instances when you or others have acted or spoken unkindly. The purpose of the meditation is not to prove that human beings are imperfect but rather, to remind us of the occasions when we act with near perfection.

Meditating on the virtues can be done literally without end. Each time you do so, you enlarge your understanding of human possibilities.

Chapter 30:
Conclusion

What does noetic magic retain of the magical tradition and what does it reject? It retains the human emphasis and the traditional magical belief in the transcendent power of will and imagination. It rejects the supernatural, the belief in a universe that is metaphysically supportive. Noetic magic begins with individuals and argues from the standpoint of our unique personal and historical situations. But noetic magic rejects the notion, fostered by scientism's world-view, of a limited human consciousness. Noetic magic offers the possibility of altered forms of consciousness, achieved through an effort of human will, that render the universe psychologically (rather than metaphysically) supportive. In this sense, noetic magic reverses the traditional formula, *as above, so below*, to *as within, so without.*

As within, so without is not a metaphysical statement about the self, capable of a logically indefinite extension culminating in solipsism, but rather, a phenomenological statement which emphasizes the potential ability of the human mind actively to participate in and alter our experience. Perhaps even more significantly, noetic magic points out that the task of revising our consciousness, of altering our world-view, cannot be carried out in isolation; our insights and illuminations must be tested and revised in the light of genuine human interchange. Only a magic that is truly intersubjective will prove to be of any lasting value in the effort to improve the human condition.

Noetic magic draws from Gnosticism the powerful doctrine of optimist gnosis, best expressed in neo-Pythagorean theurgy and Sufism. From both Sufism and Lurianic Cabala, noetic magic derives the notion of a universe that is psychologically and spiritually infinite, in which human beings are engaged in the eternal quest of creating both themselves and the universe.

If noetic magic is to he more than a form of self-amusement for an intellectual elite, its value must be recognized by those who have the ability to transform it into a genuine world-view. But where are such people to be found? In the academy, with its penchant for pedantry? In government, science, industry, etc., the bastions of a tired technocracy? Hardly. Magic has little appeal to such staunch guardians of the status quo. Where, then, is there an audience for a discipline that demands imagination and a radical denial, not only of prevailing modes of thought but of prevailing modes of perception as well?

Certainly not among the lunatic fringe of the New Age with its penchant for believing uncritically in anything that is at odds with a rationalist world-view, from channeling to alien abductions.

Not necessarily among the young with their predilection for the practical, for "good jobs" and a comfortable life-style.

Perhaps among those who have entered imaginatively into the universe of cyberspace with their rejection of the traditional, their constant quest for understanding the dimensions of communication, their relentless insistence on constructing their own realities.

It is the vision of independently constructed worlds of meaning lurking uncertainly on the mind's boundaries, that noetic magic holds out to us. Perhaps it will not fall to thoughtful rebels to bring this vision to fruition. Perhaps once again imagination and ecstasy will be forced to go into hiding to lead a surreptitious existence in a few adventurous souls. Nothing is certain; that is the basis of magic and the beauty of life. Whatever happens, we shall be responsible for it: not science, not technocracy but you and I. It is a frightening but exhilarating prospect.

This book has come, like all books thankfully must, to its end and, in the words of Silesius, "Friend, it is even enough. In case thou more wilt read, go forth and thyself become the book, thyself the reading."

Bibliographical Notes and
References to Quotations

Bibliographical Notes and References to Quotations

Preface:

Reference:
Franklin Merrell-Wolf, **Transformations in Consciousness, the Metaphysics and Epistemology** (Albany NY, 1995), 94.

Introduction: The Meanings of Magic

Bibliographical Note:
The historical and anthropological literature on magic is, of course, enormous. My suggestions for further reading are deliberately brief and intended primarily for those new to the subject.

The best one volume history of magic is Kurt Seligmann, **Magic, Supernaturalism and Religion** (New York, 1968). A breezy and entertaining overview of magic from a scientist's point of view is Anthony Aveni's **Behind the Crystal Ball, Magic, Science, and the Occult from Antiquity through the New Age** (New York, 1996). Also worthy of note is E.M. Butler's literary-historical excursus into the origins of the Faust legend, **The Myth of the Magus** (Cambridge UK, 1948). An excellent summary of anthropological and sociological theories of magic may be found in Daniel Lawrence O'Keefe, **Stolen Lightning: the Social Theory of Magic** (New York, 1982).

References to Quotations

"Magic is the art. . ." W.E. Butler, **The Magician: His Training and Work** (London, 1959), introduction and passim.

"In contrast with. . ." Willis Harman, **Global Mind Change** (Indianapolis, 1988), 94.

"society will, in only. . ." Harman, 168.

"This new position of . . ." J.R. Platt, **The Step to Man** (New York, 1966), 150.

"body of self contained acts. . ." Bronislaw Malinowski, **Magic, Science and Religion** (Garden City, NY), 98ff.

"a sort of professional pleasure. . ." Emile Durkheim, **The Elementary Forms of Religious Life** (London, 1915), 43.

"What we so casually call the Imagination. . ." Israel Regardie, **The Tree of Life** (New York, 1969), 121.

Book One: Magic Past

Part One: The Magus as Hero

1. The Birth of Dualism and the Spirit of Magic

References:

"Unquestioned and convincing. . ." Hans Jonas, The Phenomenon of Life (New York, 1966), 8.

"To the extent that life. . ." Jonas, 8.

"This is the paradox. . ." Jonas, 9.

2. The Magic of Greece

Bibliographical Note:

For a good summary of Greek magic see Seligmann and especially E.R. Dodds, **The Greeks and the Irrational** (Berkeley CA, 1951).

3. Pythagoras and Pythagoreanism

Bibliographical Note:

The life and teachings of Pythagoras have been subject to wildly varying interpretations. For a sampling of modern scholarship on Pythagoras see Walter Burkert, Lore and **Science in Ancient Pythagoreanism** (Cambridge MA, 1972); Peter Kingsley, **Ancient Philosophy, Mystery, and Magic** (Oxford, 1995); and Peter Gorman, **Pythagoras, A Life** (London, 1979). A useful summary of number mysticism and magic is Annemarie Schimmel, **The Mystery of Numbers** (New York and Oxford, 1993).

References:

"wife would bring forth. . ." Iamblichus, **Life of Pythagoras** (London, 1965), 3.

"Zaratas expounded to him. . ." Hippolytus, **Elenchos** 12 12, cited in Gorman, 65.

4. Plato and the Magical Universe

References:

"Plato's world. . ." Seligmann, 79.

5. Tales of the Magi: Apollonius of Tyana

Bibliographical Note:

Our knowledge of Apollonius derives almost entirely from Philostratus' biography. I have relied on the translation by Charles P. Eels, **Life and Times of Apollonius of Tyana** (New York, 1967). All quotations in this chapter are from the Eels translation.

6. Simon Magus and Gnosticism

Bibliographical Note:

A good, popular summary of interpretations of Christian gnosticism is John Dart, **The Jesus of Heresy and History: the Discovery and Meaning of the Nag Hammadi Gnostic Library** (San Francisco, 1988). For historical and psychological interpretations that avoid interpreting gnosticism solely as a Christian heresy see especially Hans Jonas, **The Gnostic Religion** 2nd revised edition (London, 1992) **The Gnostic Jung**, edited by Robert A. Segal (Princeton NJ, 1992) and Dan Merkur's brilliant Gnosis, **An Esoteric Tradition of Mystical Visions and Unions** (Albany, NY, 1993).

References:

". . .was not its anticosmic dualism. . . ." Merkur, 114-115.

"seven evil heavens. . . . Merkur, 124-125.

"There stood before me the angel of eternal light. . ." the Zostrianos in James

M. Robinson, ed. **The Nag Hammadi Library in English,** 3rd edition. (San Francisco, 1988), 404-405.

7. Neo-Pythagoreanism

References:

"This reminds us . . ." Philip Merlan, "Plotinus and Magic," Isis, vol. 44, (December, 1953), 341-348. For a critique of Merlan's argument see A.H, Armstrong, "Was Plotinus a Magician?" **Phronesis** I,I, 1954, 73-79.

"besides revealing past or future. . .". Dodds, **The Greeks and the Irrational,** 298.

"(1) the principle of power. . ." Georg Luck, "Theurgy and Forms of Worship in Neoplatonism" in **Religion, Science, and Magic** ed. by Jacob Neusner, Ernest S. Frerichs and Paul Virgil McCracken Flesher (New York and Oxford, 1989), 189-90.

8. Hermes Trismegistus

Bibliographical Note:

The greatest work of scholarship on Hermetism is the multi-volume study by A.J. Festugière, **La Révelation d'Hermès Trismégiste** See especially Volume I: **L'Astrologie et les sciences occultes,** 2nd edition (Paris,1950). For an excellent introduction in English to Hermetism see Frances Yates, **Giordano Bruno and the Hermetic Tradition,** (New York, 1964).

References:

"All beings are in God. . ." Yates, 32.

"The gnosis consists. . ." Yates, 33.

""That light is I myself. . ." Yates, 23.

"Now the **Nous**. . ." Yates, 23

"You are light and life. . ." Yates, 25.

"For it is possible my son. . ." Festugière, 233 ff.

"O Holy Thoth. . ." Festugière, **Ibid.**

"Man is a divine being. . ." Garth Fowden, **The Egyptian Hermes** (Cambridge, UK, 1986), 111.

"There will come a time. . ." Yates, 38-40.

Part Two: The Magus as Heretic

9. Magic in the Middle Ages

Bibliographical Note:

The fundamental work of scholarship in the history of medieval magic is Lynn Thorndike **The History of Magic and Experimental Science**, 8 vols. (New York, 1923-58). An excellent overview that integrates much modern scholarship is Richard Kieckhefer, **Magic in the Middle Ages** (Cambridge, UK, 1990)

References:

"I verily believe. . ." Ernst Kantorowicz, **Frederick the Second** (London, 1931), 355.

"A fifth part of experimental science. . ." A.G. Little, ed. **Roger Bacon Essays** (Oxford, 1914), 178.

10. The Cabala

Bibliographical Note:

The greatest modern scholar of the **Cabala** was Gershom Scholem. Among his voluminous writings, the most accessible overview is **Kabbalah** (New York, 1978).

References:

"a wonderful diagram of forces. . ." W.E. Butler, **op. cit.**, 33.

"There are similarities. . ." Shlomo Giora Shoham, **The Bridge to Nothingness, Gnosis, Kabala, Existentialism and the Transcendental Predicament of Man** (London, 1994), 94.

"The task of man. . ." Shoham, 361.

11. Sufism

Bibliographical Note:

Most previous histories of Western magic have either omitted Sufism altogether or relied on the popularized version of it found in the works of the occultist Idries Shah. An excellent scholarly introduction to Sufism is Julian Baldick, **Mystical Islam** (London, 1989). For an intriguing presentation of the psychology of Sufism see A. Reza Arasteh, **Growth to Selfhood, the Sufi Contribution** (London, 1980). See also Annemarie Schimmel's excellent bibliography, **Mystical Dimensions of Islam** (Chapel Hill, NC, 1975).

References:

"the Sufis are God's friends. . ." Baldick, 3.

"When the inner eye is opened. . ." cited in Merkur, op. cit., 224.

"Ibn Al-Arabi conceived of . . ." Merkur, 226.

"Unlike Western psychologists. . ." Arasteh, 1.

"one becomes zahid. . ." to "state of irreducible simplicity. . ." Arasteh, 61.

"knowing certainty. . ." to "This knowledge. . ." Arasteh, 90.

"the experience of An. . ." Arasteh, 107.

"To the Sufis. . ." Arasteh, 115.

"You will see your form in Him. . ." Merkur, 226-227.

"Ecstasy is akin to passing-away. . ." A.J. Arberry, trans. **The Doctrine of the Sufis** (Cambridge UK., 1977), 106

"In ecstasy delighteth he. . ." Arberry, 106.

Part Three: The Magus as Christian Humanist

12. Magic in the Renaissance

Bibliographical Note:

The key scholars in the history of Renaissance magic are Frances Yates, D.P. Walker, and Wayne Shumaker. Yates' seminal **Giordano Bruno and the Hermetic Tradition** owes much to Walker's earlier work **Spiritual and Demonic Magic from Ficino to Campanella** (London, 1958). See also Shumaker's **The Occult Sciences in the Renaissance** (Berkeley, 1972).

References:

"The whole art of magic. . ." Yates, 52.

"This was a spiritual magic. . ." Yates, 84.

"The forms of things. . ." quoted in Walker, 88.

"All action is visualized. . ." Walter Pagel, Paracelsus (New York, 1958), 111.

13. Tales of the Magi II: John Dee, Renaissance Magus and Royal Spy

References:

"before three years were ended. . ." Richard Deacon, **John Dee** (London, 1968), 8.

"thought to be older than Sanskrit" Anton Szandor LaVey, **The Satanic Bible** (New York, 1969), 155.

"more than even sense. . ." Deacon, 152.

"I say unto thee. . ." **Meric Casaubon, A True Relation of What Passed for Many Years Between Dr. John Dee and Some Spirits** (London, 1659), 31.

"The Angel of the Lord. . ." Deacon, 190-191.

"The transmutations of Kelley. . ." A.E. Waite, **Lives of Alchemystical Philoso-phers** (London, 1888), 155ff.

"to cause your Highness. . ." C. Fell-Smith, **John Dee** (London, 1904), 293.

"With Dee one sees. . ." Deacon, 277.

14. The Discovery of the Impossible

References:

"If this notion of immaterial spirit. . ." John Locke, **An Essay Concerning Human Understanding** (London, 1961), 112.

"subterraneous demons. . ." Robert Boyle, **The General History of the Air in Works**, V (London, 1772), 472.

"More than sixteen years ago. . ." William Fulke, **A Goodly Galerye with a most pleasaunt Prospect into the garden of naturall contemplation. . .** (London, 1563), B-2-B-2v.

Part Four: The Magus as Charlatan

15. Tales of the Magi III: The Comte de St. Germain: Enigma of the Enlightenment

References:

"The other day. . ." **Letters of Horace Walpole,** III (Oxford, 1903), 161.

"The author of the Brussels Gazette. . ." cited in I. Cooper-Oakley, **The Comte de St. Germain** (London, 1912), 35.

"One day madame said to him. . ." cited in Charles McKay **Extraordinary Popular Delusions and the Madness of Crowds** (London, 1852), 231-232.

"I'm afraid I cannot say. . ." to "He was well acquainted with physics. . ." to "The King ordered. . ." Cooper-Oakley, 37-39.

"Sir, I send you a letter. . ." Cooper-Oakley, 170 ff.

"If the Comte de St. Germain. . ." Cooper-Oakley, 212.

"Although the story of his life. . ." cited in E.M. Butler, op. cit., 197.

"He was perhaps. . ." E.M. Butler, 203.

"Evidence there is. . ." Cooper-Oakley, 137.

"on returning home . . ." Cooper-Oakley, 85-93.

"The other Adept. . ." E.M. Butler, 213.

16. Tales of the Magi IV: Cagliostro: Friend of Humanity or Quack of Quacks?

References:

"Fittest of visages. . ." Thomas Carlyle, **Miscellaneous Essays** (London, 1887) II, 520.

"Your soul is. . ." François Ribadeau Dumas, **Cagliostro** (London, 1967), 102.

"Would you know. . ." Bernard Fay, **Louis XVI** (Paris, 1955), 293.

"I am oppressed. . ." Ribadeau Dumas, 183.

"Am I coming back. . ." Enzo Petraccone, **Cagliostro** (Milan, 1936), 113 ff.

"In a word. . ." Ribadeau Dumas, 182.

Part Five: The Magus as Monster

17. Magic in the 19th Century

Bibliographical Note:

The only scholarly history of Tarot cards is Ronald Decker, Thierry Depaulis and Michael Dummet, **A Wicked Pack of Cards, the Origin of the Occult Tarot** (London, 1996). Previous discussions of the Tarot have been completely superseded by this superb work.

References:

"This Egyptian Book. . ." Decker et. al., 60.

"It seems unlikely. . ." Decker, et. al., 166.

"Lévi's theory is. . ." Decker, et. al., 190.

"that there are hidden powers. . ." Sylvia Cranston, **HPB, The Extraordinary Life and Influence of Helena Blavatsky, Founder of the Modern Theosophical Movement** (New York, 1993), 132.

18. Tales of the Magi V: The Anti-Victorians: Yeats, Crowley and the Golden Dawn

Bibliographical Note:

With respect to secondary works, John Symond's biography of Crowley, **The Great Beast**, (London, 1956) revised edition 1971, is entertaining and well documented. Charles Richard Cammell's **Aleister Crowley** (London, 1951) revised edition 1969, on the other hand, attempts to apotheosize the magus (an effort which I'm sure Crowley would have applauded). Israel Regardie's **The Golden Dawn** (New York, n.d.) is a compilation of many of the rituals used by that society and is, therefore, of considerable historical interest. Regardie, a former member of the principal offshoot of the Golden Dawn, the Stella Matutina, aroused considerable controversy in occult circles when he decided to publish this material in the late 1930s. Francis King's **Ritual Magic in Modern England, 1887 to the Present** (London, 1970) contains a lucid, intelligent account of the Golden Dawn and its descendants. Virginia Moore's The Unicorn (New York, 1954) is a penetrating study of the esoteric influences on the poetry of W. B. Yeats. Crowley's **The Moonchild** (London, 1972) is a marvelous occult novel, really a roman à clef, for all of the major figures in the Golden Dawn appear in the novel thinly disguised. Yeats is Gates, a seedy Irish poet. A. E. Waite is Arthwait, a locquacious pedant. S.R.M.D. is Mathers, the evil head of the Black Lodge, etc. Crowley's **Confessions** (New York, 1971) is rather long, though extremely interesting in parts. His **Magick in Theory and Practice** is perhaps the best book ever written on the philosophy and practice of magic. Crowley was a much better writer of prose than of poetry, a fact which he unfortunately never recognized.

Crowley's Poetry

Despite my description of Crowley's poetry as execrable, it is only fair to point out that a number of people have greatly admired it. In order to allow readers to judge for themselves, I have included an excerpt from Crowley's most famous poem, **Hymn to Pan.** Let me add that I would not do this were I not firmly convinced that this excerpt provides a clearer demonstration of the truth of my opinion than could any amount of literary argument.

Thrill with lissome lust of the light, 0 man! My man!
Come careering out of the night Of Pan! Io Pan!
Io Pan! Io Pan! Come over the sea From Sicily and from Arcady!
Roaming as Bacchus, with fauns and pards
And nymphs and satyrs for thy guards,
On a milk-white ass, come over the sea
To me, to me,
etc.

References:

"In 1888. . ." S. L. McGregor Mathers, **The Qabalah Unveiled** (London,1958),
viii.

"The central principle. . ." W.B. Yeats, **Essays and Introductions** (New York,
1961), 60.

"I cannot get it out of my mind. . ." Yeats, 242.

"It has been remarked. . ." Crowley, **Confessions**, 7.

"The forces of good. . ." Crowley, **Confessions**, 111.

"What hurt. . ." Crowley, **Confessions**, 157.

"Indubitably, Magick. . ." Crowley, **Confessions**, 169-170.

"In a certain sense Magick. . ." Crowley, **Magick in Theory and
Practice**, xiii.

19. Tales of the Magi VI: Rasputin, the Holy Devil

Bibliographical Note:

In addition to the works cited, important contemporary views of Rasputin may
be found in Bernard Pares, **The Fall of the Russian Monarchy** (London, 1939)
and Grand Duke Alexander, **Once a Grand Duke** (Garden City, NJ, 1932).

References:

"Gregory Efimovich Rasputin has been so blackened. . ." Alan Moorehead, **The
Russian Revolution** (New York, 1958), 69.

"There is, perhaps, no country. . ." E.A. Brayley Hodgetts, **The Court of Russia in the 19th Century** (London, 1908), I, 10.

"the possession of occult powers. . ." Edmund A. Walsh, The Fall of the Russian Empire (New York, 1928), 107.

"exotic herbs, medicinal plants. . ." Walsh, 100.

"it cannot have been only. . ." Moorehead, 65 ff.

"This pathologically shy woman. . ." Colin Wilson, **Rasputin and the Fall of the Romanovs** (New York, 1964), 52.

"He is just a good, religious. . ." M.V. Rodzianko, **The Reign of Rasputin** (London, 1927), 102.

"Little need be said about Rasputin's political views. . ." Michael T. Florinsky, **The End of the Russian Empire** (New York, 1961), 68.

"No one knows exactly what happened. . ." Wilson, **op. cit.**, 128.

"Ferdinand's death. . ." Wilson, 156.

Book Two: Magic Future

20. Introduction

Reference:

"[The first level] is as a superficial label. . ." David Spangler, **Emergence: The Rebirth of the Sacred** (New York, 1984), 78-81.

21. Tales of the Magi VII: Gurdjieff: the Magus as Trickster

Bibliographical Note:

References:

"The details of everything. . ." G.I. Gurdjieff, **Meetings with Remarkable Men** (New York, 1974), 161.

"He is God and I am God!. . ." G.I. Gurdjieff, **Life is Only Real Then: When**

'**I Am**' (New York, 1981), 23.

"I saw a man of an oriental type. . ." P.D. Ouspensky, **In Search of the Miraculous** (New York, 1949), 7.

"To meet [Gurdjieff]. . ." Gurdjieff, **Meetings**. . . Translator's Note ix.

"A strange excitement. . ." Ouspensky, 263.

"There is neither red, green. . ." Ouspensky, 262.

"The level of Gurdjieff's. . ." J.B. Priestley, **Man and Time** (London, 1964), 264.

"In principle I had to die. . ." Thomas and Olga de Hartmann, **Our Life with Gurdjieff** (New York, 1964), 139f.

"You filthy, . . ." James Webb, **The Harmonious Circle** (New York, 1980), 315.

"Every person you see. . ." Fritz Peters, **Gurdjieff Remembered** (London, 1976), 24.

"wish to fuck" Peters, 34

"the stuff. . ." Frank Lloyd Wright, "At Taliesin," **The Capital Times**, August 26, 1934.

"governs successions of events. . ." Kathleen R. Speeth, **The Gurdjieff Work** (Berkeley CA, 1976), 22-23.

"The days of the week. . ." Speeth, 25-26.

"Man is a machine. . ." Ouspensky, 21.

"It was during this summer. . ." C.S. Nott, **Journey through this World** (New York, 1969), 154.

"To destroy, mercilessly. . ." G.I. Gurdjieff, **Beelzebub's Tales to His Grandson** (New York, 1973) V, 1.

"I have already said. . ." Ouspensky, 274.

"The whole point. . ." Ouspensky, 357.

"Usually the disciple. . ." Ouspensky, 203.

"a social perception. . ." James Moore, **Gurdjieff, the Anatomy of a Myth** (Rockport, MA, 1991), 59.

"Spiritual groups. . ." Daniel Goleman, "Early Warning Signs for the Detection of Spiritual Blight," **Newsletter**, Association for Transpersonal Psychology (Summer, 1985), 11. Cited in Charles T. Tart, **Waking Up, Overcoming the Obstacles to Human Potential** (Boston, 1986), 261-262.

"a saint with balls. . ." Moore, 62.

22. The Magus as Media Maven: Carlos Castaneda and Deepak Chopra

"The name of cleargreen. . ." to "Tensegrity is the modernized. . ." infinity@webb.com

"The only way to know intent. . ." Carlos Castaneda, **The Power of Silence** (New York, 1987), 31.

"All the possible feelings. . ." Castaneda, **Tales of Power** (New York, 1976), 272.

"the point at which. . ." to "At the fourth gate. . ." infinity@webb.com

" Pure consciousness. . ." Deepak Chopra, **The Seven Spiritual Laws of Success** (San Rafael, CA, 1994), 9.

"our internal reference point. . ." Chopra, 10.

"Nature's intelligence . . ." Chopra, 55.

"Attention energizes. . ." to "The quality of intention. . ." Chopra, 70.

"says that in order. . ." Chopra, 83

"says that we have taken. . ." Chopra, 95.

23. The Coming Transformation in Human Consciousness

References:

"system of which every part . . ." to "conveyed a new recognition. . ." Floyd W. Matson, **Being, Becoming and Behavior** (New York 1967), 9-10.

"Newton's great mathematical system. . ." A.B. Arons, A. M. Bork, **Science and Ideas** (Princeton, NJ, 1964), 5.

"Let us conclude boldly. . ." Matson, 11.

"I for one. . ." R.N. Stromberg, **European Intellectual History** (New York, 1966), 33.

"Biology may be seen. . ." Stromberg, 96.

"Towards the end of his life. . ." Colin Wilson, **Beyond the Outsider** (London, 1966), 131.

"The interest of the behaviourist. . ." J.B. Watson, **Behaviourism** (Chicago, 1924), 5.

"The implication that man is not free. . ." B.F. Skinner, **Science and Human Behavior** (New York, 1953), 447.

"general principle. . . ." Skinner, 315.

"impersonal objectivity. . ." Matson, 11.

"The conception of the universe. . ." Fritjof Capra, **The Turning Point** (New York, 1982), 87.

"The existential level. . ." Capra, 370.

24. Noetic Magic

References:

"There are three main theories. . ." Crowley, **Magick in Theory and Practice**, 1.

"the philosophy which underlies magic. . ." W.E. Butler, **op. cit.**, 28.

"Satan is the grandest symbol. . ." Maximilian Rudwin, **The Devil in Legend and Literature** (London, 1931), 264f.

"Do what thou wilt. . ." to "What is a Magical operation?" Crowley, **Magick in Theory and Practice**, 107.

"it is not matter. . ." W.E. Butler, **op. cit.**, 29.

1) Deep sleep without dreams. . . Robert S. DeRopp, **The Master Game** (New York, 1968), 51.

"Man in the fourth state. . ." to "is impossible to sustain. . ." De Ropp, 67.

"that there is a third organ. . . " Merrell-Wolf, **op. cit.**, 303.

"External objects present us. . ." Merrell-Wolf, 69.

"The majority of psychologists. . ." D.H. Rawcliffe, **Illusions and Delusions of the Supernatural and the Occult** (New York, 1959), 16.

"Psychical research represents. . ." Rawcliffe, 24f.

25. The Mind as an Active Force

References:

"Experience is not simply something. . ." William A. Sadler, **Existence and Love** (New York, 1969), 12f.

"The shape in which things. . ." J.H. Van Den Berg, **The Changing Nature of Man** (New York, 1961), 191.

"suffer from emptiness. . ." to "Where Gnostics. . ." Segal, **op. cit.**, 17f.

"Once the psyche reaches. . ." Jolande Jacobi, **Complex/Archetype/Symbol in the Psychology of C.G. Jung** (Princeton, NJ, 1967), 183-85.

26. Will and Imagination

References:

"The variability of the things we observe. . ." Van Den Berg, 193.

27. Exploring the Antipodes of the Mind

28. Noetic Magic and the Other

References:

"Such a being. . ." Crowley, **Magick in Theory and Practice**, 237.

"The suffering of the other. . ." Shoham, **op. cit.**, 339.

"Self-realization cannot be made the goal. . ." Maurice Friedman, **To Deny Our Nothingness** (New York, 1967), 240.

29. Exercises in Noetic Magic

Bibliographical Note:

Charles T. Tart's **Waking Up** (Boston, 1986) provides an excellent description of active meditative exercises. For exercises using Tarot cards see Alfred Douglas, **The Tarot** (New York, 1972). Jung's approach to active imagination is well described by Dan Merkur in **Gnosis, An Esoteric Tradition of Mystical Visions and Unions** (Albany, NY, 1993).

References:

"The practice of self-observation. . ." Tart, 191.

"try to observe every thought. . ." Tart, 194.

"simultaneously sensing, looking, and listening" Tart, 201.

"These prayers are, so to speak. . ." Ouspensky, 300-301.

"open your mind to compassionate options. . ." to "can significantly restructure . . ."Tart, 277.

"This is more than a Cartesian cogito. . ." Shoham, **op. cit.**, 315f.

"led to a recurring fantasy. . ." Merkur, 39.

"I was sitting at my desk. . ." C.G. Jung, **Memories, Dreams, Reflections** (New York, 1989), 179.

"abandoned. . .restraint. . ." Jung, 177.

"systematic exercises. . ." Jung, 38.

"The whole procedure. . ." to "Critical attention must be eliminated. . ." Jung, 82f.

"A. . . danger. . ." C.G. Jung, "The Transcendent Function" in **The Structure and Dynamics of the Psyche**, trans. R.F.C. Hull, **Collected Works**, vol. 8 (New York, 1960), 68.

30. Conclusion

About The Author

Daniel L. Wick received his Ph.D. in History from the University of California. He has taught history and literature at the College of Marin, San Francisco State University, and the University of California at Davis. Dr. Wick is the international award winning author of a book on the French Revolution, a play about Lord Byron, and more than one hundred scholarly articles, essays and reviews.